JESUS AND THE OLD TESTAMENT

JESUS AND THE OLD TESTAMENT

HIS APPLICATION OF OLD TESTAMENT PASSAGES TO HIMSELF AND HIS MISSION

by

R. T. France

Lecturer in Biblical Studies,
University of Ife, Nigeria

INTER-VARSITY PRESS

INTER-VARSITY PRESS
BOX F, DOWNERS GROVE, ILLINOIS 60515

First Edition – December 1971
USA ISBN 0 87784 954 4

PRINTED IN GREAT BRITAIN BY
BILLING AND SONS LIMITED, GUILDFORD AND LONDON

FOREWORD

When we compare the New Testament documents with the literature of the Qumran community, one common feature which impresses us is the dominant part played in both by an original system of exegesis. The 'self-understanding' of the early church, as of the Qumran community, was interwoven with the interpretation of the Old Testament writings which it had received. The Qumran texts make it plain that the community owed its scheme of biblical interpretation to its first organizer, the Teacher of Righteousness, 'to whom God made known all the mysteries of the words of his servants the prophets'. Analogy, apart from anything else, might suggest that the scheme of biblical interpretation which pervades the New Testament was similarly derived from the Founder of Christianity. The New Testament biblical exegesis is not the same as that attested in the Qumran documents; both resemblances and disparities are readily recognized. But the one scheme, like the other, bespeaks the influence of one powerful mind. When we observe that the main features of primitive Christian exegesis recur independently in the works of several New Testament writers, we have to look behind them for this powerful mind, and (as C. H. Dodd has remarked in his classic treatment of this subject) we are not compelled to reject the New Testament evidence which points unmistakably to the mind of Jesus himself.

The Jesus of all four Gospels makes liberal and discriminating use of the Old Testament writings in teaching and debate, and not least in speaking of his own mission in the world. This use is so markedly characteristic that it may well be treated, as Dr France treats it in this study, as one of the criteria of authenticity to be applied to the words which the Evangelists ascribe to him.

I first read this study in its earlier incarnation as a PhD thesis, and have read it again with increasing pleasure in this revised form. In his detailed examination of Jesus' use of the Old Testament, as recorded in the Gospels, Dr France shows himself a sure-footed expert in criticism and exegesis. He lets us see how crucial Jesus' Old Testament interpretation was to his understanding of his central place in the history of salvation and the accomplishment of God's purpose. In addition to his special concentration on Daniel 7 and Zechariah 9–14, I have been impressed by his defence of the thesis that the fourth Isaianic Servant Song exercised a profound influence on Jesus' thinking about his own service and sacrifice. Such a contribution to Gospel study as this will commend itself to New Testament students without any commendatory words of mine, but I am most happy to have this opportunity of writing a few commendatory words and of wishing it well.

F. F. Bruce

CONTENTS

PREFACE

This book began life as a PhD thesis, submitted to the University of Bristol in 1966. It has since undergone the fate of most theses which aspire to become books: while account has been taken of the more important work in this field since 1966, the bulk has been reduced by the omission of some less essential detailed discussion, the footnotes have been heavily pruned, quotations in foreign languages have been rendered into English, and Hebrew and Greek translated except where the argument requires the original to be printed; in general the attempt has been made to produce a readable, though technical, book.

Even so, much detailed argument remains. In order to put as little obstruction as possible in the way of the non-specialist reader, the technical details of text-form have been removed from Chapter 2 and printed as an appendix, and a footnote at the beginning of Chapter 5 suggests that the more technical sections could profitably be skipped by those who do not wish to examine the full documentation of the argument. The heart of the work, and its most positive contribution to an understanding of Jesus' view of his mission in the light of the Old Testament scriptures, lies in Chapters 3 and 4, and, while the book is unashamedly an academic work, my aim in revising the original thesis has been that those who are not specialists in biblical study, and who do not know Hebrew and Greek, should not be debarred from following the arguments which lead to these conclusions.

The conclusions reached are not profoundly new and revolutionary. Those theologians to whom novelty is the criterion of academic respectability may not find it to their taste. At several points I have parted company with traditional exegesis or accepted opinions, but where the evidence suggested that traditional 'old-fashioned' theology was in the right, I have not been afraid to say so. Indeed, perhaps the most revolutionary suggestion that can be made in contemporary theological debate is that the traditional viewpoint is not axiomatically wrong, that even among the heady outpourings of today's avant-garde exegetes, it may still sometimes be true that the old is better, not because it is old, but because it is rooted in the sheer exegetical common sense which is one of the first casualties in the scholar's quest for originality.

Among the many who have contributed to the writing of this book, special thanks must be offered to Professor K. Grayston, who supervised the original research, and to whose shrewd guidance the present form of the work is much indebted, even though he would not wish to be associated with all its conclusions. Professor F. F. Bruce has given much encouragement, particularly by honouring the book with a Foreword. My thanks are also due to the Council and Staff of Tyndale Hall, Bristol, who first gave me the enthusiasm and the opportunity for this study, and to the Tyndale Fellowship for Biblical Research, through whose assistance and support it was completed: without the excellent research facilities of the Tyndale Library, Cambridge, and the ever-ready help of its then Librarian, Mr A. R. Millard, this book would probably not have seen the light of day. Finally, I am grateful to the Publishers for taking on a difficult and unrewarding task, and for carrying it through with impressive skill and patience.

R. T. France

University of Ife,
Nigeria.
September 1970.

ABBREVIATIONS

AG	W. F. Arndt and F. W. Gingrich, *A Greek–English Lexicon of the New Testament* and other Early Christian Literature (Chicago, 1957)
BDB	F. Brown, S. R. Driver and C. A. Briggs, *A Hebrew and English Lexicon of the Old Testament* (Oxford, 1906)
BJRL	*Bulletin of the John Rylands Library*
CBQ	*Catholic Biblical Quarterly*
ET	English Translation
ExpT	*Expository Times*
EVV	English Versions
JB	The Jerusalem Bible, 1966
JBL	*Journal of Biblical Literature*
JTS	*Journal of Theological Studies*
LXX	The Septuagint
MT	The Massoretic Text
NEB	The New English Bible, 1961 and 1970
NT	*Novum Testamentum*
NTS	*New Testament Studies*
RB	*Revue Biblique*
RSV	The Revised Standard Version, 1946 and 1952
RV	The Revised Version, 1885
SB	H. L. Strack and P. Billerbeck, *Kommentar zum neuen Testament aus Talmud und Midrasch*, vols. 1–4 (München, 1922–28); vols. 5–6 (Indices) by J. Jeremias and K. Adolph (München, 1956, 1961)
SJT	*Scottish Journal of Theology*
ST	*Studia Theologica*
TDNT	*Theological Dictionary of the New Testament*, ET of *TWNT* by G. W. Bromiley (Grand Rapids, 1964–)
Tg	Targum
Thdt	Theodotion
TLZ	*Theologische Literaturzeitung*
TWNT	*Theologisches Wörterbuch zum neuen Testament*, ed. G. Kittel, G. Friedrich (Stuttgart, 1933–)
Vg	The Vulgate
VT	*Vetus Testamentum*
ZATW	*Zeitschrift für die alttestamentliche Wissenschaft*
ZNTW	*Zeitschrift für die neutestamentliche Wissenschaft*

Citations from the Old Testament are by chapter and verse of the MT unless otherwise indicated. Rabbinic and other citations follow the customary notation. A reference to the Palestinian Talmud is indicated by p before the name of the tractate; other talmudic references are to the Babylonian Talmud.

Bibliographical details of modern works are given in the footnotes only at the first citation of a work. Thereafter *op. cit.* is used, or, in the case of an author more than one of whose works is cited, an abbreviated title. The index of modern authors may be used to find the first reference to a work. Commentaries are generally cited, after the first reference, by the name of the biblical book. Titles of periodical and Festschrift articles are included only if there is special reason to do so.

Biblical quotations in English are generally taken from the RSV.

CHAPTER ONE

INTRODUCTION

1. THE SUBJECT

Recent years have seen a spate of works on the use of the Old Testament by the writers of the New.[1] Much valuable work has been accomplished, but as the study has proceeded a remarkable hiatus has appeared. The use of the Old Testament by the founder of the New Testament church has been relatively neglected. The reason is not far to seek. The prevalent attitude to the words of Jesus recorded in the Gospels is one of scepticism as to their dominical origin. The quotations of the Old Testament attributed to him are tacitly, and sometimes explicitly, regarded as reflecting the scriptural interpretation not of Jesus himself, but of the churches in which the Gospels emerged. The thought of the founder is allowed to recede behind the screen of that of his followers.

The attempt to penetrate this screen must seem a rash, and perhaps hopeless, quest. That, however, is the aim of this present thesis. It is directed towards a filling, however partial, of the hiatus that has appeared.

We aim, then, to study the use of the Old Testament by Jesus. The field is too large to be covered in full, and the following restrictions have been imposed. (i) We shall study only the teaching of Jesus as presented in the Synoptic Gospels, leaving the Fourth Gospel out of account. (ii) We have not, except where the argument required it, discussed Jesus' principles of

[1] The following are of particular importance: C. H. Dodd, *According to the Scriptures*: the Sub-structure of New Testament Theology (London, 1952); K. Stendahl, *The School of St. Matthew* and its Use of the Old Testament (Uppsala, 1954; second edn. Philadelphia, 1968: references are to the first edn.); E. E. Ellis, *Paul's Use of the Old Testament* (Edinburgh, 1957); B. Lindars, *New Testament Apologetic*: the Doctrinal Significance of the Old Testament Quotations (London, 1961); R. H. Gundry, *The Use of the Old Testament in St. Matthew's Gospel*, with Special Reference to the Messianic Hope (Leiden, 1967).

exegesis, nor the suggested use of the exegetical devices of Qumran or the Rabbis, but have confined ourselves to his *application* of the Old Testament. (iii) Even in this restricted field the material is too extensive. We have accordingly concentrated on the Old Testament passages applied by Jesus to his own status and mission. His use of, *e.g.*, the legal and ethical teaching of the Old Testament is considered only in so far as it bears on this subject. Even with these restrictions, not all points can be discussed in detail, and much must inevitably be taken for granted, or assumed from the work of other scholars.

The question we shall be discussing, therefore, is, How did Jesus see his mission in the light of the Old Testament Scriptures? What does his choice and use of Old Testament passages reveal of his conception of his own place in the purpose of God, and indeed of his own person? By considering these questions we hope to explore one route which leads to an understanding of Jesus' thought about himself and about the significance of his work, an understanding which is the essential foundation of New Testament Christology. And in view of the frequency of reference to the Old Testament attributed to Jesus, we feel that this route is more than a bypath.

The significance of Jesus' use of the Old Testament depends largely on two factors, whether it was an original development within the contemporary Jewish scene, and whether it formed the pattern for the use of those same Scriptures in the Christian church of the New Testament and beyond. A tendency in some recent writing to suggest a cautiously affirmative answer to both these questions, though not supported by detailed argument, is exemplified by the famous words of C. H. Dodd quoted below.[2] Our final chapter aims to provide some of the evidence required to justify this affirmative answer.

II. THE MATERIALS

We shall not confine our attention to formal quotations of the Old Testament. The tendency to do so has marred some recent work, for it inevitably results in an incomplete picture. To discover how Jesus understood and used the Old Testament, we must go beyond verbatim quotations, whether introduced

[2] *Op. cit.*, pp. 109–110, quoted below, p. 262.

by a set formula or not, to include references to Old Testament teaching or events, verbal allusions, and even, in a few cases, significant actions which seem to have been intended to call attention to prophecies of the Old Testament. The importance of the less formal allusions in particular is that they often betray the Old Testament models around which the speaker's or writer's thinking formed itself, and in many cases they are deliberately framed to suggest a particular Old Testament passage or idea.[3]

It is not easy, however, to decide what constitutes an allusion to the Old Testament. There is no rule of thumb by which intentional allusions can be detected, and it is possible to see references to the Old Testament in the most innocent everyday language.[4] We have attempted in an appendix[5] a classification of quotations and allusions attributed to Jesus, including as 'clear' allusions and references those cases where it cannot reasonably be doubted that the Old Testament passage concerned is in mind, and as 'possible' allusions and references, by no means all that could be suggested, but those where we feel that an intentional use of Old Testament language or ideas could reasonably be postulated. The quotations and allusions thus selected form the basis of our study; where we have occasion to include cases in the 'possible' category in our argument, the reality of the allusion is generally discussed at the appropriate point.

III. THE QUESTION OF AUTHENTICITY

We have mentioned the widespread belief that we can have only the most shadowy idea of what Jesus actually said and did, that the teaching of Jesus has not reached us without being considerably altered, adapted, edited and supplemented in the process which culminated in its incorporation in the Gospels. While few would deny that we possess at least some authentic teaching of Jesus, many are sceptical as to our chances of detect-

[3] See the discussion of this subject by R. H. Gundry, *op. cit.*, pp. 2–5, and below, pp. 112–114.

[4] For an example of the attempt to discover the maximum number of allusions see E. Hühn, *Die alttestamentlichen Citate und Reminiscenzen im NT* (Tübingen, 1900).

[5] Appendix C, below, pp. 259–623.

ing it in the haystack of later accretions, and attempts to do so have resulted in widely differing conclusions.

This is the legacy of form-criticism, or rather of its extension, especially by R. Bultmann, into a method of historical criticism. As long as it confines itself to the literary analysis of the Gospel material, and the forms into which it was cast and in which it was transmitted, form-criticism has little to say on the origin of the material it considers. But in the hands of Bultmann, the search for the *Sitz im Leben* of the form of a saying becomes the search for the originator of its contents. A saying which is adapted to the needs of a particular community is presumed to owe its origin to that community.

The inevitable result has been a loss of interest in 'the historical Jesus', and a concentration instead on the faith and teaching of the apostolic church. A distinction between 'the Jesus of history' and 'the Christ of faith' has become the starting-point of much modern research into Christian origins. For Bultmann the former, a Jewish eschatological prophet, is of secondary importance; the latter is the basis of Christian faith. The beginning among Bultmann's followers of *A New Quest of the Historical Jesus*[6] has done little to reverse this trend, for though the desire is to stress the continuity between 'the Jesus of history' and 'the Christ of faith', this very fact tends to drive Jesus as he actually was more deeply into the shadows behind the portrait of him set up by his followers. While to these scholars the faith of the church was built on what Jesus really was and said, the record of him which they compiled is an interpretation, not a transcription, of his words and deeds, and their scepticism with regard to the authenticity of any given saying is hardly less than that of their master.

This scepticism leads to the setting up of criteria which can be used to establish the authenticity of certain sayings over against the creative work of the Christian church. To these criteria and their validity we must turn shortly, but a few words must first be said about the presuppositions on which they are based.

It is generally recognized that an objective approach to

[6] The book of this title by J. M. Robinson (London, 1959) provides a useful survey of this movement, esp. pp. 12–19. *Cf.* also R. H. Fuller, *The New Testament in Current Study* (London, 1963), pp. 33–67.

history is impossible. H. E. W. Turner, in a slight but significant book,[7] discusses this question with special reference to the study of the Gospels. He distinguishes two opposite approaches to the Gospels, which he labels respectively 'historicist' and 'interpretative'.[8] The distinction lies in their respective view of the purpose and nature of the Gospels: for the historicist they are primarily intended as historical records, and may fairly be taken as such unless there is evidence to the contrary; for the interpretative school they are essentially propaganda, written to present a certain view of Jesus, and relatively unconcerned with 'bare history'. For this latter school, therefore, unless stringent criteria of authenticity are fulfilled, the Gospel records present not the life and words of Jesus, but the theology of the church in which they originated. We cannot pursue Turner's argument here; essentially it is a plea for the rehabilitation of the historicist approach, which has been in retreat before the sceptical onslaught of Bultmann and his followers. Our purpose is simply to draw attention to the fact that the different estimates of the Gospels arise not from the use of conflicting evidence, but from fundamentally opposed presuppositions. Only when these presuppositions are recognized rather than assumed can progress be made.

The conflict crystallizes into the question of the burden of proof. Members of the interpretative school assume that it has now been transferred to their opponents. 'We can no longer assume the general reliability of the Synoptic tradition about Jesus. . . . The obligation now laid upon us is to investigate and make credible not the possible unauthenticity of the individual unit of material but, on the contrary, its genuineness.'[9] Granted the validity of their presuppositions this would indeed be true, but that is precisely what the historicist cannot grant. We have not space here for a discussion of the relative merits of the opposing presuppositions,[10] but a fruitful consideration of the

[7] *Historicity and the Gospels* (London, 1963).

[8] *Ibid.*, p. 30 and *passim.*

[9] E. Käsemann, *Essays on New Testament Themes* (ET London, 1964), p. 34. The point is made even more forcefully by N. Perrin, *Rediscovering the Teaching of Jesus* (London, 1967), see esp. p. 39. *Cf.* J. M. Robinson, *op. cit.*, pp. 37–38 and 38–39 note.

[10] See below, p. 22 n. 26.

proposed criteria of authenticity depends on the recognition of the roots of this conflict.

IV. CRITERIA OF AUTHENTICITY

The basic criteria for determining the authenticity of a saying adopted by Bultmann and his school are twofold. '(1) If it reflects the faith of the church after the resurrection, it must be regarded as a creation of the church, rather than an authentic saying of Jesus. (2) If there is a parallel saying attributed to a Rabbi, it must be held as a Jewish tradition which has erroneously been attributed to Jesus. But if it is neither – if it is clearly distinct both from the faith of the church and from Judaism – then it may be safely accepted as authentic.' [11] This is a useful summary of principles that emerge repeatedly in the writings of Bultmann and the post-Bultmannians; the two criteria together make up what N. Perrin calls the 'criterion of dissimilarity'.[12] In practice the application of these criteria tends to take the form of drawing up a picture of Jesus as far as possible in direct contrast with both contemporary Judaism and the church, and assessing the genuineness of a saying by its coherence with this picture. (Perrin elevates this practical application into a second principle, the 'criterion of coherence'.[13]) For Bultmann this means the acceptance of sayings which express the 'distinctive eschatological temper which characterised the preaching of Jesus'.[14]

The Old Testament quotations attributed to Jesus come out of this scrutiny particularly badly. While Bultmann[15] allows that 'now and again' Jesus may have used a given Old

[11] R. H. Fuller, *Interpreting the Miracles* (London, 1963), pp. 26–27.

[12] *Op. cit.*, p. 39. The first criterion was already inherent in P. W. Schmiedel's famous selection of nine 'foundation-pillars for a truly scientific life of Jesus', *Encyclopaedia Biblica* (London 1899–1903), vol. 2, *s.v.* 'Gospels', §§ 139–140. For Bultmann's own statement of these criteria see, *e.g.*, his *The History of the Synoptic Tradition*[3] (ET Oxford, 1963), p. 205.

[13] *Op. cit.*, p. 43. Perrin's book is one of the most thoroughgoing recent attempts in English to refine and apply the Bultmannian criteria, but in fact it makes no significant departure from Bultmann's critical approach.

[14] *History*, p. 205; *cf. ibid.*, p. 162, and for a fuller list of 'characteristic' sayings, p. 105. H. E. Tödt's list of characteristics of authentic Son of man sayings is essentially a refinement of the same approach: *The Son of Man in the Synoptic Tradition* (ET London, 1965), pp. 224–226.

[15] *History*, p. 49.

Testament text (though 'that is something it is no longer possible to establish'), Käsemann[16] is less optimistic, and Tödt[17] regards lack of appeal to Scripture as a mark of the 'sovereign certainty' of Jesus' words, which need no other legitimation.

The basic twofold criterion of the Bultmannian school has been extended both by those who sympathize with Bultmann's approach and by those who do not. R. H. Fuller has added the important criterion that a saying is more likely to be authentic if 'it has a Palestinian flavour and the characteristics of Aramaic speech',[18] but this criterion is proposed only to corroborate the findings of the basic twofold criterion, not as valid by itself.

On the other hand, H. E. W. Turner, an avowed protagonist of historicism, presents the following list of criteria. In addition to the standard twofold criterion of Bultmann, he proposes to regard as probably authentic sayings which show (i) a 'marked difference in the scale of treatment' between Jesus and the early church, even though the theme is a common one,[19] (ii) certain characteristics of Jesus, especially as 'an authoritative Person, . . . teacher, healer, controversialist, and sufferer', (iii) certain formal and stylistic characteristics, which are listed, and (iv) 'the style and idiom of contemporary Aramaic'.[20]

Turner[21] believes that this extension of the Bultmannian criteria justifies him in claiming authenticity for a considerable body of the Gospel material. Certainly he has relaxed the stringency of Bultmann's tests. But the presumption is still that no saying may be treated as authentic unless it passes tests to distinguish it from the teaching of Judaism or early Christianity. If a satisfactory *Sitz im Leben* for a saying can be found elsewhere than in the teaching of Jesus, it must be presumed spurious. The search for criteria of authenticity, whether in the

[16] *Op. cit.*, p. 40; *cf.* p. 43.

[17] *Op. cit.*, p. 224.

[18] *Miracles*, p. 27: *cf.* his *Current Study*, pp. 41–42; N. Perrin, *op. cit.*, pp. 37–38.

[19] Turner instances 'the Church, or the community of the disciples, and the passages which bear upon our Lord's mission to the Gentiles' as themes of great importance to the apostolic church which appear much less prominently in the teaching of Jesus. The presumption is that if these 'sayings of Jesus' were produced by the apostolic church, they would be fuller and more emphatic.

[20] *Historicity*, pp. 73–78 (our summary).

[21] *Ibid.*, p. 78.

hands of a Bultmann or of a Turner, rests on the assumption that the tradition is suspect, and that the burden of proof is on those who would maintain the authenticity of any given saying. The conditions of proof required may vary, but the approach is essentially the same.

Certain observations may be made on this approach:

(i) Both the basic approach and the details of its application can tell us more about the presuppositions of the exponents of this method than about the material under consideration. The basic approach reveals a sceptical attitude to the question of authenticity, such as we outlined above; the aim is to salvage at least a few sayings from the general suspicion which hangs over the tradition as a whole. Given such an attitude, the method is a valid one, but for the historicist, who does not share these presuppositions, the approach has no objective validity. It begs the question. The application of the twofold criterion is no less exposed to subjective elements. Thus the antitheses of the Sermon on the Mount, which are pronounced indubitably authentic because of the 'unheard-of implication of the saying',[22] could as well be rejected as a reflection of the anti-Jewish apologetic of the early church, created to establish the originality and authority of Jesus over against the scribes.[23] This contradiction cannot be resolved by the criteria in themselves, but only by the presupposed understanding of the character and teaching both of Jesus and of the early church. Thus these criteria can operate only within the presuppositions of the individual who uses them. They cannot be expected to produce agreement between those who are not agreed already.

(ii) The twofold criterion rests on a most improbable view both of Jesus and of the early church. It requires a Jesus who was utterly eccentric, in that he took nothing from his environment, never endorsed a proverb or maxim of Jewish wisdom, and, most unlikely of all, seldom if ever simply endorsed the teaching of the Old Testament. And it requires a church which was utterly unfaithful to its master's teaching, in that it hardly ever simply preserved and endorsed anything that he

[22] E. Käsemann, *op. cit.*, pp. 37–38.

[23] A good case can be made out for the exegesis which sees in all six antitheses a contradiction not of the Mosaic law, but of the scribal interpretation of it.

said, but altered and adapted it to such an extent that its teaching stands in sharp contrast with the few remaining genuine sayings of Jesus. Even Fuller is compelled to admit that 'these methods . . . yield no complete certainty, for on some points Jesus *could* have agreed with the post-Easter church . . . Jesus might also have quoted or used with approval Rabbinic teaching.'[24] What Fuller reluctantly concedes would seem self-evident to most readers of the New Testament.

(iii) Fuller's answer to the preceding criticism is that if the twofold criterion excludes much that may be the genuine teaching of Jesus, at least that which passes so stringent a test is likely to be a reliable minimum.[25] The production of such an indubitable, if limited, corpus of sayings of Jesus, if it can be achieved, is no doubt desirable, but it cannot be too strongly stressed that this corpus will represent, in the nature of the case, *not* the central message of Jesus, but that which was extraordinary, and which the church felt able to ignore. It is quite illegitimate to set up this minimum collection of sayings as enshrining the essential and characteristic teaching of Jesus, and to use this as a touchstone by which the authenticity of other sayings may be determined. This procedure would be legitimate only if there were reason to believe in the image, mentioned in the last paragraph, of an eccentric Jesus and an unfaithful church.

Yet this is how these criteria are generally used. Thus when, on the basis of these criteria, Bultmann pictures Jesus as an eschatological prophet, he may be right; but when he proceeds to reject sayings as 'not characteristic of Jesus' when they fail to enshrine this emphasis, he is certainly wrong. Bultmann's eschatological prophet is no more the whole Jesus than Harnack's liberal moralist. A half truth cannot be set up as the whole truth without resulting in untruth. Nor is this criticism confined to Bultmann; whatever portrait of Jesus may be isolated by such criteria may be reliable, but it will not be exhaustive, and will be characteristic only if the early church failed to perpetuate the essential teaching of its master, an assumption which requires more than bare assertion to carry any weight.

We conclude that such criteria *may* help us to affirm posi-

[24] *Current Study*, p. 41.
[25] *Ibid.*

tively the authenticity of certain unusual sayings, but they cannot legitimately be used negatively to exclude any saying. Even the less stringent criteria of Turner can provide confirmation for only a partial account of the teaching of Jesus; they provide no grounds on which other sayings can be pronounced unauthentic. The only justification for this is sheer scepticism, which involves a most unlikely view both of Jesus and of his followers.

V. THE PROPOSED APPROACH

Our criticisms of the sceptical approach to the Gospels are essentially twofold. (i) Methodologically, the use of the criteria of authenticity discussed above to exclude certain sayings as unauthentic is illegitimate; they inevitably produce a truncated, and therefore inaccurate, account of Jesus and his teaching. (ii) Historically, this approach assumes an unreliability and licence in the transmission of Jesus' sayings which is not in accordance with what may be known of tradition in the contemporary Jewish scene and in Christianity itself.[26]

As an alternative to this approach, we propose to start from the other end: not to assume the unreliability of the tradition, but to assume its essential reliability unless there are good reasons for questioning it.[27] This approach we believe to be a truer expression of 'historicist' principles than Turner's extension of the Bultmannian criteria. It is similar to what G. E. Ladd[28] calls 'Biblical Realism', the approach which aims

[26] Considerations of space have led to the omission of a long appendix to the original thesis in which the question of the reliability of the tradition of the sayings of Jesus was discussed. Without wishing to endorse the whole thesis of B. Gerhardsson's *Memory and Manuscript* (Uppsala, 1961), we feel that it is unrealistic to ignore the milieu of Palestinian Judaism, in so far as its character in the first century AD can be reconstructed, in assessing the likely character of the early Christian transmission of the sayings of Jesus. For this reason we feel that the approach of such British scholars as V. Taylor, T. W. Manson and C. F. D. Moule is better grounded in historical probability, not to mention factual evidence, than that of those German scholars who attribute to the disciples of Jesus a sublime disregard for what their Master actually said and did on earth.

[27] We are not, of course, arguing that the present order and arangement of the sayings should be accepted as original. But the evidence of a large-scale regrouping is no argument against the authenticity of the material thus rearranged.

[28] *Jesus and the Kingdom* (London, 1966), pp. xiii–xiv. Ladd's book is

primarily 'to interpret the gospels as they stand as credible reports of Jesus and his preaching'.

It may be objected that this approach is too credulous. Such charges are dependent on the presuppositions of those who make them, and it could be argued that the role ascribed by the 'interpretative' school to the early church in the formation of the tradition is no easier to believe. But what this approach does offer is at least the possibility of gaining a truly historical view of the teaching of Jesus. The sceptical approach can lead us neither to the Jesus of history, since it rejects much relevant material which it cannot prove to be unauthentic, nor to the Christ of early Christian faith, since it discounts all that is parallel to what the early church believed. Perhaps ours is a hazardous approach, but we believe that it is necessary if any progress is to be made towards an understanding of the teaching of Jesus; and we suspect that the element of hazard can be exaggerated.

The validity of this approach, and of the presuppositions on which it is based, may be tested by certain data which will emerge from our study.

(i) If the pattern of the use of the Old Testament which emerges from a study of the quotations and allusions attributed to Jesus is a consistent one, forming a coherent and credible whole, this will be an indication that it reflects the work of one mind.[29]

(ii) If this pattern presents not only consistency but originality, in comparison with other known uses of the Old Testament at the time, this favours more strongly the suggestion that we are confronted with the work of a single mind.

(iii) If in addition this pattern is found at any point to be different in content or emphasis from the use of the Old

---

built on a historicist approach to the Gospels, and provides a fine demonstration of the value of such an approach.

[29] This is J. A. Baird's test of 'internal continuity' (*The Justice of God in the Teaching of Jesus* (London, 1963), pp. 30–32). He believes that such consistency 'demands either a theory of apostolic agreement and deliberate concurrence beyond belief or a theory of verbal inspiration that outdoes the literalists. The law of parsimony would seem to demand a simpler answer: behind this unity stands Jesus of Nazareth, whose authentic mind has come through the exigencies of Gospel formation reasonably intact' (*ibid.*, pp. 30–31).

Testament in the preaching and writing of the early church, it will be hard to deny that it reflects the true teaching of Jesus, rather than that of the early church.[30]

(iv) The Old Testament quotations and allusions are susceptible of a test of authenticity not open to us for the other sayings, that of the text-form. If a saying embodies and depends on a text of the Old Testament which could not have been available to Jesus, it cannot be authentic. Specifically, if a saying is found to depend on the LXX version of an Old Testament passage, and could not have been derived from any known Semitic version of that passage, the presumption is that it is not a saying of Jesus.

The data for the first of these tests will be provided by the work as a whole; that for the second and third will emerge in the final chapter.[31] We turn now to the fourth, and proceed in our next chapter to a study of the text-form of the Old Testament quotations.

[30] These last two points constitute, of course, the twofold criterion of the school of Bultmann (and also J. A. Baird's test of 'internal discontinuity', *ibid.*, pp. 32–34). Here, however, they are suggested not as criteria able in themselves to determine the acceptance *or rejection* of certain sayings, but as confirmation of an authenticity already suggested on other grounds. So used, they are not open to the objections raised above (pp. 20–22) against their use by the school of Bultmann.

[31] See esp. below, pp. 222–226.

CHAPTER TWO

THE TEXT-FORM OF THE OLD TESTAMENT QUOTATIONS

It is generally agreed that Jesus spoke normally in Aramaic, and that his quotations of the Old Testament would therefore also normally be in that language. It has, however, been argued[1] that certain of the Old Testament quotations attributed to Jesus in the Synoptic Gospels depend on the LXX (or, in the case of Daniel, a version akin to Theodotion). The conclusion is drawn that these cannot be authentic words of Jesus, but must originate in a Greek-speaking milieu where the LXX was the version in common use.

This argument must, however, be used with care. It is clearly unrealistic to ask that the translator of Jesus' words from Aramaic into Greek should either be ignorant of the LXX or studiously avoid any assimilation to it. Where the LXX was a fair translation of the version quoted by Jesus, it would be natural for the Greek translator to use the LXX words familiar both to himself and to his readers. Sometimes this assimilation might be almost unconscious, from his memory of the LXX; at other times, especially in the case of longer and more formal quotations, the translator might be expected to look up the relevant passage in the LXX and transcribe that version exactly. B. M. Metzger gives a parallel in Rabbula's translation into Syriac of Cyril's *De Recta Fide*, in which the quotations from the Gospels are assimilated to the Syriac version.[2] Metzger suggests two possible reasons why assimilation to the LXX might *not*

[1] *E.g.* by T. F. Glasson, *ExpT* 69 (1957/8), pp. 213–215. *Cf.* R. H. Fuller, *The Foundations of New Testament Christology* (London, 1965), p. 19.

[2] B. M. Metzger, *ExpT* 65 (1963/4), p. 125. The same procedure is commonly followed in translations of modern works which quote from the Bible: see the Translator's Preface in, *e.g.*, G. Bornkamm, *Jesus of Nazareth* (ET London, 1960) or O. Cullmann, *The Christology of the New Testament* (ET London, 1959).

occur: (a) that the Greek translator did not remember the LXX exactly, or (b) that he was struck by a difference in meaning between the Aramaic text and the LXX, in which case he would render the Aramaic literally.[3]

The mere fact of LXX form in an Old Testament quotation ascribed to Jesus is therefore no argument against its authenticity. Such a conclusion could be drawn only when the LXX differs from known Semitic texts (both Hebrew and Targumic), and the text-form in the Gospels is that of the LXX.

But even this conclusion needs qualification. The LXX is full of minor differences from the Hebrew, addition of articles, change of tense or number, addition of explanatory words and glosses, *etc.* It would be unreasonable to demand that the translator should pedantically correct all these deviations to conform to the Aramaic version in front of him, *when nothing depended on the points of difference.* If, then, the LXX differs from the Semitic versions at a point which in no way affects the sense or the use of the quotation in its Gospel context, the fact that the Gospel version follows the LXX (where this is the case; it is by no means invariable, as we shall see) is again no proof that the quotation is not an authentic saying of Jesus. This argument can be admitted only in cases where the Gospel text follows the LXX against the Semitic versions *at a point which affects the use of the quotation by Jesus.* In other words, where the argument attributed to Jesus *depends on* a LXX text-form, then, and then only, can the text-form be admitted as an argument against the authenticity of the saying.[4]

[3] K. Stendahl (*The School of St. Matthew*, pp. 143ff.) attempts to assess the respective tendencies of the Synoptic writers to assimilate to the LXX. He finds the process well advanced in Mark, though a strong Semitic element remains in many of the quotations (see below, p. 37). Where Matthew takes over Marcan quotations the tendency is more marked, and in quotations deriving from Q there is little deviation from the LXX. The tendency in Luke is the same, though less obvious. In all three writers the tendency to assimilate to the LXX is greater when recording the sayings of Jesus than in editorial quotations (*ibid.*, p. 162). Stendahl's findings are, therefore, in accordance with what we have postulated as the likely method of a Greek translator.

[4] The above argument has been expressed in terms of translation from a written Aramaic source. If, as is quite likely, the Greek version was made from the Aramaic tradition at a stage when this was still oral, the argument is stronger still. Assimilation of a quotation orally received to the LXX would seem to be almost inevitable, except in a case where the argument depended on a text foreign to the LXX.

In order not to weary the reader with masses of linguistic detail, we have printed in an appendix our detailed survey of the text-form of the Old Testament quotations and allusions attributed to Jesus in the Synoptic Gospels.[5] In this chapter we shall simply summarize those findings, and indicate what light they throw on the question of authenticity.

We may divide the quotations and allusions into five groups from the point of view of their text-form, and it is under these five headings that they are considered in the appendix:

i. Those which agree with both the LXX and the MT;[6]
ii. Those which differ from both the LXX and the MT;
iii. Those which agree with the MT against the LXX;
iv. Those which agree with one text of the LXX against another;
v. Those which agree with the LXX against the MT.[7]

I. QUOTATIONS WHICH AGREE WITH BOTH THE LXX AND THE MT

These cases are far too numerous to detail. Nor would this be of any value for our purpose, as these passages can tell us nothing about the origin of the sayings involved. A study of the sixty-four quotations or allusions attributed to Jesus in the Synoptic Gospels which we regard as certain or virtually certain[8] reveals that in more than half of these cases the LXX is a fair translation of the MT, and the Gospel text follows the LXX (except that there are occasionally minor grammatical adjust-

[5] Appendix B, pp. 240–258.

[6] The use of the Massoretic Text as our authority for the Hebrew OT is not meant to suggest that the Hebrew text available to Jesus and the NT church was identical with our present MT. This is not the place to go into the intricacies of the textual criticism of the Hebrew OT, but current scholarship in this field, especially since the discovery of the Qumran texts, places a high value on the MT as a witness to the standard Hebrew text of the first century AD. At the risk of occasional oversimplification, we shall take it as a reliable indication of the Hebrew text available to Jesus except where there is evidence to the contrary.

[7] No account is taken of merely grammatical alterations necessitated by the insertion of the OT words into their NT context, unless these in some way affect the sense of the original.

[8] See above, p. 15, and below, Appendix C, pp. 259–263, for the classification of passages for this study. Classes A, B and C make up our sixty-four cases.

ments necessitated by the context). This is what our argument concerning the natural use of the LXX by a Greek translator would lead us to expect, and the LXX form can throw no light on the question of the authenticity of such sayings. This question will be raised only in those cases where the LXX and the MT differ.

II. QUOTATIONS WHICH DIFFER FROM BOTH THE LXX AND THE MT

Twelve such cases are considered in the appendix.[9] All contain some textual feature which differs from both the LXX and the MT (in most cases only a minor grammatical or stylistic variation), though in two cases the Lucan version is assimilated to the LXX, and in two further cases the New Testament wording, while different from other texts of the LXX, is found in LXX A.

That these were not necessarily entirely independent translations is shown by the fact that the departure from LXX and MT in Mark 4:12 is supported by the Targum of Jonathan, and the variation in Matthew 4:10 may also be explained by reference to the Targum of Onkelos. It is tempting to infer that this is evidence that the form of Jesus' original Aramaic saying is preserved in these two cases.

The least that may be said of these twelve passages is that they give the lie to any suggestion that the Old Testament quotations in the Synoptic Gospels are drawn entirely from the LXX. Indeed, they are sufficiently numerous, and sufficiently varied in character, to make us cautious of any attempt to discern a regular and standard procedure in selecting the text-form for the quotations. They bear all the marks of being what they purport to be, that is, records of a 'live' use of the Old Testament (as opposed to the products of a scholar's study), transmitted and translated by those familiar with the LXX, but with a reverence for their material sufficient to prevent a wholesale assimilation to the LXX. This impression becomes stronger as we proceed.

[9] See pp. 240–241.

III. QUOTATIONS WHICH AGREE WITH THE MT AGAINST THE LXX

Here too we examine in the appendix twelve cases from among our sixty-four certain or virtually certain quotations and allusions. In addition we consider nine cases of agreement with the MT against the LXX in allusions which are less certain; if in some of these no intentional allusion is admitted, they may still betray an underlying familiarity with the Semitic as against the Greek text in the original sayings. Finally, one further passage is mentioned in which a well-supported textual variant would yield a further case of a non-LXX quotation.[10]

In many of these passages the LXX form would have served to convey the allusion adequately, without altering the sense of Jesus' words, but the New Testament text prefers a Greek wording which is closer to the MT, and independent of the LXX. This suggests that these sayings arose independently of the LXX, and most likely in a Semitic milieu where the Hebrew Old Testament or an Aramaic version derived from it was in use. More significantly, in nine of the cases studied[11] the LXX could not have served as the basis for the allusion, either because it translates the Hebrew in a sense quite different from that taken up by Jesus, which would make the allusion meaningless, or, in one case, because the phrase alluded to is absent from the LXX. In such cases there can be little doubt that the allusion was originally made in a Semitic milieu, and that the original form of the saying of Jesus has resisted assimilation to the LXX even in the process of translation into Greek.

Summarizing the results so far, we may now say that of the sixty-four Old Testament quotations in the sayings of Jesus which may be regarded as certain or virtually so, twenty are to some degree independent of the LXX, and of these twenty, twelve are closer to the MT at this point. The addition of a further ten cases of likely or possible allusions to the MT against the LXX further strengthens the impression that it is wrong to speak of the Old Testament quotations in the sayings of Jesus as basically in LXX form. That a process of assimilation to the LXX is under way, both before the composition of the Gos-

[10] See below, pp. 242–245.

[11] Mk. 4:29; 11:15; 14:24; Mt. 6:11, 23; 11:10, 29; 13:41; Lk. 20:18.

pels and in the later textual tradition, is both clear and natural. But that these quotations originated in a Greek-speaking milieu, and from a LXX text, is clearly untrue. The remarkable fact is not the amount of assimilation to the LXX, but the amount that remains independent of it, indicating an original Semitic form of these sayings which has resisted alteration in the course of transmission at a considerable number of points.[12]

IV. QUOTATIONS WHICH AGREE WITH ONE TEXT OF THE LXX AGAINST ANOTHER

We have suggested that divergence from the LXX in the quotations attributed to Jesus may serve as evidence for the authenticity of these sayings, particularly when the text agrees with the MT against the LXX. This argument depends, however, on the assumption that we can speak meaningfully of 'the LXX' as a standard Greek text of the Old Testament used by the Christian church in New Testament times. This assumption has been challenged particularly by P. E. Kahle,[13] who postulated an original luxuriant variety of 'Greek Targums', which were gradually reduced to a standard LXX text. On this view, divergence from our present LXX text need not imply that the quotation concerned originated in a non-Greek milieu, and represents an *ad hoc* translation of a Hebrew or Aramaic original; it could as well indicate use of a Greek Targum different from that eventually standardized as the LXX, and now lost.

It would clearly be wrong to postulate a single LXX tradition without textual variation in the first century; the variants in the New Testament quotations, as well as in those by Philo and Josephus, are sufficient to prove that. But it is also clear that the New Testament shows a predominant agreement with a certain type of LXX text, best represented in codices A and Q and in the Lucianic revision. It used to be commonly said that such

[12] *Cf.* the conclusion of K. Stendahl (*op. cit.*, p. 146) that the recurrent Semitic features of the OT quotations in Mark seem 'to be a survival of that Aramaic form in which the words and deeds of Jesus were originally recounted'.

[13] *The Cairo Geniza*[2] (Oxford, 1959), pp. 209–264. Kahle's view has not found wide support; for a convenient summary of scholarly reaction see S. Jellicoe, *The Septuagint and Modern Study* (Oxford, 1968), pp. 59–63.

agreement is to be explained by A, *etc.* having been corrected to agree with the New Testament, but this explanation is not now generally accepted. It does not do justice to several cases in the New Testament (why, for instance, should LXX A of Zc. 13:7 be corrected at several points to agree with Matthew, but not in the striking variant πατάξω?), nor does it explain the agreement with the A text found in Josephus and Philo, as well as in most early Christian writers.

A study of the quotations within our field which agree with one text of the LXX against another[14] shows that in almost every case the New Testament favours the A type of text; the one clear exception is Mark 13:25, where the clause in question is absent from most MSS other than B. One must, of course, reckon with the possibility that A has been assimilated to the New Testament text, and where A stands alone this is often the most probable explanation. But, deciding each case on its own merits, our examination strongly supports the view that the New Testament writers used fairly consistently a Greek text which was close to that of LXX A, supported by Q and the Lucianic revision, and distinct from that of B and, to a lesser extent, א.

Thus, while we must certainly be cautious in attributing divergence from the LXX to *ad hoc* translation of a Semitic original, the evidence of the quotations studied suggests that this is a more likely explanation than that a lost 'Greek Targum' has been used. Our argument that a non-LXX text-form, particularly one which agrees with the MT, is evidence for the authenticity of an Old Testament quotation ascribed to Jesus, may therefore be allowed to stand. The consideration of textual variants within the LXX tradition has shown the need for caution in using this argument, but has not significantly detracted from its results.[15]

[14] See below, pp. 245–246.

[15] Of the quotations studied under headings II and III above, only two (Mt. 4:10 and Lk. 23:30, both in section II) would be eliminated by the recognition of A as a first-century Palestinian text; and in both these cases A stands alone, which throws it under strong suspicion of being corrected to the NT. In two further cases (Mk. 9:48; 10:19) one point of 'divergence from the LXX' is in agreement with A, but a second point shows independence of all LXX texts. The conclusion reached on pp. 29–30 above is, therefore, not affected.

V. QUOTATIONS WHICH AGREE WITH THE LXX AGAINST THE MT

The classes of text-form so far studied have tended to *support* the authenticity of the sayings concerned, as independent of the LXX and probably originating in a Semitic form. We turn now to cases where the text-form may be expected to provide evidence *against* the authenticity of the quotations as sayings of Jesus.

In order to assess the validity of such an argument, we must bear in mind a point which we have made above.[16] We maintained that it is only to be expected that someone translating Aramaic quotations into Greek would tend to assimilate his translations to the Greek version with which he was familiar. Thus where the LXX was a fair translation of the Aramaic, he would naturally use it, and even where there were points of difference between the LXX and the Aramaic, it would be pedantic to expect him to retain scrupulously the peculiarities of the Aramaic where nothing depended on the points of difference. Only where the use of the quotation *depends on* its LXX form, and could not have been based on the Hebrew or Aramaic text, can text-form be admitted as evidence that the quotation was first made in a Greek-speaking milieu.

We have accordingly divided the quotations and allusions under this heading into two groups:[17] *a.* those where the difference from the MT clearly in no way affects the sense of the passage, or its application; *b.* those where it may be argued that the use of the Old Testament passage attributed to Jesus depends on its LXX form. We shall then treat separately *c.* the allusions in the Synoptic versions of Jesus' Apocalyptic Discourse, which have been the subject of a special study in this connection.

a. Quotations where the LXX *form does not affect the sense or the application of the passage*

This first group comprises ten passages.[18] All contain only very minor discrepancies from the MT, mere questions of grammar

[16] Above, pp. 25–26.

[17] We have included in this section all relevant passages, even where the allusion is not a certain one.

[18] See below, pp. 247–248.

and style, sometimes turning on as little as a single letter in the Hebrew. In the case of Mark 10:8 it seems virtually certain that the LXX has in fact preserved the original Hebrew text, and Mark 10:19 displays a rich variety in the textual tradition, both Semitic and Greek. Further, five of these ten quotations, while they differ from the MT at one point, differ from the LXX at another. All this suggests caution. But in any case the differences involved are so insignificant that they can give no guidance as to whether Jesus could have made these quotations: the appropriateness of the quotation in no case depends on the point of difference.

b. Quotations whose appropriateness may be said to depend on their LXX *form*

The five quotations and allusions in this group bring us to the heart of the question of authenticity, and so, while full discussion is printed in the appendix,[19] a brief résumé of the argument in each case is given here.

Mark 7:6–7. Jesus' quotation of Isaiah 29:13 includes the phrase 'in vain' (μάτην), which is peculiar to the LXX. But a study of the argument of Jesus in which this quotation occurs shows that nothing is made of the idea that the Pharisees worship *in vain;* the whole point is that they place their human tradition above the commandment of God, and this point is made as clearly by the Hebrew text as by the LXX, perhaps even more clearly. Thus the original quotation could properly have been made from the Hebrew text, and does not depend on the LXX for its force.

Mark 9:12. The allusion to Malachi 3:23–24 (EVV 4:5–6) uses the LXX verb ἀποκαταστήσει in the sense 'restore', whereas the MT verb which it translates is והשיב, 'cause to turn back'. In context it refers to 'turning the hearts of fathers to their children', and the Hebrew text does not carry the sense of 'restoring all things' which the New Testament allusion requires. But the words in question are part of Jesus' quotation of what *the scribes* teach. Whatever the source of this well-attested scribal interpretation of Malachi, there is no reason why Jesus should not have known and quoted it. The source of Jesus' allusion is not the LXX, but Jewish teaching.

[19] Below, pp. 248–254.

Matthew 21:16. In Psalm 8:3 עז, which normally means 'strength', is translated by the LXX as αἶνον ('praise'), and is so quoted by Jesus to defend the children who praise him. However, the psalm speaks of God using what comes out of the mouths of children to silence his enemies, and this sense would be very appropriate to the use Jesus makes of it, even if עז could not bear the meaning 'praise'. In fact a study of the use of עז in the Old Testament indicates that this meaning is not improbable in such a context.

Luke 4:18. The phrase τυφλοῖς ἀνάβλεψιν ('recovering of sight to the blind') in the quotation of Isaiah 61:1 follows the LXX wording, whereas the corresponding MT phrase לאסורים פקח־קוח is normally taken to mean 'the opening of the prison to those who are bound' (so RSV). פקח, however, is regularly used of opening *eyes*, never of opening doors, *etc.*, so that the LXX translation may well reflect the intention of the mixed metaphor in the Hebrew. In any case, either metaphor would have been equally appropriate to Jesus' use of the quotation as a prediction of his work of deliverance; there is no question of its use *depending on* the LXX phrase.

Matthew 11:5. The same phrase in Isaiah 61:1 is in question here, and the same argument that the LXX may in fact reflect the intention of the Hebrew is therefore relevant. In this case the allusion is a composite one to Isaiah 35:5 and 61:1, and in the former passage the idea of healing for the blind is unquestionably present in both MT and LXX. Again, therefore, the Hebrew Old Testament is a totally adequate source for the allusion attributed to Jesus.

Thus the five passages studied under section *b.* provide no case of a quotation which is shown by its text-form to have originated in a Greek-speaking milieu. In some cases the LXX version may sharpen the point of Jesus' saying, but in no case does the appropriateness of the quotation depend on it.

c. The Apocalyptic Discourse

T. F. Glasson has argued that the LXX form of several Old Testament allusions in Mark 13 is evidence 'that genuine words of Jesus have been expanded with material from elsewhere'.[20]

[20] 'Mark xiii and the Greek Old Testament', *ExpT* 69 (1957/8), pp. 213–215. *Cf.* J. A. T. Robinson, *Jesus and His Coming* (London, 1957), pp. 56–57.

We therefore discuss in the appendix [21] the various allusions in the Apocalyptic Discourse (including, for completeness' sake, passages peculiar to Matthew 24 and to Luke 21) which are said to follow the LXX against the MT. All are allusions rather than formal quotations.

The results of our examination may be summarized in the form of four objections to Glasson's argument: (i) Only in the case of Mark 13:14 is the New Testament wording, at least in Mark, an exact quotation of that of the LXX (or Thdt). Even where the exact LXX wording would have been appropriate, it is not used (*e.g.* in Mark 13:25, *ἔσονται πίπτοντες* for *πεσεῖται*, *αἱ δυνάμεις αἱ ἐν τοῖς οὐρανοῖς* for *αἱ δυνάμεις τῶν οὐρανῶν*, *οἱ ἀστέρες* for *τὰ ἄστρα*, *etc.*); this weighs against the theory of a deliberate composition from the LXX. Whereas Matthew has tended to assimilate more closely to the LXX, the earlier version of Mark is further from it. The motion seems to be *towards* the LXX, not from it. (ii) The supposed allusion is in two cases very doubtful (Mk. 13:7, 13), and in two others cannot be restricted to the single Old Testament passage adduced (Mk. 13:27; Lk. 21:24). (iii) The supposed difference in meaning between the LXX and the MT is in most cases either non-existent, or only discernible by one who demands the type of literal translation that might be produced by a computer. The only cases of real discrepancy discovered were in Mark 13:27 and Luke 21:24, *i.e.* precisely those points at which Glasson had illegitimately restricted a composite allusion to a single Old Testament passage. (iv) The most important objection is that Glasson has started from a false premise. It seems that LXX form in itself is to him evidence of a Greek origin. The only evidence he would admit, apparently, of a Semitic origin would be divergence from the LXX in favour of the MT, such as we did in fact discover in Mark 13:24. But merely to state this position unambiguously is to see its weakness. We are asked to assume that a Greek translator, who knew his LXX, should deliberately refrain from using its terminology, and produce a pedantically literal translation of the Aramaic, even where the LXX rendered the sense adequately.[22] If we may assume that the Greek trans-

[21] Below, pp. 254–258.

[22] *Cf.* Glasson's words on Mk. 13:19: 'The Greek words represent quite fairly the meaning of the Hebrew; but *they are not the only words possible* . . .

lator was aware that the words concerned were an allusion to the Old Testament (and the LXX form would be a remarkable coincidence if this were not so!), the obvious method of ensuring that his Greek readers saw the point would be to use the familiar LXX version, in passing allusions no less than in extended quotations.

Glasson's argument, then, rests on a most unlikely view of the technique of translation. His case would be supported if at any point the New Testament definitely followed the LXX *against* the MT, where the appropriateness of the allusion depended on the LXX form. But such cases we have failed to discover. The text-form of the Old Testament allusions is no argument against any part of the Apocalyptic Discourse as the authentic teaching of Jesus.

VI. CONCLUSIONS

Our aim has been to discover Old Testament quotations attributed to Jesus where the text-form of the quotation is that of the LXX, where the latter differs materially from any known Semitic text, and where the use of the passage attributed to Jesus depends on this difference. Only in such cases can the text-form be admitted as evidence that the saying is unauthentic.

We have considered five passages outside the Synoptic versions of the Apocalyptic Discourse where this has been or could be maintained, and have found that in no case is it impossible, or even improbable, that Jesus' use of the quotation could be based on the MT or some related Semitic text. In some of these cases the LXX provided a more forceful or clear-cut expression of the thought involved, but in no case did it give rise to an argument or application which could not have arisen from the Hebrew text.[23] It is hardly to be expected that a translator, finding that the LXX expressed the idea even more clearly than the Hebrew, should studiously avoid using it. The evidence with regard to the Apocalyptic Discourse has

---

and this close agreement supports the suggestion that parts of this Marcan section rest upon the Greek OT.' (Our italics.)

[23] The case of Mk. 9:12 is particularly instructive, for there an argument which appeared at first sight to be based on the LXX was found in fact to be a scribal interpretation evolved in a purely Semitic milieu.

also been considered, and we have come to the same conclusion, that here too there is no evidence for a Greek origin for the sayings ascribed to Jesus.

On the other hand, we have noted at several points divergence from the LXX, often in the direction of the MT. These cases are far more significant than those where the agreement is with the LXX. For whereas we might expect a translator to conform the text to the familiar version in the language into which he is translating, we could hardly expect the producer of an original composition in Greek to introduce gratuitous Semitic features. Agreement with the MT against the LXX is, therefore, an indication of the Semitic origin of the sayings in which it occurs; and such agreement is in fact as frequent as agreement with the LXX against the MT. Indeed, with regard to Mark, T. W. Manson concludes, 'When Mark records our Lord's quotations from the Old Testament they usually agree with the Hebrew or the Targum against the LXX in cases where the witnesses to the Old Testament text are divided.'[24] Our investigation has confirmed that, of cases where the Old Testament witnesses are divided, Mark follows the MT and/or the Targums against the LXX in more than half.[25] When we bear in mind the strong and increasing tendency in the Synoptic writers to greater conformity with the LXX,[26] these survivals of a Semitic original are doubly significant.

We conclude, then, that whereas in no case does the evidence of the text-form demand a Greek origin for the Old Testament quotations attributed to Jesus, there are many cases where a Semitic origin seems certain. That is as far as the argument from text-form will allow us to go, but it strongly suggests that it would be rash to deny the authenticity of any saying of Jesus, especially of those involving quotation from the Old Testament, unless there is evidence to the contrary in that particular case. When there is no such evidence, we may with confidence assume that the sayings of Jesus have been faithfully preserved.

[24] *BJRL* 34 (1951/2), p. 318.

[25] Agreement with MT and/or Targums against LXX: 4:12; 8:38; 11:15; 12:30; 13:8; 13:24; 14:24. Agreement with LXX against MT and Targums 7:6–7; 9:12; (10:8); 12:1; 13:25. Divergences in *both* directions: 4:29; 10:19.

[26] See above, p. 26 n. 3.

CHAPTER THREE

TYPOLOGICAL USE OF THE OLD TESTAMENT

I. INTRODUCTION

The last twenty-five years have seen a significant increase in interest in typology.[1] The subject is still, however, rendered unnecessarily complex by a lack of agreement on the proper use of this term. It is necessary, therefore, before considering what is here described as Jesus' typological use of the Old Testament, to indicate what meaning is being given to the term, and the justification for it.

An analysis of the use of τύπος and its derivatives, even in the New Testament alone, is beyond the scope of this study.[2] K. J. Woollcombe[3] concludes that 'the word τύπος invariably has the primary meaning of "model" or "pattern" '. Typology will, therefore, be concerned with persons, events, *etc.* which are viewed as models or patterns for other persons, events, *etc.*

With specific reference to Christian typological use of the Old Testament, F. Foulkes[4] proposes the following definition: 'We may say that a type is an event, a series of circumstances,

[1] On the subject of NT typology see the following: L. Goppelt, *Typos* (Gütersloh, 1939); A. Richardson, *Christian Apologetics* (London, 1947), pp. 188–198; R. Bultmann, 'Ursprung und Sinn der Typologie als hermeneutischer Methode', *TLZ* 75 (1950), pp. 205–212; J. Daniélou, *Sacramentum Futuri* (Paris, 1950; ET *From Shadows to Reality*, London, 1960); G. von Rad, 'Typological Interpretation of the Old Testament' (1952; ET in *Interpretation* 15 (1961), pp. 174–192); G. W. H. Lampe, 'Typological Exegesis', *Theology* 56 (1953), pp. 201–208; E. E. Ellis, *Paul's Use of the Old Testament* (Edinburgh, 1957), pp. 126–139; G. W. H. Lampe and K. J. Woollcombe, *Essays on Typology* (London, 1957); F. Foulkes, *The Acts of God* (London, 1958); R. P. C. Hanson, *Allegory and Event* (London, 1959), pp. 65–73; W. Eichrodt, 'Is Typological Exegesis an Appropriate Method?' in *Essays on Old Testament Interpretation*, ed. C. Westermann (1960; ET London, 1963), pp. 224–245; A. T. Hanson, *Jesus Christ in the Old Testament* (London, 1965).

[2] It is also largely irrelevant: see below, p. 77 n. 120. For such an analysis see K. J. Woollcombe, *op. cit.*, pp. 60–65.

[3] *Ibid.*, p. 65. [4] *Op. cit.*, p. 35.

or an aspect of the life of an individual or of the nation, which finds a parallel and a deeper realization in the incarnate life of our Lord, in His provision for the needs of men, or in His judgments and future reign. A type thus presents a pattern of the dealings of God with men that is followed in the antitype, when, in the coming of Jesus Christ and the setting up of His kingdom, those dealings of God are repeated, though with a fulness and finality that they did not exhibit before.'

This statement, with which our agreement will become apparent in what follows, indicates the conviction which lies at the root of New Testament typology. It is that there is a consistency in God's dealings with men. Thus his acts in the Old Testament will present a pattern which can be seen to be repeated in the New Testament events; these may therefore be interpreted by reference to the pattern displayed in the Old Testament. New Testament typology is thus essentially the tracing of the constant principles of God's working in history, revealing 'a recurring rhythm in past history which is taken up more fully and perfectly in the Gospel events'.[5] The New Testament writers are aware not only of being involved in this continuous process, but also of being witnesses of the climax and culmination of it.

This same conviction is already apparent in the Old Testament. The prophets frequently looked forward to a 'repetition of the acts of God'.[6] The Exodus especially provided a model for prophetic predictions both of acts of deliverance within the national history of Israel, and of the more glorious eschatological work of God. Following the lead of the prophets, Jesus and the New Testament writers saw in the coming of Jesus a parallel and yet greater redemption.

Typology is thus to be distinguished from two other methods of applying the Old Testament: the appeal to prediction, and allegory.[7]

A type is not a prediction;[8] in itself it is simply a person, event, *etc.* recorded as historical fact, with no intrinsic reference

[5] G. W. H. Lampe, *Essays*, p. 27.

[6] This last phrase is the heading of the first chapter of Foulkes' monograph (*op. cit.*), where the OT basis of typology is fully treated.

[7] *Cf.* K. J. Woollcombe, *op. cit.*, pp. 40–42.

[8] *Cf.* for the distinction W. Eichrodt, *loc. cit.*, p. 229. See further, below, p. 83.

to the future. Nor is an antitype the fulfilment of a prediction; it is rather the re-embodiment of a principle which has been previously exemplified in the type. A prediction looks forward to, and demands, an event which is to be its fulfilment; typology, however, consists essentially in looking back and discerning previous examples of a pattern now reaching its culmination.

On the other side, typology is not allegory.[9] It is grounded in history, and does not lose sight of the actual historical character of the events with which it is concerned. Typology may be described as 'the theological interpretation of the Old Testament history'.[10] Allegory, on the other hand, has little concern with the historical character of the Old Testament text. Words, names, events, *etc.* are used, with little regard for their context, and invested with a significance drawn more from the allegorist's own ideas than from the intended sense of the Old Testament. No real correspondence, historical or theological, between the Old Testament history and the application is required.

In contrast with these two methods of applying the Old Testament, typology appears as a distinct discipline. It is essentially the recognition of a correspondence between New and Old Testament events, based on a conviction of the unchanging character of the principles of God's working, and a consequent understanding and description of the New Testament event in terms of the Old Testament model. The idea of fulfilment inherent in New Testament typology derives not from a belief that the events so understood were explicitly predicted, but from the conviction that in the coming and work of Jesus the principles of God's working, already imperfectly embodied in the Old Testament, were more perfectly re-embodied, and thus brought to completion. In that sense, the Old Testament history pointed forward to Jesus. For the Old Testament prophets the antitypes were future; for the New Testament writers they have already come.

Our discussion of the difference between typology and

[9] *Cf.* W. Eichrodt, *loc. cit.*, pp. 227–228; G. W. H. Lampe, *Essays*, pp. 30–35. The distinction has been attacked by J. Barr, *Old and New in Interpretation* (London, 1966), pp. 103–111.

[10] F. Foulkes, *op. cit.*, p. 35.

allegory uncovers one feature essential to true typology: that is a real correspondence between type and antitype. This correspondence must be both historical (*i.e.* a correspondence of situation and event) and theological (*i.e.* an embodiment of the same principle of God's working). The lack of a real historical correspondence reduces typology to allegory, as when the scarlet thread hung in the window by Rahab is taken as a prefiguration of the blood of Christ;[11] both may be concerned with deliverance, but the situations and events are utterly dissimilar. On the other hand, the lack of a real theological correspondence destroys what we have seen as the very basis of typology, the perception of a constant principle in the working of God.[12] This is not, of course, to demand a correspondence in every detail of the two persons or events, but simply that the same theological principle should be seen operating in two persons or events which present a recognizable analogy to each other in terms of the actual historical situation. Only where there is both a historical and a theological correspondence is a typological use of the Old Testament justified.

It is therefore clearly essential to typology that a correct exegesis of the Old Testament text should be made; only so can a real correspondence of later events with those there recorded be established. Typology may, indeed must, go beyond mere exegesis. But it may never introduce into the Old Testament text a principle which was not already present and intelligible to its Old Testament readers. Sound exegesis, and a respect for the sense of the Old Testament text thus discovered, will prevent typology from degenerating into allegory.

But while strict exegesis is a prerequisite of typology, it is not correct to describe typology itself as a method of exegesis. Exegesis is the establishment of the true meaning and intention of the original text; it is 'drawing out from a passage what the human author understood and intended as he wrote'.[13] As such it is distinct from interpretation or application, which are concerned with what is seen in the text, and what use is made of it, by later readers.[14] If every type were originally intended

[11] 1 Clem. 12.7.

[12] A. T. Hanson (*op. cit.*, pp. 162–163) rightly distinguishes between 'parallel situation' and 'typology'.

[13] F. Foulkes, *op. cit.*, p. 39.

[14] *Cf.* for the distinction E. Fuchs, *Studies of the Historical Jesus* (ET

explicitly to point forward to an antitype, it might be correct to class typology as a style of exegesis. But this is not the case. There is no indication in a type, as such, of any forward reference; it is complete and intelligible in itself. Thus Deuteronomy 6–8 makes perfect sense as it stands, as a historical record, and a correct exegesis need make no mention of types and antitypes; there is no indication that the author had any such intention. Yet Jesus used the passage typologically.[15] Was this then illegitimate? If typology were merely a question of exegesis this would be so, for the author surely had no such intention. But typology is not exegesis, but application. It is theological reflection in the light of later events which sees the experiences of the people of Israel as an apt parallel to those of Jesus in the wilderness, and interprets the latter in terms of the former, as an exemplification of the same principles. The story of Jonah is likewise quite intelligible in itself, with no forward reference to 'a greater than Jonah'; the typological use of Jonah rests on theological reasoning, not on the Old Testament author's intention. It is a matter of application, not of exegesis.[16]

Thus the decision on whether a given use of the Old Testament in the New is typological or an appeal to prediction will reduce itself to a question of Old Testament exegesis. If a forward reference was intended in the Old Testament (even if, as in the Royal Psalms, there is a primary reference to a contemporary figure or event[17]), we are not concerned with typology, but with the appeal to prediction. Clearly border-line cases will arise. The use of the covenant theme is an example. Where the New Testament speaks of 'the blood of the covenant', this may fairly be classed as typology, for the reference is apparently to Exodus 24, a passage which is a simple historical account of the covenant ceremony, with no future reference. But when the

London, 1964), pp. 84–87. W. Eichrodt (*loc. cit.*, pp. 241–243) argues against this terminological point, and would describe typology as exegesis, which for him is virtually equivalent to 'exposition', and so includes application. It makes for clarity, however, if 'exegesis' is restricted to (in Eichrodt's words) 'the bringing out of that which lies in the text itself'.

[15] See below, pp. 50–53.

[16] *Cf.* below, pp. 68–69 on Is. 6:9–10; 29:13, neither of which had any forward reference, but both of which are taken explicitly as predictions of the reactions of Jesus' contemporaries, on a typological principle.

[17] For the eschatological reference of such passages see below, pp. 85–86.

New Testament speaks of 'the new covenant', whether simply by the use of these words, as in 1 Corinthians 11:25, or by explicit quotation, as in Hebrews 8:8ff., the reference is clearly to Jeremiah 31:31ff., a direct prediction of the new covenant. Here, then, we have the appeal to prediction. Jeremiah was, of course, thinking typologically when he framed his prophecy; it is he, rather than the New Testament writers who refer to his words, who has made the typological application in this case. To press the distinction to the point of mutual exclusion is clearly unrealistic, but the example serves to illustrate the principle on which this study of Jesus' typology is compiled.

We must beware of limiting typology to a small number of recognized types. We are not dealing with a homogeneous group of Old Testament passages which one could label 'typical', but with a theological conviction on the part of the New Testament writers, manifested in their use of the Old Testament. The method is fluid, sometimes less and sometimes more explicit;[18] it will not always be easy to decide whether a given passage is an example of typology, or a mere illustration, or quotation of a general maxim culled from the Old Testament. Our concern is not with a rigid catalogue of Old Testament types, but with the practical application of the conviction that God works in a consistent manner, and that in the coming of Jesus his Old Testament acts are repeated and consummated. This is New Testament typology.

II. TYPES OF JESUS

Our next section will bear more directly on the *work* of Jesus. Here we are concerned with his typological application of the Old Testament to himself, his status and experiences. These he saw foreshadowed both in individuals in the Old Testament history, and in the people of Israel as a community.

a. Individuals as types of Jesus

(i) *Jonah* (Mt. 12:39–41; Lk. 11:29–30, 32; *cf.* Mt. 16:4). This is probably the most obvious example of typology attributed to

[18] *Cf.* E. E. Ellis, *Paul*, p. 134; what he writes there of Paul is as true of the other NT writers, and of Jesus himself.

Jesus.[19] The crucial verse, Matthew 12:40, is commonly rejected as later 'Christian midrash', which introduces a typological interest foreign to Jesus' original intention. We maintain, however, that it represents the true intention of the 'sign of Jonah', and is most probably authentic. The arguments are set out in an excursus.[20]

The commonly advocated exegesis, which sees the 'sign of Jonah' as consisting in his preaching, is dependent on the rejection of Matthew 12:40, verse 41 being then taken as the explanation of verse 39. Quite apart, however, from the probable authenticity of verse 40, this exegesis is open to the objection that Jewish use of the book of Jonah was focused entirely on chapters 1–2, so that a reference to Jonah would inevitably be interpreted of his miraculous deliverance, not of his preaching.[21] J. Jeremias also points out[22] that preaching would hardly constitute a 'sign', and that the future tense which appears in Luke 11:30 as well as in Matthew 12:40 precludes a reference to his present preaching.

It seems then that even without Matthew 12:40, the point of the reference to Jonah must lie in his miraculous deliverance, regarded as a type of the resurrection of Jesus. Matthew 12:40 makes the correspondence explicit. The transition to the preaching of Jonah and the repentance of the Ninevites is not a *non sequitur*: Jonah was a 'sign' to the Ninevites in that he appeared as one delivered from death. It was the knowledge of this which attested his preaching and caused their repentance.[23] The point of the comparison with Jonah lies, therefore, in 'the authorization of the divine messenger by deliverance from death'.[24] Jesus' preaching, which his hearers are rejecting, will

[19] It is recognized as such even by R. Bultmann, *TLZ* 75 (1950), p. 210, and is the only case of typology recognized in the Synoptic Gospels by A. T. Hanson, *op. cit.*, p. 175.

[20] Excursus 1, pp. 80–82.

[21] See P. Seidelin, *ST* 5 (1951), pp. 119–131.

[22] *TDNT* III, p. 409.

[23] So J. Jeremias, *TDNT* III, p. 409, and *ibid.*, n. 26; S. Amsler, *L'Ancien Testament dans l'Église* (Neuchatel, 1960), p. 88. The same connection is implied in Justin, *Dial.* 107–108. P. Seidelin, (*loc. cit.*, pp. 121–122) argues that the probability or otherwise of the Ninevites' knowing of Jonah's deliverance would not occur to the Jews, and therefore must not affect our exegesis.

[24] J. Jeremias, *TDNT* III, p. 409.

in due course be attested by a still greater deliverance; therefore their condemnation will be the greater (verse 41).

Verses 40 and 41 of Matthew 12 thus introduce two separate, though connected, points of historical correspondence between Jonah and Jesus. In verse 40 the correspondence lies in the 'imprisonment' of both men, for the same length of time, in a situation from which no deliverance could naturally be expected, and in their deliverance by the supernatural work of God; in verse 41 it is in their preaching of repentance. At other points there is contrast rather than correspondence, in that Jonah was 'imprisoned' as a punishment for disobedience, and as the beginning of his effective ministry, which led to the repentance of his hearers, whereas Jesus' death and resurrection were the culmination of a ministry of utter obedience, but one which met with little acceptance. But typology does not depend on equivalence at every point, and Jesus' argument establishes the correspondence in what was, for the Jew, the essential point of the story of Jonah.[25]

The theological correspondence, the repeated principle of God's working, lies in the sending of a preacher of repentance, whose mission is attested by a miraculous act of deliverance. As God sent Jonah to the Ninevites, so Jesus is sent to the Jews of his day. The typology thus places Jesus in the succession of God's prophetic messengers to men. Now, in the sending of a 'greater then Jonah' (verse 41), this long-continued method of God's working has reached its climax, and in a greater act of deliverance God will accredit this supreme call to repentance. Nineveh had repented at the preaching of Jonah; Jesus' hearers are thus challenged to do likewise. But the antitype is greater than the type; failure to repent will, therefore, incur a greater condemnation than that which Nineveh's repentance averted.

(ii) *Solomon* (Mt. 12:42; Lk. 11:31). The use of the story of Solomon and the Queen of Sheba is exactly parallel to the use of that of Jonah and the Ninevites, both in form and purpose. There seem to be two points: (a) the response of Gentiles to God's Old Testament messengers must put to shame the impenitence of Jesus' Jewish hearers, and (b) the presence of

[25] See P. Seidelin, *loc. cit.*, p. 130.

something greater[26] than Jonah or Solomon renders their guilt yet greater. A typological element is not essential to the argument, but it is suggested both by the clearly typological use of Jonah in the previous verses, and by the formula 'something greater than Jonah (Solomon) is here', which captures exactly the idea of repetition on a higher plane which we have seen to be essential to typology. The appropriateness of such typology in the case of Jonah has been demonstrated. In the case of Solomon we have a son of David, proverbial for wisdom, to whom Jesus corresponds as the greater Son of David and the wisest of teachers. The principle of God's working seen in both cases is his sending of a royal teacher to win the allegiance of men. Perhaps the future response of the Gentiles is not absent from Jesus' mind. The typological element is not explicit, but the close connection of the allusion to Solomon with that to Jonah suggests that it is not absent.[27]

(iii) *David* (Mk. 2:25–26; Mt. 12:3–4; Lk. 6:3–4). Jesus' defence of his disciples' alleged violation of the Sabbath by citing the story of David and the shewbread is not simply an appeal to precedent, claiming that since David once broke the law, and Scripture did not condemn his action, therefore any legal requirement may be set aside. This would be both inadequate reasoning, and inconsistent with Jesus' scrupulous attitude to the law as witnessed elsewhere in the Gospels. Nor is there any explicit repudiation of the Pharisees' interpretation of the law of the Sabbath. It is a question of authority. Mark 2:28 claims that Jesus has the right to regulate Sabbath observance. The appeal to the example of David therefore has the force: 'If David had the right to set aside a legal requirement, I have much more.'[28] The unexpressed premise is 'a greater than David is here': indeed the parallel argument in Matthew 12:5–6 introduces an equivalent formula.

[26] πλεῖον; the neuter perhaps lays the emphasis on Jesus' work rather than his person, but that the reference is to him is clear. *Cf.* (on the parallel formula in Mt. 12:6) B. Gärtner, *The Temple and the Community in Qumran and the New Testament* (Cambridge, 1965), pp. 115–116.

[27] *Cf.* S. Amsler, *op. cit.*, pp. 88–89; writing of the use of Jonah and Solomon, he speaks of 'the connection established by Jesus between the revelatory events of the old covenant and himself, involving at the same time resemblance and progression'.

[28] So S. Amsler, *op. cit.*, p. 88; B. Gärtner, *op. cit.*, p. 116.

This argument from the authority of David to the greater authority of Jesus is best explained by an underlying typology.[29] If David, the type, had the authority to reinterpret the law, Jesus, the greater antitype, must have that authority in a higher degree. Without the idea of the superiority of Jesus to David (or at least his equality in status), the argument is a *non sequitur*, and that superiority (or equality) is best established by a typological relationship. When so much of Jewish Messianic expectation was based on a David-typology, the conclusion seems warranted that Jesus the Messiah sees David as a type of himself, and thus claims a status equal to or above that of David.

(iv) *The Priesthood* (Mt. 12:5–6). This Old Testament allusion, though not directly concerned with an individual, may be considered here as it is directly parallel to the one just discussed. Again Jesus' authority to modify the law is established by an argument of the *a fortiori* type: if the Old Testament priests had the right to 'profane the Sabbath', how much more has Jesus the right to interpret the Sabbath law. Here, however, the assumption of Jesus' superiority to the Old Testament pattern, on which again the argument depends,[30] is explicit; 'something greater than the temple is here'. The typological element is thus more explicit here than in the case of David. It is the beginning of the typology which the Epistle to the Hebrews develops so fully, in which the Old Testament cultic institution and its officers are seen as 'symbolic for the present age', 'a shadow of the good things to come'.[31] The principles of mediation and reconciliation with God demonstrated in the Old Testament cult find their antitype and fulfilment in Jesus, the mediator of the new covenant.

(v) *Elisha* (Mk. 6:35ff.; Mt. 14:15ff.; Lk. 9:12ff.). The narrative of Jesus' feeding of the five thousand bears many resemblances to Elisha's miraculous feeding of a hundred men with twenty loaves (2 Ki. 4:42–44), not only in the wording,

[29] So A. Richardson, *An Introduction to the Theology of the New Testament* (London, 1958), p. 126.
[30] *Cf.* further, B. Gärtner, *op. cit.*, pp. 115–116.
[31] Heb. 9:9; 10:1.

which would be evidence of the Evangelists' desire to point out the parallel, but in the nature and manner of the act itself. The presumption is that Jesus was consciously re-enacting on a vastly greater scale the miracle of Elisha.[32] If so, a typological element in Jesus' use of the Old Testament story is probable. Again the note of the superiority of the antitype is in evidence, in that whereas Elisha fed a hundred men with twenty loaves, Jesus fed five thousand with five. Elisha was a mighty prophet of God, but Jesus claims to be a mightier. As in the case of Jonah, Jesus claims a continuity with the status of the Old Testament prophet, but at the same time manifests himself as the culmination of the prophetic line.

(vi) *Elijah and Elisha* (Lk. 4:25–27). The application of the stories of Elijah and Elisha to Jesus' practice is not explicitly typological; it could be just a matter of quoting precedent. Yet their function in Jesus' defence against the presumed objection that he was neglecting those who had the first call on him (verse 23) depends on what is, as we have seen, the basic idea behind typology, that the principles of God's working are constant. God had sent Elijah and Elisha to the aid of a Phoenician and a Syrian respectively, when they could have found ample scope for similar work among their own people. So now he was sending Jesus to work outside his own town of Nazareth. The pattern is repeated, and Jesus, as God's messenger, stands in a position analogous to Elijah and Elisha. There is in this case no implication of superiority, but the typological use of Elisha just considered encourages us to see a typological way of thought behind the choice of these two Old Testament examples.[33] The implication is clear, and it is the same as that which we have already seen in the references to Jonah and Elisha, that Jesus stands in the line of the prophets through whom God's purpose has been accomplished. It is this that justifies his unpopular course of action.

[32] 'The striking coincidence of the circumstances under which the commands of Jesus and Elisha were uttered – the hungry crowd, the small supply of food, the surprised question of the servant and the disciples, the multiplication of the loaves, and the superabundance with some left over – demands that Jesus' choice of these particular words was a conscious allusion to this OT passage' (R. H. Gundry, *op. cit.*, p. 36, on Mt. 14:16).

[33] *Cf.* S. Amsler, *op. cit.*, p. 89.

(vii) *Isaiah* (Mk. 4:12; Mt. 13:13; Lk. 8:10). We shall argue below[34] that this application by Jesus to his own day of a prophecy which had already been fulfilled in the experience of Isaiah and his hearers, is based on a typological equivalence between the rejection of Isaiah's message by his contemporaries and the Jewish failure to accept the teaching of Jesus. There is, however, the further implication of an analogy between the prophet Isaiah and Jesus. Both were sent by God to a rebellious people, and their preaching produced not understanding and repentance, but a greater blindness. Again we see God's working repeated; and again we see Jesus as standing in line with the true prophets of God.

Obviously not all the above can be claimed as clear examples of typology. In some cases the analogy of a parallel passage, or of another reference to the same Old Testament figure in a more explicitly typological vein, encourages us to see a typological significance where we might otherwise not have been justified in postulating it. But through the examples given the twin themes of correspondence and fulfilment (including the idea of the superiority of Jesus to the Old Testament figure) seem to exhibit a consistent pattern which is the essence of typology.

It is interesting that the Old Testament persons whom we have reason to believe Jesus saw as types of himself fall into the three categories classically combined as a summary of the saving work of Christ, viz. prophet, priest and king. This is not accidental. For it was on these three classes that the Messianic hope both of the Old Testament itself and of later Judaism was based. These were the three classes who in the Old Testament performed a mediatorial function between God and his people, and thus constituted types of the future Mediator. It is to these, therefore, that Jesus looks for the 'pedigree' of his mediatorial work. In him the three classes come together, and the types find their fulfilment.

An interesting case of typology not specifically relating to Jesus himself, but closely connected, may be mentioned here. In Mark 9:13b[35] Jesus states that what was done to John the

[34] P. 68.

[35] For Mk. 9:12–13a see below, pp. 91–92, 155.

Baptist, who is here identified with Elijah *redivivus* of Malachi 3:23–24, was written about him. Malachi contains no prediction of the persecution, let alone the death, of Elijah *redivivus*, who is an authoritative, commanding figure; and there is no other prediction of the return of Elijah. How then could it have been written about him that he was to suffer? It seems that the answer lies in typology.[36] The prediction of Malachi was based on a typological idea: one was to come who would re-embody the spirit and work of Elijah, who would stand to Elijah as antitype to type. Jesus, therefore, goes behind the explicit prediction to the typology which underlies it, and draws out the corollary that the persecution of Elijah must be re-enacted in the antitype; so the fate which was intended for Elijah (1 Ki. 19:2, 10, 14) had overcome Elijah *redivivus*. So seriously does Jesus take the necessity for a repetition of the pattern, that he can class the experience of the type as equivalent to a prediction of that of the antitype. So John the Baptist, the antitype, must suffer, and had suffered, what was written of Elijah, the type.

b. Israel as a type of Jesus

(i) *The temptation narrative* (Mt. 4:1–11; Lk. 4:1–13).[37] The passages of Scripture with which Jesus answers the three temptations (Dt. 6:13, 16; 8:3) are drawn from a passage where Moses, at the close of the forty years of wandering in the desert, addresses Israel on the threshold of the promised land, calling them to a more whole-hearted devotion and obedience to God, and a trust in his care and provision for them. While each verse quoted might be seen as an appropriate expression of a moral principle which happened to come to Jesus' mind, the fact that the choice was in all three cases made from this single small section of the Old Testament suggests that the

[36] *Cf.* H. B. Swete, *The Gospel according to St. Mark*[3] (London, 1909), p. 194.

[37] For a similar account to the following see G. H. P. Thompson, *JTS* 11 (1960), pp. 1–12; also J. A. T. Robinson, 'The Temptations', *Theology* 50 (1947), pp. 43–48, reprinted in his *Twelve New Testament Studies* (London, 1962), pp. 53–60 (references below are to the latter publication). More fully, B. Gerhardsson, *The Testing of God's Son*, chapters 1–4 (Lund, 1966) interprets the whole temptation narrative as a 'Christian midrash' based primarily on Dt. 6–8.

passage was especially in Jesus' mind at the time, as a prefiguration of his own experience. He was learning the lessons which God had intended Israel to learn in the desert.

It is to be noticed that here, if anywhere, we are in touch with the true self-estimation of Jesus. The narrative can hardly have come from anyone except himself, and it shows him not in public debate, but alone with the tempter. His use of Deuteronomy here is, therefore, no mere teaching device, but reflects his own basic conception of his status and ministry. And it is in typological terms: he not only wished to be seen, but saw himself, as Israel, tested and taught in the desert as God's 'son' Israel had been.[38]

This exegesis is confirmed by the very considerable parallels between the situation of Jesus and that of Israel in the desert. Both are times of hardship and testing, preparatory to the undertaking of a special task (the conquest of the promised land, and the ministry of Jesus). Both suffer hunger, a hunger deliberately inflicted by God to teach a lesson.[39] The forty days of Jesus' fast reflects the forty years of Israel's wandering. A study of the context of the verses quoted by Jesus reveals further echoes.[40]

The principle involved is in each case one of 'testing'.[41] In each case the one tested was the 'son of God' (Mt. 4:3, 6, and Dt. 8:5, *cf.* Ex. 4:22).[42] In each case God tested his son (the one fresh from the deliverance from Egypt, the other just commissioned for his redeeming work in baptism), to prove

[38] Some have seen in the forty days' fast a parallel to the similar fast of Moses at Sinai, and so see Jesus here as the new Moses rather than Israel (*e.g.* J. Dupont, *NTS* 3 (1956/7), pp. 295–298). It is possible that such an idea was in the mind of the Evangelists, though even this is doubtful (see W. D. Davies, *The Setting of the Sermon on the Mount* (Cambridge, 1964), pp. 45–48); it certainly does not appear in the recorded words of Jesus.

[39] So Dt. 8:3, to which Jesus refers.

[40] For a detailed study to this effect see J. Dupont, *loc. cit.*; note esp. his isolation of verbal and situational echoes of Dt. 8:2–4 in the Synoptic accounts (*ibid.*, pp. 288–289).

[41] *Cf.* the stated purpose of Jesus' period in the desert, *πειρασθῆναι ὑπὸ τοῦ διαβόλου* (Mt. 4:1), and of the wanderings of Israel, *ὅπως ἂν . . . ἐκπειράσῃ σε* (Dt. 8:2, the previous verse to that quoted by Jesus; *cf.* also 8:16).

[42] *Cf.* B. Gerhardsson, *Testing*, pp. 21–22, 54–56. Also J. A. E. van Dodewaard, *Biblica* 36 (1955), pp. 487–488. Gerhardsson (*ibid.*, pp. 19–35) throws much light on the connection between sonship and testing in Deuteronomy.

his loyalty, and to teach him to trust and obey and worship God alone, in preparation for his special task.

The correspondence is seen in more detail in each of Jesus' three quotations, especially as seen in relation to their Old Testament context.

The first temptation is generally seen as a suggestion that Jesus should test his supposed sonship, and at the same time satisfy his hunger, by attempting a miracle. This may, indeed, be involved. Jesus' reply, however, is not concerned with the misuse of miraculous power, nor with doubt of either the reality of his sonship or God's provision. It picks on just that lesson which Israel's hunger had been intended to teach them, that physical food is not the most important thing, but rather the reception of, and obedience to, the word of God (Dt. 8:2–3). This, then, is for him the essence of the temptation, and this lesson he, like Old Testament Israel, must learn, if he is to be worthy of the title 'Son of God'.

In the second temptation (following the Matthean order) the testing of the reality of Jesus' sonship may again be involved, but it is not explicit in Jesus' answer. Still less is there the suggestion that the spectacular effect of an uninjured fall from the pinnacle of the Temple would be a quick road to power; neither the temptation nor the reply supports such an exegesis. The temptation is to test God to see whether he will prove true to his promise in the Old Testament. Deuteronomy 6:16 furnishes a most appropriate reply, for it is not only a command not to test God, but specifically a command not to test God as they had tested him at Massah. The reference is to Exodus 17:2–7, when the people, demanding water, and threatening to stone Moses, 'put the Lord to the proof (נִסִּתֶם, hence מסה) by saying, "Is the Lord among us or not?" ' Jesus likewise is tempted to force God's hand to see whether he really is with his Son, and will meet his need as he has promised.[43]

The third temptation is to achieve power by the worship of God's rival. Old Testament Israel, too, was confronted by rival claimants to worship, and in Deuteronomy 6:13–15 God demanded an undivided allegiance to himself. Again, 'what

[43] *Cf.* J. A. T. Robinson, *Twelve New Testament Studies*, pp. 54–56. On the significance of the Massah episode and its relevance to the temptation of Jesus see B. Gerhardsson, *Testing*, pp. 28–31, 60–61.

was wrong for God's "son" Israel is wrong for God's Son Jesus'.[44]

Jesus then saw himself as God's son, undergoing prior to his great mission as Messiah the testing which God had given to his 'son' Israel before the great mission of the conquest of Canaan. Israel then had failed the test; now, in Jesus, was found that true sonship which could pass the test, and be the instrument of God's purpose of blessing to the world which Old Testament Israel had failed to accomplish. 'The history of Israel is taken up by him and carried to its fulfilment.'[45] The antitype, as always, is greater than the type. Old Testament Israel had failed; Jesus must succeed.[46]

(ii) *Predictions of the resurrection.* The Gospels record several predictions by Jesus of his death and resurrection,[47] all of which contain a reference to the resurrection as occurring 'after three days'[48] or 'on the third day'.[49] In two of these cases[50] the word 'must' introduces the prediction, implying that an Old Testament authority lies behind the statement;[51] in two further cases[52] the prediction is explicitly attributed to the Old Testament. It seems clear, then, that Jesus found in the Old Testament ground for the prediction that (i) he would rise from the dead, and (ii) this would be on the third day, or after three days. On what Old Testament passages could these predictions have been based?

For the prediction of the resurrection itself there is no single clear Old Testament source. Such passages as Psalm 16:10–11; 118:17–18 and Isaiah 52:13; 53:10–11 have been suggested, and other 'resurrection' passages from the Psalms and Job

[44] A. H. McNeile, *The Gospel according to St. Matthew* (London, 1915), p. 40.

[45] J. Dupont, *loc. cit.*, p. 304.

[46] *Cf.* more fully, J. A. T. Robinson, *Twelve New Testament Studies*, pp. 59–60.

[47] Mk. 8:31 (Mt. 16:21; Lk. 9:22); Mk. 9:31 (Mt. 17:23); Mk. 10:34 (Mt. 20:19; Lk. 18:33); Lk. 24:7; 24:46. (This last is, of course, *post eventum.*) Note also his opponents' citations of predictions apparently of the resurrection, supposed to have been uttered by Jesus: Mk. 14:58 (Mt. 26:61); Mk. 15:29 (Mt. 27:40); Mt. 27:63.

[48] Mk. 8:31; 9:31; 10:34.

[49] Mt. 16:21; 17:23; 20:19; Lk. 9:22; 18:33; 24:7; 24:46.

[50] Mk. 8:31 (Mt. 16:21; Lk. 9:22); Lk. 24:7.

[51] See below, p. 126.

[52] Lk. 18:31; 24:46.

might be added, but none is convincing as *the* source of Jesus' expectation.

For the third day, on the other hand, the field is more restricted. Only three passages are suggested with any plausibility:

Jonah 2:1 (EVV 1:17). If, as we shall argue,[53] Matthew 12:40 is authentic, there can be no doubt that Jesus saw Jonah's experience as a type of his own. This, then, is at least a partial basis for his prediction.

2 Kings 20:5. The prediction that Hezekiah will be healed of his illness, and go up to the house of God 'on the third day' could be typologically applied to Jesus. Since, however, the correspondence would be minimal, and Jesus nowhere else makes any reference to Hezekiah, this is unlikely.

Hosea 6:2. Hosea 6:1–3 gives the words of a half-repentant Israel, resolved to return to God in the belief that, 'After two days he will revive us; on the third day he will raise us up, that we may live before him.' The hope is of a national restoration in the near future, this being the sense of the idiom 'on the third day'.[54] Verbally, this verse is the nearest parallel the Old Testament offers to Jesus' predictions of his resurrection, and its influence on them is widely accepted.[55]

If Hosea 6:2 were the only Old Testament background, we would be justified in concluding that Jesus' reference to 'the third day' was in the same idiomatic sense that it bears in Hosea, viz. 'in the near future'. Since, however, as we have argued, Jonah 2:1 was also in Jesus' mind in this connection, a literal three-day period seems to be intended, as there is no evidence that the longer and more precise phrase 'three days and three nights' was ever used in this idiomatic way. Jesus, expecting on the basis of Jonah 2:1 a resurrection after literally three days, would naturally, while recognizing the idiomatic sense of Hosea 6:2, see the literal applicability of 'on the third day' to the resurrection which Jonah 2:1 had already led him to expect.[56]

[53] See below, Excursus 1, pp. 80–82, also above, pp. 44–45.

[54] *Cf.* V. Taylor, *The Gospel according to St. Mark* (London, 1952), p. 378, and 2 Ki. 20:5 above.

[55] *Cf.* C. H. Dodd, *Scriptures*, p. 77; B. Lindars, *op. cit.*, pp. 60–61; M. Black, *ZNTW* 60 (1969), pp. 4–5, 8.

[56] B. Lindars (*op. cit.*, pp. 60–64) does not allow for the influence of

We may then see the Old Testament source of Jesus' prediction of his resurrection in three days as a combination of Jonah 2:1 with Hosea 6:2.[57] The application of Jonah 2:1 to himself has been discussed above; it remains to discuss the principles underlying the use of Hosea 6:2.

As in the temptation narrative, a reference to the people of Israel is here applied to Jesus himself. The hope of national restoration in the near future is applied to his speedy restoration to life. The assumption is that in Jesus the destiny of Israel finds its completion, and in his resurrection the hopes of Israel's restoration are to be fulfilled. 'The resurrection of Christ *is* the resurrection of Israel of which the prophet spoke.'[58] It is not so much that Israel was a type of Jesus, but Jesus *is* Israel.

Again, as in the temptation narrative there is the implication of the superiority of Jesus to the Old Testament Israel. Hosea 6:1–3 records a profession of repentance which in verses 4ff. is declared to be of no value. The hope of verse 2 that this 'repentance' will result in restoration was not fulfilled. Before many years had passed Samaria had fallen, and the Northern Kingdom had no 'resurrection'. But where Old Testament Israel had failed, Jesus would succeed; their groundless hope of 'resurrection' would come to fruition in him. We may then see here the twin ideas of correspondence (in the hope of 'resurrection') and superiority or fulfilment (in that what Israel had groped towards but failed to find, Jesus is to achieve), which are the basis of typology. But the principle on which the application is made is less that of typology proper, viz. a recurrent pattern, than an idea of *continuity*. Jesus *is* Israel, and in his resurrection Israel's destiny is fulfilled.

(iii) *Psalms of suffering and vindication.* We are concerned here with four psalms to which Jesus alluded as prefiguring his

---

Jonah 2:1, and so concludes that not only 'the third day' but also the 'raising up' would be as figurative in Jesus' expectation as it was in Hosea, *i.e.* that Jesus meant a national restoration in the near future. This thesis would be invalidated by the recognition of Jonah 2:1 as a source of Jesus' resurrection predictions. It is in any case hard to reconcile with the context in which these predictions occur, where there is no word of national fortunes, but only of his own imminent betrayal, suffering and death.

[57] *Cf.* J. W. Doeve, *Jewish Hermeneutics in the Synoptic Gospels and Acts* (Assen, 1954), p. 149.

[58] C. H. Dodd, *Scriptures*, p. 103.

own experience, viz. 22, 41, 42–43, and 118. The first three of these are psalms of the righteous sufferer, cast in the form of an individual lament, through which breaks the hope of deliverance by God; the last alternates between an individual and a corporate form, and celebrates a recent deliverance from distress. Our inclusion of them at this point depends on the belief that all, to some degree, represent the experiences of the community of Israel as a whole.

Psalm 118 is generally regarded as a national thanksgiving, the speaker even in the section expressed in the singular being Israel as a nation,[59] or at least an individual, *e.g.* the king, speaking in the name of the nation.[60] The stone of verse 22 is Israel, and those blessed in verse 26 are the worshippers rejoicing over their national deliverance.

The other three psalms, however, are expressed entirely in individual terms. But Psalm 118 shows that the use of individual language is no warrant for limiting the reference of a psalm to the author's own experiences. The psalms do not allow any rigid distinction between the individual and the corporate, and the cultic use of many of them depends on the corporate interpretation of individual language. The psalms of the righteous sufferer may properly be regarded as 'national psalms of lamentation in the I-form'.[61] Even if their original intention was individual, their incorporation in the national collection indicates that a corporate interpretation was felt to be appropriate.[62] We therefore class these four psalms together as ones in which Jesus saw his experiences prefigured not only in those of unknown psalmists, but in those of the nation.

Psalm 22 (Mk. 15:34; Mt. 27:46, quoting verse 2 (EVV verse 1)). Whatever the full theological implications of Jesus'

[59] *Cf.* C. A. Briggs, *The Book of Psalms* (Edinburgh, 1906–1907), vol. 2, pp. 402ff.; E. J. Kissane, *The Book of Psalms* (Dublin, 1953–1954), vol. 2, p. 216.

[60] *Cf.* S. Mowinckel, *The Psalms in Israel's Worship* (ET Oxford, 1962), vol. 1, pp. 38, 180. For a more strictly individual interpretation, see A. Weiser, *The Psalms*[5] (ET London, 1962), pp. 724ff.

[61] This is the title of a section in S. Mowinckel, *Psalms*, vol. 1, pp. 225ff., which includes Ps. 22.

[62] *Cf.* further on Ps. 22, A. F. Kirkpatrick, *The Book of Psalms* (Cambridge, 1892–1901), p. 114; on Ps. 42–3, S. Mowinckel, *Psalms*, vol. 1, pp. 219, 242. Even the strongly individual Ps. 41 is classed by Briggs (*Psalms*, vol. 1, p. 361) as a 'national' psalm.

'cry of dereliction', it is clear that he saw the suffering of the psalmist (or of Israel) as an apt parallel to his own. It is perhaps too bold to deduce a full-blown typological interpretation from a momentary cry of agony, but that the words of Psalm 22 came into Jesus' mind at all at such a time may well indicate that he recognized in the suffering described in this psalm a pattern which must be repeated in his case. The amazingly close correspondence of this psalm with the suffering of Jesus in the crucifixion can hardly have escaped him, any more than it escaped later Christian thought.

Psalm 41 (Mk. 14:18, alluding to verse 10 (EVV verse 9)). The Synoptic Gospels do not contain an explicit quotation of this verse, as does John 13:18. But the idea of betrayal by a close friend is close to that of the psalm, and the wording in Mark and Matthew at least is reminiscent of this verse. The Marcan *ὁ ἐσθίων μετ' ἐμοῦ* ('one who is eating with me') is probably an intentional allusion to the words אוכל לחמי (LXX *ὁ ἐσθίων ἄρτους μου*), but even if this verbal allusion is seen as a gloss,[63] it seems likely that this psalm was in Jesus' mind, and influenced the wording of his prediction of the betrayal. This is further supported by the clause 'as it is written of him' (Mk. 14:21; Mt. 26:24; *cf.* Lk. 22:22, 'as it has been determined') referring to the betrayal.[64] The psalm describes a sad experience of unnatural treachery, and in this Jesus sees a prefiguration of his betrayal by a close friend and disciple. The unnamed sufferer of the psalm, whether Israel or an individual, was a type of a more righteous man, whose suffering was to be greater.

Psalm 42–3 (Mk. 14:34; Mt. 26:38, alluding to the refrain 42:6, 12 (EVV verses 5, 11), 43:5). The clause *περίλυπός ἐστιν ἡ ψυχή μου* ('my soul is very sorrowful') is probably drawn from the words מה־תשתוחחי נפשי (LXX *ἵνα τί περίλυπος εἶ, ψυχή;*).[65] As in the case of Psalm 22:2, this need be no more than the selection of an appropriate form of words from the Old Testa-

[63] *Cf.* V. Taylor, *Mark*, p. 540.

[64] *Cf.* A. George in *À la Rencontre de Dieu*: mémorial A. Gelin (Le Puy, 1961), pp. 304–305.

[65] *Cf.* V. Taylor, *Mark*, pp. 552–553; A. George, *loc. cit.*, p. 305. The infrequent occurrence of *περίλυπος* supports this derivation: see R. Bultmann, *TDNT* IV, p. 323; *cf.* R. H. Gundry, *op. cit.*, p. 59 and n. 3, *ad loc.*

ment to express Jesus' feelings. But the nature of the psalm, with its rise from a despairing agony of mind to a calm assurance of God's continuing care, so exactly suits Jesus' state of mind at Gethsemane that it is not unlikely that he saw the psalm as a prefiguration of his own experience.

In each of these three cases, then, Jesus saw his sufferings in terms of those of the psalmists, or, as they may well be interpreted, those of Israel as portrayed in the psalms. In each case the psalm describes a vivid experience of the speaker in the present, or the recent past; there is no suggestion that general maxims or principles are being expressed. What Jesus applies to himself, therefore, are not truths of general application, but specific incidents and experiences. Nor is there any suggestion that the psalms are intended to be predictive. This means that, unless these allusions are mere catchwords with no further implications, a view which the high relevance of the Old Testament context in each case renders improbable, we are left with a typological principle as the most likely explanation of Jesus' use of these three psalms.

Psalm 118 (Mk. 12:10–11; Mt. 21:42; Lk. 20:17, quoting verses 22–23 (verse 22 only in Luke); Mt. 23:39; Lk. 13:35 quoting verse 26). Verse 22 is couched in the form of a proverbial saying. Here, then, there might be justification for seeing in Jesus' quotation no more than the statement of a general truth, that God favours and delivers the oppressed, or that the despised may make good later. But it is clearly the fortunes of Israel specifically which are the subject of the psalm, and the language suggests that a specific recent deliverance is in mind (see especially verse 23). Again, therefore, a typological reference best explains Jesus' application of the psalm to himself. As Israel, scornfully oppressed by her enemies, had been delivered by God, so must Jesus, after being oppressed and rejected by the authorities, prove the eventual victor. Jesus recapitulates the history of Israel.

Verse 26a is cited by Jesus as the greeting with which he will eventually be received by those who now reject him. In the original context it is the greeting of the priests in the Temple to the worshippers as they arrive; it is part of the processional 'dialogue' of the psalm. The blessing is therefore applied to the same subject as the 'stone'-proverb in verse 22, viz. the nation, rejoicing over a great deliverance by God. The application of verse 26 to himself by Jesus is therefore parallel to his use of verse 22. He is to repeat the experience of Israel. He too must come, victorious and exalted, to Jerusalem, to receive the greeting and homage of its religious authorities, as in his vindication they recognize the perfect antitype of God's vindicated people, the fulfilment of God's purposes for Israel.[66]

None of these uses of the psalms exhibits a strict typology. But the similarity of the four psalms chosen, each of which describes the suffering and subsequent, or expected, deliverance of one who may, with varying degrees of probability, be seen to represent Israel, suggests that in this pattern of suffering and deliverance Jesus saw a prefiguration of his own experience, both in the general pattern, and in some of the details, notably of Psalms 22 and 41. God's dealings with his chosen people were now finding their counterpart, their true realization and fulfilment, in the life, death, and vindication of Jesus.[67] If these cases do not exhibit a developed typology, they at least illustrate that conception of his place in the purpose of God on which a true typology must rest.

In this section two related principles of application have come to light: (i) typology proper, in which the history of Israel is seen as a pattern which is repeated, though on a higher plane, in the life of Jesus (the clearest example of this was the use of Deuteronomy 6–8 in the temptation narrative); (ii) the conception of Jesus as himself *being* Israel, taking over Israel's destiny, and carrying it to its intended fulfilment (this we saw especially in the use of Hosea 6:2). In the first category the basic idea is one of correspondence, or repetition; in the second it is one of continuity. But while distinguishable in theory, these two ideas are closely related, and it is seldom possible to isolate one from the other. This twofold principle of interpretation will reappear in our next section, where we consider Jesus' application of Old Testament passages about Israel to his disciples. Them too he sees as Israel, possessing the privileges

[66] This renders unnecessary the suggestion (see below, p. 97 n. 50) that Jesus' use of v. 26 was due to a Messianic use of the title *ὁ ἐρχόμενος*, which would involve an uncharacteristic disregard of the OT context.

[67] *Cf.* S. Mowinckel, *He That Cometh* (ET Oxford, 1956), pp. 11–12.

and responsibilities of the Old Testament people of God, and carrying their destiny to its fulfilment.

III. TYPES OF THE DISCIPLES OF JESUS

Several of the allusions already considered imply that the people of Israel has found its fulfilment in Jesus. But Jesus gathered round himself a band of disciples to receive his message and to continue his work. Did he then see them as the continuing people of God, the true Israel, in whom the hopes and the destiny of the Old Testament Israel were to find fulfilment? In this section we consider the evidence for such a view in Jesus' application of Old Testament passages to his disciples.[68]

We are not concerned here simply with the obvious fact that Jesus transferred much of the teaching of the Old Testament, both theological and moral, wholesale into the Christian community. To indulge in an extended demonstration of the way Jesus' life and teaching were founded on the ideas and even phrases of the Old Testament would be superfluous. The validity of the Old Testament for his disciples as for the other Jews is assumed without question, however unusual Jesus' interpretation of its requirements may be. Thus the Sermon on the Mount, though it contains few formal quotations from the Old Testament, is so permeated with both Old Testament words and ideas that hardly any part of its teaching is not to some degree modelled on, or at least paralleled in, the Old Testament.[69]

This fact does not in itself demand a view of the disciples as the true Israel; it may simply reflect a belief in the *universal* validity of the Old Testament law for all men at all times, not

[68] A valuable treatment of this subject is to be found in G. E. Ladd, *op. cit.*, pp. 239–257. P. Richardson (*Israel in the Apostolic Church* (Cambridge, 1969), pp. 48–69) argues against such an idea in the teaching of Jesus, but takes no account of the implications of the OT allusions; he also gives insufficient attention to Jesus' predictions of the fall of Jerusalem and their significance.

[69] The Beatitudes, for instance, contain only one explicit allusion to the OT (Mt. 5:5, alluding to Ps. 37:11), but never move far from OT ideas. Thus Mt. 5:3–4 echoes Is. 61:1–3 (see below, pp. 134–135); for Mt. 5:6 *cf.* Is. 55:1ff.; Je. 31:25; for Mt. 5:7 *cf.* Jb. 22:9–10; Pr. 21:13; for Mt. 5:8 *cf.* Ps. 24:4.

exclusively for the Jewish and Christian communities. But the cases to be discussed will not bear such an interpretation; they demand the view of the Christian community as the true people of God, with the privileges, the responsibilities, and the destiny of Israel. In the light of these passages, therefore, it is not unlikely that such an idea underlies also the wholesale transference of Old Testament teaching to the nascent church.

In his teaching Jesus indicates in several places that the true people of God is not to be found in the Jewish leaders of his day, but in the Christian community.[70] This was, for instance, the purpose of the parable of the tenants (Mk. 12:1–9), where the men who refused the overtures of God's messengers, and finally of his Son, are rejected and replaced by other tenants.[71]

This idea appears strikingly in *Matthew 15:13*, 'Every plant which my heavenly Father has not planted will be rooted up', which refers to the Pharisees, whose hostile reaction to his teaching has just been reported. The terminology is probably a conscious allusion to the Old Testament figure of Israel as God's plant (Is. 61:3; *cf.* Is. 60:21). Jesus is therefore denying that the Pharisees belong to God's true people; they were not planted by God.[72] To be a Jew is no longer automatically to be one of God's people. The Jewish leaders have no privileged position; they are not Israel.

The complementary idea appears in *Matthew 5:48*, where the disciples have taken over this privileged position. The words *ἔσεσθε οὖν ὑμεῖς τέλειοι ὡς ὁ πατὴρ ὑμῶν ὁ οὐράνιος τέλειός ἐστιν* ('You, therefore, must be perfect, as your heavenly Father is perfect') are based on Leviticus 19:2 קדשים תהיו כי קדוש אני יהוה אלהיכם (LXX *ἅγιοι ἔσεσθε ὅτι ἐγὼ ἅγιος, κύριος ὁ θεὸς ὑμῶν*) and the parallel formulae (Lv. 11:44, 45; 20:7, 26). It was the distinctive mark of Israel as the people of God that they were set apart for him, and must reflect his character. Leviticus 20:26 makes the point particularly clearly: 'You shall be holy to me; for I the Lord am holy, and have separated you from the peoples, that you should be mine.'

[70] *Cf.* G. B. Caird, *Jesus and the Jewish Nation* (London, 1965), pp. 16–17.

[71] *Cf.* W. D. Davies, *Sermon*, p. 290; he classes the parable among 'those passages in which Matthew makes clear that the Old Israel has been rejected in favour of a new community'. *Cf.* also G. E. Ladd, *op. cit.*, p. 245.

[72] *Cf.* R. V. G. Tasker, *The Old Testament in the New Testament*[2] (London, 1954), pp. 30–31.

Israel's likeness to God was to be the result and mark of their unique status. This status Jesus attributes to his disciples;[73] *they* are God's chosen people, so now *they* must be perfect.[74]

In *Matthew 5:5* a promise to Israel is applied to the disciples. The allusion is to Psalm 37:11, a psalm which draws a contrast between the wicked and the righteous. Though the wicked may prosper for a time, in due course 'the meek shall possess the land' (ענוים יירשו־ארץ; LXX οἱ πραεῖς κληρονομήσουσιν γῆν). The contrast is a familiar one, and it is recognized that the righteous meek and the wicked oppressors are more than merely moral categories. The ענו or עני is the pious Israelite, oppressed by those who do not fear God, *i.e.* probably other nations. Some hold that the ענוים are a party of pious Israelites, the wicked being the opposing party within Israel, but S. Mowinckel[75] argues strongly for their identification with the nation as a whole. Here then Jesus is deliberately applying to his disciples a promise made to Israel. (If Mowinckel's arguments were not accepted, the promise would have been to the pious remnant within Israel, which would make the application perhaps even more significant.) The disciples are the ענוים, the people of God, and it is to them that the destiny predicted of the ענוים now applies.

This leads us on to a group of allusions to Old Testament predictions of the future gathering together of the dispersed people of God. This common theme of Old Testament prophecy is seen by Jesus as about to be fulfilled in the gathering of Gentile believers into the Christian community, the true Israel.[76]

[73] See Mt. 5:1–2 for the audience.

[74] R. H. Gundry (*op. cit.*, p. 73) suggests that the use of τέλειος rather than ἅγιος may be due to the influence of Dt. 18:13.

[75] Originally in his *Psalmenstudien* I (Kristiania, 1921), pp. 113ff., and now in *Psalms*, vol. 1, pp. 30, 229; vol. 2, p. 251. *Cf.* BDB, p. 776.

[76] For Jesus' intention that Gentiles should be included in his kingdom, see T. W. Manson, *Jesus and the Non-Jews* (London, 1955); J. Jeremias, *Jesus' Promise to the Nations* (ET London, 1958). Both discuss Jesus' restriction of his own mission and that of his disciples during his lifetime to Israel. Manson concludes that this was to prepare a Jewish church which should then become the missionary force to bring in the Gentiles, while Jeremias sees the inclusion of the Gentiles as a purely eschatological expectation, of which Jesus' mission to Israel and his vicarious death were necessary conditions.

Matthew 8:11–12 (Lk. 13:28–29). The allusion is to an Old Testament idea rather than to one particular passage. Jesus predicts a gathering of Gentiles into the kingdom of God, in place of the rejected Jews.[77] The passages which may be reflected in his wording, with its geographical details, fall into two groups: (i) Descriptions of a gathering of *Israel* from all quarters of the earth (Ps. 107:3; Is. 43:5–6; 49:12); (ii) Predictions of the worship of God *by Gentiles* in all parts of the earth (Is. 45:6; 59:19; Mal. 1:11).[78] If group (ii) were the source of Jesus' saying, there would be no typology involved, nor any idea of the rejection of the Jews and their replacement by an Israel drawn from all nations. This last idea is, however, clearly implicit in Jesus' saying. None of the above passages in themselves suggests this idea, but it could have been drawn from a typological application of group (i); the Old Testament gathering of Israel is to find its New Testament counterpart and fulfilment in the gathering of the Gentiles into the kingdom, the true Israel. This suggestion is strengthened by two observations: (a) the idea of coming or being gathered in is present only in the first group of passages; (b) the fourfold geographical division of the Lucan version ('from east and west, and from north and south') is paralleled only in Psalm 107:3 and Isaiah 43:5–6, the former being the closer verbal parallel. (*Cf.* also the inclusion of the north in Is. 49:12.)

There seems then to be good reason for concluding that the source of the wording of Matthew 8:11 lay in descriptions of the gathering of Israel back into their own land in Old Testament times. (Ps. 107:3 describes a gathering which is already in the past; Is. 43:5–6 and 49:12 look forward to a future gathering, but one which was fulfilled, at least partially, in Old Testament times, in the return from the Exile.) As Israel had been gathered from foreign lands in Old Testament times, so the true Israel was now to be gathered from all the world.

Mark 13:27 (Mt. 24:31). As is shown below,[79] this verse

[77] *Cf.* J. Jeremias, *Promise*, p. 51. For the authenticity of the saying see *ibid.*, pp. 56, 62.

[78] Predictions of the coming of the Gentiles to Jerusalem, such as Is. 2:2–3; 60:3–4, might have contributed to the *idea* expressed in Jesus' saying, but they do not present the verbal parallel in the specification of east and west which is found in the passages cited.

[79] Pp. 256–257.

contains a composite allusion to Deuteronomy 30:4 and Zechariah 2:10 (EVV verse 6). Both passages are explicitly concerned with a regathering of dispersed Israel. The former promises that when God drives his disobedient people into exile, and they repent, he will restore them to their land. The latter is a call to Zion (*i.e.* those who remained in Babylon after 538 BC) to 'flee from the land of the north'.[80] In applying these passages to the gathering of the Gentile church in the age succeeding the fall of Jerusalem,[81] Jesus is again taking up Old Testament predictions which had been, partially at least, fulfilled in Old Testament times, and regarding that partial Old Testament fulfilment as a type of the greater gathering in of the people of God which he has come to inaugurate.

Matthew 24:31. The Matthean version of this saying includes the phrase *μετὰ σάλπιγγος μεγάλης* ('with a loud trumpet call'). In a passage so riddled with Old Testament language, it is likely that this too is an allusion to the Old Testament. Exodus 19:16 introduces a trumpet blast as a mark of the awesome appearing of God. But a closer verbal parallel[82] is found in Isaiah 27:13 (itself possibly based on Ex. 19:16) יתקע בשופר גדול (LXX *σαλπιοῦσιν τῇ σάλπιγγι τῇ μεγάλῃ*). Isaiah 27:12–13 predicts the end of a period of disaster and dispersion for Israel, when the true Israel will be weeded out within the ideal limits of the promised land (verse 12), and the great trumpet will summon those dispersed to Assyria and Egypt to return and worship Yahweh in Jerusalem. The context is thus closely similar to those of Deuteronomy 30:4 and Zechariah 2:10, and the application is made on just the same principles.

This group of Old Testament allusions, then, shows a close connection in the mind of Jesus between the people of Israel in the Old Testament and the community of his followers. The historical gathering of Israel into their own land, predicted

[80] The clause here alluded to is a parenthesis indicating the extent of the dispersion from which they are to be gathered. The LXX mistranslation *συνάξω* must be due to a failure to recognize its parenthetical nature, and a consequent feeling that the clause was incompatible with a context of the return of the nation.

[81] For this interpretation see below, pp. 238–239.

[82] *φωνῆς*, found in several texts of Mt. 24:31, is probably an intentional echo of LXX Ex. 19:16, but is almost certainly not original.

and already fulfilled in Old Testament times, supremely in the return from the Exile in 538 and the following years, is seen as a type of the future gathering of men from all nations into the Christian community. The quotations and allusions studied in this section thus show the same relationship between the Christian community and Israel as those in the last section showed between Jesus and Israel, correspondence and continuity. The disciples of Jesus both correspond to the Old Testament people of God in that in their experience the history of Israel is repeated, and they also assume and carry to completion the destiny which in the Old Testament was to be Israel's. This is due to the close relationship between Jesus and his disciples. To use the Pauline terminology, they are 'in Christ'. It is because he himself sums up in his own person the status and destiny of Israel that his disciples come to share that position. As the people of the Messiah of Israel they are themselves the true Israel.[83] The two following quotations exhibit this connection.

Mark 14:27 (Mt. 26:31), quoting Zechariah 13:7. The meaning of this passage in Zechariah, and Jesus' use of it, will be fully discussed below.[84] We shall there argue that the shepherd is a Messianic figure, and the flock is Israel, the people of God. The passage is a dramatic prediction of a suffering or persecution of Israel, consequent on the 'smiting' of their Messiah, to be followed by the restoration of a part of them ('one third'), refined and purified, to be the true people of God. In Jesus' application the flock becomes his disciples, who, after the 'smiting' of their leader, will be scattered. The remainder of the passage in Zechariah, though not explicitly cited, is also relevant: this temporary reverse will prove a test for the disciples, of whom those who pass the test will be restored, purified and strengthened, to constitute his true people. Since then Jesus is the Messiah, the shepherd of Zechariah 13:7, his disciples must fulfil what was written of the Messiah's people, Israel, because they are the Israel of the Messianic age.

Matthew 19:28, alluding to Daniel 7. The whole verse is modelled on various features of Daniel 7. Echoes of it may be

[83] *Cf.* C. H. Dodd, *The Old Testament in the New* (London, 1952), pp. 20–21.

[84] See below, pp. 107–109, 154.

seen in the term 'Son of man', the ideas of thrones, glory, and judgment, and the reign of the saints. The last is our concern here. According to Daniel 7:18, 22, 27 the 'saints of the Most High' are to receive the kingdom from God, this being the interpretation of the vision of the reception of power by the 'Son of man' (verses 13–14), who is a representative figure standing for Israel.[85] Jesus saw himself as this 'Son of man',[86] but, true to the representative sense of the original, he here attributes to his disciples that dominion which is his own. When he sits on his throne, they too (or rather the Twelve, as representatives of the whole community) will sit in judgment.[87] Thus, because Jesus is the true representative of Israel, they assume the predicted function of Israel.

The conception of the Christian community as the true Israel, which we have been considering, is summed up in the idea of a new covenant. *Mark 14:24* (Mt. 26:28; Lk. 22:20) alludes to Exodus 24:8.[88] *τὸ αἷμά μου τῆς διαθήκης* ('my blood of the covenant') echoes the MT דם־הברית (LXX *τὸ αἷμα τῆς διαθήκης*).[89] In taking the sacrificial blood of the burnt-offerings and peace-offerings of Exodus 24 as a type of his own blood soon to be shed in the final sacrifice of the cross, Jesus is giving expression to that line of typology which finds its fullest expression in the Epistle to the Hebrews, where Jesus' one perfect and complete sacrifice is seen as fulfilling the whole sacrificial system of the Old Testament. But the relevance of the allusion for our present purpose is that the covenant at Sinai is thereby seen as a type of Jesus' own work. As the blood

[85] For the interpretation of Daniel 7, see Excursus 3, below, pp. 169–171.

[86] See below, pp. 135ff.

[87] Even though Dn. 7:22 is probably to be translated 'judgment was given *for* the saints' (see below, p. 157 n. 286), a function of judgment is implicit in Dn. 7 in the dominion given to them.

[88] The phrase 'the new covenant' in Lk. 22:20 clearly alludes to Je. 31:31 (see below, p. 94), but the mention of blood cannot be derived from that source.

[89] This is a closer verbal parallel than Zc. 9:11 בדם־בריתך (LXX *ἐν αἵματι διαθήκης*), which B. Lindars (*op. cit.*, pp. 132–133) sees as the earliest source of such language in the NT. His argument depends on the belief that such typology as a reference to Ex. 24:8 would demand is not found earlier than the Epistle to the Hebrews. Our study has already given us much cause to doubt this belief. The typology involved is in fact in close harmony with the other examples we have studied in the teaching of Jesus. The considerably closer verbal form in Ex. 24:8 should be decisive.

of those sacrifices was the sign and seal of a covenant between God and his people Israel, so now, by the blood of Jesus, God is making a new covenant. In Old Testament times the people of God had been the nation, redeemed from Egypt under Moses; now it is to consist of those who through the sacrificial death of Jesus are brought into a covenant relationship with God. Though Jeremiah 31:31 is not explicitly referred to, the prophecy of a new covenant cannot have been far from the mind of Jesus. And the implication is, as Hebrews 8:13 explicitly states, that the old covenant is now obsolete. The community founded by the death of Jesus is now the covenant people of God.

We find then in these uses of the Old Testament by Jesus a consistent view of the community which he came to found as the true Israel.[90] In our last section we saw how Jesus regarded himself both as the antitype of the experiences of Israel and as the one in whom Israel's destiny must find its fulfilment. We have now seen this same conception transferred to his disciples; they too are related to the Old Testament people of God by the twin principles of correspondence and continuity. The implication is that the Jewish nation has no longer a place as the special people of God; that place has been taken by the Christian community, and in them God's purposes for Israel are to be fulfilled.

In our next section the idea of the rejection of the Jewish nation from its favoured position becomes more explicit.

IV. TYPES OF JEWISH UNBELIEF AND ITS PUNISHMENT

Frequently in the Old Testament an unbelieving and rebellious element arose within Israel, and Jesus applies some Old Testament statements about such people to his Jewish opponents. But it is not only their actual unbelief which he sees foreshadowed in the Old Testament, but also the act of God by which he predicts that their rebellion will soon be punished and brought to an end. This too is seen foreshadowed in the punishments of Israel described in the Old Testament, but

[90] For other evidences of this conception see G. E. Ladd, *op. cit.*, pp. 246–248.

also on one occasion in similar judgments on Gentile nations. We therefore divide our treatment into the two groups, concerned with Jewish unbelief and with its imminent punishment.

a. Jewish unbelief

Mark 4:12 (Mt. 13:13; Lk. 8:10), an abbreviated allusion to Isaiah 6:9–10. Those who fail to understand and accept Jesus' teaching ('those outside') are seen as equivalent to those who rejected Isaiah's message in the eighth century BC. Isaiah's mission, with its result in the greater blindness of those to whom he was sent, is being repeated in that of Jesus.[91] There is no cause for surprise in the lack of response, for the type must find its antitype. Not that Isaiah 6:9–10 was a prediction for any time beyond Isaiah's own, but Jesus takes it as a type, and so can expect a fulfilment. If we may take Matthew 13:14a as authentic,[92] the formula 'with them is fulfilled the prophecy of Isaiah' reveals a strong sense of the forward-looking nature of the type; in the antitype, here contemporary Jewish unbelief, it finds its fulfilment or completion, almost as if it were in itself incomplete.[93]

Mark 7:6–7 (Mt. 15:8–9), quoting Isaiah 29:13. This quotation is closely parallel to that just considered. Again a description of Israel in the eighth century is transferred to Jesus' contemporaries. The shallowness and hypocrisy of the worship

[91] *Cf.* above, p. 49.

[92] R. H. Gundry (*op. cit.*, pp. 116–118) argues convincingly for Mt. 13:14–15 as an original part of the Gospel. That the verses did not originate with Matthew may be indicated by the following facts: (i) The formula of verse 14a is built round two words not found elsewhere in Matthew, ἀναπληροῦν and προφητεία (Matthew has his own equivalents for these terms often elsewhere); (ii) The pure LXX form of the quotation would be unique among the Matthean formula-quotations; (iii) The verses are closely linked to the following Q saying (vv. 16–17), making up a carefully balanced contrast, and may well have formed with them a single unit of tradition, existing independently of Mk. 4:12, which could be inserted complete into this context in Matthew, but from which Luke would necessarily drop the first half, which would be irrelevant to his context in chapter 10. Even if the formula did not originate with Jesus, it clearly conveys his intention in referring to Is. 6:9–10.

[93] R. H. Gundry (*op. cit.*, p. 213) suggests that ἀναπληροῦν here means 'to fulfil *again*', the words having been already fulfilled in Isaiah's time. Elsewhere in the NT, however, ἀναπληροῦν means simply 'to fulfil' (or, in 1 Thes. 2:16, 'to bring to completion'); its one other use in connection with prophecy is 1 Esdras 1:54, where it is not discernibly different from πληροῦν.

condemned by Isaiah is repeated in the Pharisees and scribes. Again the words quoted bear no more than a purely contemporary application. But again Jesus takes them as virtually predictive: 'well did Isaiah prophesy *of you*. . . .' In both these cases the conviction is clearly present that even what was originally of purely contemporary application in Scripture is no mere period piece, but embodies principles of God's dealings which do not change, and are as applicable in the first century AD as in the eighth BC. Therefore the words of Isaiah were concerned with Jesus' contemporaries.

In the following three cases this conviction is not explicit. It could, therefore, be argued that the Old Testament language used by Jesus was the result of mere coincidence, due to common Semitic thought-forms and phraseology, or at least the use of appropriate wording without any intention to draw a specific parallel with the Old Testament passage concerned. In Matthew 17:17 this could be so; but the other references are to passages which are too specific and unique to be thus dismissed.

Mark 11:17 (Mt. 21:13; Lk. 19:46), alluding to Jeremiah 7:11. Jeremiah used the phrase 'a den of robbers' in accusing his contemporaries of a disregard for the moral requirements of the Temple. Jesus' use of the same phrase against the traders in the Temple in his day indicates that they are repeating the dishonouring of God's house which Jeremiah had condemned.

Mark 12:1 (Mt. 21:33), alluding to Isaiah 5:1–2. This is more than mere pictorial detail. The use of the idea of a vine or vineyard in a parable must in itself inevitably have been construed as an allusion to Israel, which was commonly so described in the Old Testament.[94] But the wording is modelled in some detail on Isaiah 5:1–2. There God condemns Israel's failure in the picture of a vineyard which yielded no returns;

[94] Ps. 80:9ff. (EVV vv. 8ff.); Is. 5:1ff.; Je. 2:21; Ezk. 15:2ff.; 19:10ff. This fact discredits the argument of J. Jeremias, *The Parables of Jesus*[6] (ET London, 1963), pp. 70–71, that the absence of the detailed allusion to Is. 5:1–2 in the versions of Luke and the Gospel of Thomas points to an original 'non-allegorical' parable, later 'allegorized' by the addition of these details. The vine idea alone ensures that a reference to Israel is understood. Jeremias' argument against the authenticity of the allusion on the grounds of its LXX form is considered below, p. 247 (and *cf.* the argument of pp. 25–26 above).

here Jesus condemns contemporary Judaism in similar terms.[95] The Jewish nation which now refuses the overtures of God's son is only repeating the failure of the Israel of Isaiah's day; only now the failure is more disastrous, and the condemnation final, as the rest of the parable shows.[96]

Matthew 17:17 (Lk. 9:41). γενεὰ ἄπιστος καὶ διεστραμμένη ('faithless and perverse generation') is a probable echo of Deuteronomy 32:5 דור עקש ופתלתל (LXX γενεὰ σκολιὰ καὶ διεστραμμένη; *cf.* also verse 20). The phrase occurs in a description of the faithlessness with which Israel responded to the faithfulness and justice of God. Jesus' application of it to his contemporaries (the disciples, though no doubt included in the rebuke, are not its primary object; γενεά extends it far wider) is parallel to those just considered. The faithlessness and rebellion of Israel in Old Testament times is repeated and brought to its head in the Jewish response to Jesus.

The same point is made incidentally in *Matthew 9:13; 12:7*, quoting Hosea 6:6. The primary purpose is to enforce the moral teaching of that verse, but its applicability depends on the view that the religion of the Pharisees, against whom it is quoted on each occasion, is a repetition of the superficial emphasis on ritual which Hosea had attacked.

Jesus thus saw the unbelief and hostility of the Jews towards his message prefigured in several different phases of Old Testament history. Unbelief and rebellion were recurrent reactions of Israel to the revelation and requirements of God, and this pattern Jesus saw repeated in his own time. It had to be so, for Jesus regarded the types as having little less than the force of predictions. They were bound to react as they had always reacted. But this was the final and culminating rebellion, as the parable of the tenants so clearly warned them. As we have seen before, the antitype is not only a repetition of the type, but is its fulfilment, on a higher plane. The one they are now rejecting is not merely a prophet, but God's son. Jesus' ministry is the last and strongest of God's appeals to his people, and its rejection is the last and greatest in the long succession of their acts of rebellion. The sequel is inevitable.

[95] The details are different: in Isaiah it was the fruit which failed, in Jesus' parable the tenants. But the echo is unmistakable.

[96] *Cf.* S. Amsler, *op. cit.*, pp. 89–90.

b. The imminent punishment of Jewish unbelief

Jesus' predictions of the destruction of Jerusalem and its Temple are too many and varied to be dismissed as *vaticinia ex eventu*. Often they are expressed in Old Testament language which implies a typological use of the Old Testament closely related to what we have so far examined. Jewish unbelief, and the fact that it is no longer they, but Jesus and his disciples, who are the true people of God, find their logical outcome in the destruction of the Temple and capital of the nation, and this destruction, no less than these other results of the coming of Jesus, finds its types in Old Testament history. They are now to be repeated on a scale more drastic even than the Old Testament catastrophes.

(i) The destruction of Samaria, 722 BC. *Luke 23:30*, quoting Hosea 10:8. The passage in Hosea is a prediction of the inevitable destruction of the Northern Kingdom for its wickedness, which did in fact occur in 722 BC. Jesus uses the words in his warning to the women of Jerusalem of what is to happen to their city. Its fall will be like that of Samaria. In quoting the prediction, Jesus is using a convenient method of referring to the event predicted, which is a type of that event which he himself foresees.

(ii) The destruction of Jerusalem, 587 BC. *Matthew 23:38* (Lk. 13:35). In the words ἀφίεται ὑμῖν ὁ οἶκος ὑμῶν ἔρημος (lit. 'your house is abandoned to you desolate') there is a probable allusion to Jeremiah 22:5 לחרבה יהיה הבית הזה (LXX εἰς ἐρήμωσιν ἔσται ὁ οἶκος οὗτος). If ἔρημος is a later gloss, as it clearly is in Luke, though not so likely in Matthew,[97] the reference might be rather to Jeremiah 12:7 עזבתי את־ביתי (LXX ἐγκαταλέλοιπα τὸν οἶκόν μου), with its idea of abandonment rather than desolation. Both passages are descriptions of what God is about to do[98] to his house at Jerusalem, predictions of the

[97] The support of the MSS is strong in Matthew. It is often rejected as an assimilation to LXX Je. 22:5, but (i) it does not echo directly the LXX construction, and (ii) the Matthean text without ἔρημος hardly bears sufficient resemblance to Je. 22:5 to induce a scribe to assimilate it to that verse.

[98] The perfect of Je. 12:7 should probably be construed as a 'prophetic perfect', vividly describing a future event as having already occurred.

disaster of 587 BC. Again a prediction is used as a convenient reference to the event. What Jeremiah predicted for Jerusalem, Jesus now predicts for her again. Nebuchadrezzar's destruction of the Temple is to be repeated, a further punishment by God of the apostasy of the nation.

(iii) The desecration of the Temple, 167 BC. *Mark 13:14* (Mt. 24:15). The phrase 'the desolating sacrilege' (AV 'the abomination of desolation') is an allusion to Daniel 11:31; 12:11; (9:27). The three parallel expressions in Daniel are השקוץ משומם (11:31), שקוץ שמם (12:11), and על כנף שקוצים משומם (9:27). The difference between the first two is a minor grammatical variation; in the last the construction is different and the sense disputed, leading some to suggest emendation.[99] Since, however, the New Testament text is verbally closer to 11:31 and 12:11, we may safely leave 9:27 out of account.

The phrase in Daniel 11:31 and 12:11 is a description of the desecration of the Temple by Antiochus Epiphanes in 167 BC, when he erected in the Temple both an image of Zeus Olympius (whose Hebrew name בעל־שמים may be contemptuously parodied in שומם[100]), and an altar for his worship. Whether the specific reference is to one or other of these, or to the whole act of defilement, is not important. In alluding to this phrase, therefore, Jesus is predicting that something analogous to the desecration of 167 BC is to occur, the prediction[101] of Daniel being used, as in the two previous quotations considered, as a convenient means of reference to the event. Jesus is not saying that Daniel's prediction will be fulfilled, but rather looking for a repetition of the event in which it has already been fulfilled.

We cannot discuss here exactly what sort of repetition Jesus envisaged, or how, if at all, his prediction was fulfilled;[102] but the context makes it clear that at any rate the reference is to

[99] *E.g.* S. R. Driver, *The Book of Daniel* (Cambridge, 1900), p. 142, reading כנו for כנף.

[100] So E. Nestle, *ZATW* 4 (1884), p. 248, and many since.

[101] The date and nature of the book of Daniel need not be considered here, as there is no doubt that *for Jesus* the book was of exilic date, and the prophecies were genuine predictions.

[102] G. R. Beasley-Murray (*A Commentary on Mark Thirteen* (London, 1957), pp. 59–72) gives a useful survey of suggested interpretations, but dismisses too lightly the suggestion of, *e.g.*, M.-J. Lagrange, *Évangile selon Saint*

an event connected with the coming destruction of Jerusalem. This destruction is, therefore, for Jesus the antitype not only of the disasters of 722 and 587 BC, but also of the desecration of the Temple by Antiochus Epiphanes.[103] Thus the three greatest national disasters known to the Old Testament are rolled together by Jesus into a single terrible picture of the final and complete destruction which confronts his nation.

Luke 21:24. The idea of the trampling of Jerusalem is a common one in the Old Testament.[104] Reference has been made especially to Psalm 79:1; Isaiah 63:18; Zechariah 12:3 (LXX), but the closest parallel to this verse is again in Daniel. A reference to the desecration by Antiochus in Daniel 8:13 (using the phrase הפשע שמם, *cf.* 9:27; 11:31; 12:11) includes the making of the sanctuary into a מרמס (LXX *καταπάτημα*), 'a trampling-ground', for a limited period (2,300 days), after which it will be reconsecrated. This was what in fact happened: for a time Antiochus 'trampled on' the sanctuary, but under the Maccabees the Temple was cleansed and the sacrifices restored. This period of Gentile domination probably lies behind Jesus' prediction of the 'times of the Gentiles' during which Jerusalem will be trampled on. In that case, here, as in Mark 13:14, Jesus is taking the desecration of 167 BC as a type of the coming fall of Jerusalem. As Antiochus not only desecrated the Temple, but exposed it to profanation ('trampling') by Gentiles for a long, though limited, period, so the coming capture and destruction of the Temple will be succeeded by a long but limited period of continued profanation, the 'times of the Gentiles'.

But Jesus does not only take the three greatest national disasters of Israel in the Old Testament as types of the coming fall of Jerusalem. He even describes it in terms drawn from Old Testament descriptions of the fall of Gentile nations. As God has destroyed these nations for their wickedness and arrogance (for it was the message of the prophets that this, too, was the work of the God of Israel), so he would judge his own

---

Matthieu[7] (Paris, 1948), pp. 461–462, that Jesus' prediction was fulfilled in the Zealot desecration of the Temple in AD 67/8 as recorded by Josephus (*BJ* 4.3.6–8 and thereafter). In our view this interpretation best matches the original reference of the phrase in Daniel.

[103] *Cf.* C. H. Dodd, *Journal of Roman Studies* 37 (1947), p. 53.

[104] See below, p. 257.

people's rebellion. The complete rejection of the Jews as the people of God could hardly be more graphically presented than by this typology.

Mark 13:24–25 (Mt. 24:29) is a compilation of astronomical metaphors which in the Old Testament denote the fall of nations. The terms used are standard Old Testament apocalyptic imagery.[105] But the actual phrases of Mark 13:24–25 are drawn entirely from Isaiah 13:10, referring to Babylon, and Isaiah 34:4, referring to Edom.[106] Thus Jesus describes the coming fall of Jerusalem[107] in terms drawn from Old Testament predictions of the fall of Babylon and of Edom. In both cases, as in other uses of similar imagery, it was the final overthrow of the nation which was thus described. As those nations were finally destroyed by God, so now he will not only reject the Jews from being his people, but will bring to an end their existence as a nation, and that in a disaster as terrible as that which befell Babylon and Edom.

Finally, we may mention a unique case of the application of an Old Testament threat against a Gentile nation not to the Jews as a whole, but to an individual community which refused to accept Jesus' teaching. *Matthew 11:23* (Lk. 10:15), alluding to Isaiah 14:13, 15. The Old Testament context is a taunt uttered over the fall of arrogant Babylon, personified in its king; he had aspired to exalt himself to heaven, to be equal with God himself (verses 13–14), but God has dashed him down to Sheol (verse 15). The same is to be true of Capernaum, which, like other Galilean towns, has rejected Jesus' message. Their judgment will be worse than that of Tyre, Sidon and Sodom. The arrogant self-exaltation of Babylon, and its challenge to the authority of God, was a type of all who reject God's lordship, and all such must be cast down. Thus the unrepentant self-sufficiency of Capernaum, and its rejection of the claims of Jesus, will meet a similar retribution.

It is interesting to notice that Capernaum was not the only antitype which Jesus saw of the pride and punishment of

[105] For examples see below, p. 233.

[106] For the reading see below, p. 233 n. 24. For details of the verbal links with Is. 34:4 see below, pp. 255–256.

[107] For the reference see below, Appendix A, esp. pp. 233–234.

Babylon. In Luke 10:18 he says 'I saw Satan fall like lightning from heaven', probably alluding to Isaiah 14:12. The type is the same, but the antitype is now not Capernaum, but Satan, who embodies in a still higher degree that spirit of arrogant self-exaltation against God which was the essential principle in the type. His fate is therefore the same.

V. CONCLUSIONS

a. Survey of types

Jesus' types are drawn from a wide range of aspects of Israel seen in the Old Testament; they are not restricted to any one period or any single class. Thus he uses *persons* in the Old Testament as types of himself (David, Solomon, Elijah, Elisha, Isaiah, Jonah)[108] or of John the Baptist (Elijah);[109] he refers to Old Testament *institutions* as types of himself and his work (the priesthood and the covenant);[110] he sees in the *experiences* of Israel foreshadowings of his own;[111] he finds the *hopes* of Israel fulfilled in himself[112] and his disciples[113] and sees his disciples as assuming the *status* of Israel;[114] in Israel's *deliverance* by God he sees a type of the gathering of men into his church,[115] while the *disasters* of Israel are foreshadowings of the imminent punishment of those who reject him,[116] whose *unbelief* is prefigured in that of the wicked in Israel[117] and even, in two instances, in the arrogance of the Gentile nations.[118]

In all these aspects of the Old Testament people of God Jesus sees foreshadowings of himself and his work, with its results in the opposition and consequent rejection of the majority of the Jews, while the true Israel is now to be found in the

[108] Mk. 2:25–26; Mt. 12:42; Lk. 4:25–27; Mk. 6:35ff.; 4:12; Mt. 12:40–41.

[109] Mk. 9:13.

[110] Mt. 12:6; Mk. 14:24.

[111] Mt. 4:1–11; Mk. 12:10–11, and the other uses of psalms.

[112] The resurrection predictions, based on Ho. 6:2.

[113] Mt. 5:5; 19:28.

[114] Mk. 14:27; Mt. 5:48; 15:13.

[115] Mk. 13:27; Mt. 8:11; 24:31. Here, and in the following group, OT predictions are alluded to, but the reference is to the event predicted, which has already occurred.

[116] Mk. 13:14; Mt. 23:38; Lk. 21:24; 23:30.

[117] Mk. 4:12; 7:6–7; 11:17; 12:1; Mt. 9:13; 12:7; 17:17.

[118] Mk. 13:24–25; Mt. 11:23.

new Christian community. Thus in his coming the history of Israel has reached its decisive point. The whole of the Old Testament is gathered up in him. He himself embodies in his own person the status and destiny of Israel, and in the community of those who belong to him that status and destiny are to be fulfilled, no longer in the nation as such.

b. Is this 'typology'?

If we examine the above list to find a uniform method of application, we shall look in vain. The typological method, while sometimes explicit and used in detail, is at other times at most implicit, in passages which need carry no more than a verbal echo or a mere illustration of a general truth. Certainly we should be wrong to try to extract from the above list a set catalogue of types and their antitypes. We are confronted by a far looser method than that. An Old Testament figure may be taken as type of more than one New Testament counterpart where the same principle is involved (as Is. 14:12–15 is applied both to Capernaum and to Satan); conversely, several events in the Old Testament may be seen as prefigurations of a single New Testament occurrence (as the fall of Jerusalem is seen prefigured both in the Israelite disasters of 722, 587, and 167 BC, and even in the fall of Gentile nations). Is it then correct to class all these varied applications under the heading of 'typology'? Certainly typology as we originally described it, an explicit drawing of both historical and theological parallels between Old and New Testament persons and events, does appear in some of the above cases. But more often the parallels, though present, are unexpressed, and the typological intention must be inferred from the selection of that particular Old Testament passage for that particular occasion.

We stated, however, at the outset, that typology is essentially the expression of a conviction of the unchanging principles of the working of God, and of the continuity between his acts in the past and in the present. It is 'an historical approach to the understanding of the saving acts of God'.[119] That such a conviction, such a 'historical approach', governed Jesus' use of Old Testament texts in the passages considered above, is the

[119] K. J. Woollcombe, *op. cit.*, p. 69.

reason for our classing them together under this heading. This, while it differs from the developed technique of patristic typology, is the typology of the New Testament.[120] It is less a hermeneutical technique than a theological conviction working itself out in practice.

The conviction expresses itself in various ways, from the more sophisticated application of the experiences of Jonah (Mt. 12:39–41) to the citation of apparently mere illustrations. The reference to Elijah and Elisha in Luke 4:25–27 could be seen as such, but the purpose of the reference is to establish the pattern of Jesus' ministry as in line with the way God worked in the Old Testament. It is not a long step from this conviction to a statement of full typological correspondence. Jesus can even take what might seem again to be mere illustrations, and confer on them the status of predictions of a similar state of affairs in his own time (Mk. 7:6–7; 9:13; Mt. 13:14). The point of the illustrations was that they embodied a principle which must be repeated in Jesus and his work. It is the presence of this conviction, rather than any one manner of expressing it, which unites the above passages into a single class which we can fairly call 'typological'. On this basis, an incidental verbal reference to an Old Testament person or event which is seen as the counterpart of a New Testament person or event may be no less truly typological than the elaborate construction of parallels. And to this basic idea of the 'recurring rhythm of the divine activity'[121] all the above passages, in different ways, bear witness.

c. Implications of Jesus' typology

It remains to note three implications which we have seen recurring in Jesus' typological use of the Old Testament, which are of some importance for his conception of his own

[120] We would thus not accept A. T. Hanson's strictures (*op. cit.*, esp. pp.172–178) on the 'typological' approach to the NT use of the OT. He thinks in terms of a conscious and developed mode of interpretation like that of patristic typology, and has little difficulty in showing that in general the words for 'type' which occur in the NT do not 'convey what the later church meant by typology' (p. 172). The question is one of terminology; we feel that his restriction of 'typology' to a sophisticated technique is unjustified.

[121] G. W. H. Lampe, *Essays*, p. 29.

mission, especially in its relation to the Old Testament Scriptures.

(i) *Jesus is in line with the Old Testament.* In the face of accusations of being a revolutionary, and setting himself up against God and his people, Jesus claimed, by means of this typology, a continuity between God's working in the Old Testament and his own work. He was simply working out patterns already seen in the Old Testament. If in the Old Testament God worked through prophets, priests and kings, then Jesus could point to all three as types of himself. If in the Old Testament God chose out a people to whom he made promises of blessing, then Jesus could claim that in himself and his disciples that people was embodied, and those promises would find their fulfilment. Jesus understood the Old Testament Christologically: in its essential principles, and even in its details, it foreshadows the Messiah whom it promises. The whole theological system of the Old Testament points forward to his work, and in his coming the whole Old Testament economy finds its perfection and fulfilment.

(ii) *Jesus is superior to the Old Testament.* God's working is not only repeated, but repeated on a higher plane, and with a greater glory and significance.[122] We have seen how three times Jesus states this superiority of the antitype to the type in so many words: 'Something greater than the temple is here' (Mt. 12:6); 'Something greater than Jonah is here' (Mt. 12:41); 'Something greater than Solomon is here' (Mt. 12:42). In Mark 2:25–26, a parallel argument to Matthew 12:6, although the superiority is not explicit, the argument depends on it. In Mark 6:35ff. Jesus repeats Elisha's miracle, but on a vastly greater scale. Twice he succeeds where Old Testament Israel, the type, had failed (the temptation, and the resurrection, where Israel's vain hope comes to fruition in him). And since Jesus is superior to the Old Testament types, the Jewish refusal to accept him as God's messenger must carry a greater condemnation. Their punishment, in the destruction of Jerusalem and the final rejection of the nation from their privileged

[122] F. Foulkes (*op. cit.*, pp. 23–33) traces this idea as already present in the typological thinking of the OT itself.

status as the people of God, will be on a scale higher even than the most terrible disasters known to the Old Testament: 'In those days there will be such tribulation as has not been from the beginning of the creation which God created until now, and never will be' (Mk. 13:19). The rejection of the Old Testament prophets brought severe condemnation, but, as the parable of the tenants shows, something greater than the prophets is here.

(iii) *Jesus is the fulfilment of the Old Testament.* The eschatological implication, that the occurrence of the antitype is the mark of the new, golden age, which Bultmann notes as the distinguishing mark of true typology,[123] is strongly present in the typology of Jesus. In him the age of fulfilment has come. The patterns discerned in the Old Testament are not only repeated on a higher plane, but they are now finding their final and perfect embodiment. All God's working in the Old Testament is now reaching its culmination, and the Old Testament economy is at an end. The new, Messianic age has dawned.

This is seen, paradoxically, in the fact that Jewish unbelief has now reached its highest point, so that its punishment must this time be final and complete. The true Israel of this eschatological age is no longer the nation of the old covenant, but the Christian community, inaugurated by a new covenant through a mediator greater than the Israelite priesthood; for Jesus not only repeats the work of prophet, priest and king, but in him it is perfected. In this new community the hopes of the Old Testament Israel are fulfilled. We shall see more of this eschatological element in Jesus' view of his mission when we study his use of Old Testament predictions; but it runs strongly through his typology as well. The glorious fulfilment to which the Old Testament looked forward *has* come; these are the 'last days'. The words of Paul in 1 Corinthians 10:11 sum up the conviction of Jesus: 'Now those things happened to them as a warning (τυπικῶς), but they were written down for our instruction, *upon whom the end of the ages has come*.'

Thus Jesus saw his mission as the fulfilment of the Old Testament Scriptures; not just of those which predicted a coming redeemer, but of the whole sweep of Old Testament

[123] *TLZ* 75 (1950), pp. 207–208.

ideas. The patterns of God's working which the discerning eye could trace in the history and institutions of Israel were all preparing for the great climax when all would be taken up into the final and perfect act of God which the prophets foretold. And in the coming of Jesus all this was fulfilled. That was why he could find 'in *all* the scriptures the things concerning himself'.

EXCURSUS I

THE AUTHENTICITY OF MATTHEW 12:40

The principal arguments against the authenticity of this verse are threefold.

1. It is alleged that verse 40 breaks the continuity between verses 39 and 41. In verse 39 Jesus refuses any sign except the 'sign of Jonah', and in verse 41 he condemns his hearers for not repenting at his preaching as the Ninevites repented at the preaching of Jonah. The 'sign of Jonah' is, therefore, the preaching. The reference to Jonah's three days in the fish's belly is out of place, and must be a later addition by someone who misunderstood Jesus' intention.

This argument depends on the exegesis which sees the preaching as constituting the 'sign'. We have, however, seen reason to reject this exegesis.[1] Our discussion of the passage above shows that the 'sign' must refer to the miraculous deliverance of Jonah, and that this in no way breaks the continuity of Jesus' argument, which is concerned with the attestation of his preaching by the miracle of the resurrection. Verse 40 is in fact integral to this argument. Where a passage presents a coherent argument as it stands, it is rash to propose an exegesis which involves the elimination of the central part of it.

2. Verse 40 is absent from the parallel passage, Luke 11:29–32; it is therefore claimed that it was not in Q, and was an addition either by Matthew or by an early hand to his Gospel.

The case is not so simple. The Lucan version differs from the Matthean at two points: (i) In place of Matthew 12:40 (*i.e.*

[1] See above, p. 44.

immediately following the reference to the 'sign of Jonah'), Luke has 'For as Jonah became a sign to the men of Nineveh, so will the Son of man be to this generation', a verse peculiar to Luke; (ii) The saying about Solomon is placed *before* that about the repentance of the Ninevites, *i.e.* between the two references to Jonah. Two conclusions may be drawn: (a) The supposed continuity between verses 39 and 41 in Matthew 12 can certainly not be supported from Luke, where it is deliberately broken not only by the peculiarly Lucan verse 30, but also by the reference to Solomon. Luke clearly did not see the preaching as being the 'sign'; he has deliberately separated the two ideas. The Lucan explanation of the 'sign' is verse 30, not verse 32. (b) It seems clear that either Matthew 12:40 is a later specification of an originally cryptic explanation of the 'sign' preserved in Luke 11:30, or Luke in verse 30 is deliberately veiling the explicit typology of Matthew 12:40. Which of these is the more likely? The wording of Matthew 12:40 seems to settle the question, for the reference to three days and three nights is in startling contrast with the actual length of Jesus' lying in the tomb, which covered two nights, and one whole day with parts of two others. To a Jewish reader the idiom might be familiar,[2] and the saying cause no difficulty, but Luke, a Gentile writing for Gentiles, might be embarrassed by the apparent discrepancy. The cryptic wording of verse 30 would be a safer form. At all events, it is most improbable that the wording of Matthew 12:40, which could so easily be misunderstood, would be invented subsequent to the resurrection, when it was common knowledge that Jesus was in the tomb for only two nights. We conclude that Matthew 12:40 is the original form of the saying.

3. Justin (*Dial.* 107:1), aiming to establish from Jonah an Old Testament testimony for the resurrection, quotes Matthew 12:39, but instead of continuing with verse 40, says rather that Jesus was speaking 'cryptically' (παρακεκαλυμμένα), but his

[2] For the use of 'three days and three nights' as a Jewish idiom to denote a period covering only two nights, see SB I, p. 649. The same words occur in 1 Sa. 30:12, to describe a period which began היום שלשה, 'today three (days)' (v. 13), *i.e.* 'the day before yesterday' (*cf.* LXX σήμερον τριταῖος, Vg. *nudius tertius*, both of which bear this meaning); the period is thus exactly parallel to that of Jesus' lying in the tomb. *Cf.* also Esther 4:16 with 5:1.

words were intended to be interpreted of the resurrection. Why the use of *παρακεκαλυμμένα*, if in verse 40 he had an explicit prediction of the resurrection?

One answer might be that his quotation was taken not from Matthew 12:39, but from Matthew 16:4 (Justin omits the words *τοῦ προφήτου*, which occur in 12:39 but not in 16:4), where there is no explicit reference to the resurrection. More likely, however, Justin, a Gentile with a Greek upbringing, failed to recognize the Semitic idiom, and so found Matthew 12:40 an embarrassing verse. He explicitly states that Jesus rose 'on the third day', and that Jonah was disgorged by the fish 'on the third day'; to have quoted Matthew 12:40 would have seemed damaging to his case. He therefore contented himself with a mention in his own words of Jesus' typological understanding of this incident in the story of Jonah.

We conclude that Matthew 12:40 not only represents the true intention of Jesus' reference to Jonah,[3] but is an original part of the saying.[4] Theories of its interpolation into the tradition in the post-resurrection period raise more difficulties than they solve.

[3] This is agreed by, *e.g.*, J. Jeremias, *TDNT* III, pp. 408–410; P. Seidelin, *loc. cit.*, pp. 130–131; B. Gärtner, *op. cit.*, pp. 112–113.

[4] So *e.g.* O. Cullmann, *Christology*, pp. 62–63 (and see further references *ad loc.*); M.-J. Lagrange, *Matthieu*, pp. 249–250; P. Bonnard, *L'Évangile selon Saint Matthieu* (Neuchatel, 1963), p. 184. See *contra* K. Stendahl, *op. cit.*, pp. 132–133.

CHAPTER FOUR

THE USE OF OLD TESTAMENT PREDICTION

I. INTRODUCTION

We have distinguished between types and predictions[1] on the principle that whereas the former have no intrinsic forward reference, the latter demand a future fulfilment. To claim that a prediction is fulfilled is not simply to affirm a discernible correspondence, but to assert that the Old Testament passage concerned, whether expressed in the future tense or not, intentionally pointed forward to that which has occurred. There is, of course, a close connection between the appeal to prediction and typology. Both spring from a belief in the essentially forward-looking nature of the Old Testament, and in the continuity of the working of God in both Old and New Testaments. Prediction, we may say, is where this forward reference comes to the surface. It is to Jesus' use of the explicit predictions that we now turn. They are drawn largely from the prophetic books, notably Isaiah and Zechariah, and from the Psalms and the book of Daniel.

Before embarking on this study, however, two preliminary questions must be considered. The first concerns the place and nature of eschatology in the prophets and psalms, and the second, the definition of the term 'Messianic', and the place of Messianism in the future hope of the Old Testament.

a. Eschatology[2]

G. B. Caird[3] draws attention to the prevailing confusion in the use of the term 'eschatology'. It is used on the one hand to denote that which happens after death, or the end of the world,

[1] See above, pp. 39–40.

[2] See G. E. Ladd, *op. cit.*, pp. 41–71 for a valuable treatment of this subject.

[3] *Op. cit.*, pp. 17–19.

and on the other hand to describe the future hope of the Old Testament. The result is that the unwary reader is in danger of assuming a note of finality in the future hope of the Old Testament which is in fact foreign to it. The 'eschatology' of the Old Testament prophets is not concerned with the end of the world, but with that decisive act of God which will bring to an end the existing order of things in the world, and inaugurate a new era of blessing, of a totally different order. Thus, for the Old Testament prophets, the 'eschaton' was not a full stop, but an end followed by a new beginning. But the terminology is firmly entrenched; with Caird we must regret its ambiguity, but cannot dispense with it.

It is this ambiguity which accounts for much of the disagreement over the place of eschatology in Israel. For while many, if not most, modern scholars recognize an eschatological element in the prophetic message from the eighth century on, S. Mowinckel[4] denies any eschatology until after the Exile. This is because he would define 'eschatology' in terms of a more or less developed dualistic scheme, involving a universal cosmic drama of destruction, followed by a restoration of the perfection of the original creation,[5] and so distinguishes the prophetic 'future hope' sharply from this apocalyptic 'eschatology'. That the content of the future hope developed considerably after the Exile is indeed clear; but Mowinckel himself recognizes in the pre-exilic prophets a hope of a 'day of Yahweh', when by a decisive intervention he will give Israel victory over her enemies, and make a new covenant with his people, ruling over them in peace and prosperity, a day which can be described in terms of a new creation.[6] This hope, no less than that of the apocalyptists, envisages an end of the present order, and a new beginning, even though the character of the end is differently conceived. The term 'eschatology', therefore, in the sense outlined above, seems an appropriate one for the future hope of the prophets.

We must, however, beware of importing an alien chronological precision into prophetic thought. A clear distinction between an eschatological hope and a future hope confined to the current historical situation may be convenient, and indeed

[4] *He That Cometh*, pp. 125–154.
[5] *Ibid.*, pp. 125–126.
[6] *Ibid.*, pp. 143–149.

essential, for modern Western thought; but the Hebrew prophet did not make it his business to distinguish between the near and the distant future, and to label his predictions accordingly. At root, the hope of God's saving activity in the history of the imminent future and that of his eschatological acts are very much the same. Both spring from a conviction of the sovereign rule of Yahweh, and his hostility against all that would oppose his will and his purposes of blessing for his people. Whether these result in his work of judgment and salvation within the contemporary historical scene, or in the final catastrophic demonstration of his sovereignty, it is the work of the same God, based on the same principles, and for the same purpose. The difference is one of degree rather than of kind.

Thus the fact that many of the so-called 'Messianic' prophecies of the Old Testament appear to have a primary reference to the prophet's own historical situation, and express his hope for the near future, does not rule out a further eschatological reference. The fulfilment may not come as soon as the prophet hopes, but come it will, and it is the fact of the fulfilment, not the time of it, that matters.[7]

This feature may be seen also in the Royal Psalms. These psalms, written with reference to particular historical kings, and expressing the hopes and prayers of the people for his reign, do so in what seems impossibly extravagant language. It could hardly have been seriously believed that any given Israelite king would have 'the ends of the earth for his possession' (Ps. 2:8), occupy his 'divine throne for ever and ever' (Ps. 45:7, EVV verse 6), and 'live while the sun endures, and as long as the moon, throughout all generations' (Ps. 72:5). This seems to go beyond pious optimism or flattering hyperbole. 'While they may have been royal psalms, used in the royal rites of the temple, they were also "messianic". They held before the king the ideal king, both as his inspiration and guide for the present, and as the hope of the future.'[8]

[7] Thus J. Klausner (*The Messianic Idea in Israel*[3] (ET London, 1956), pp. 57–58) takes as Messianic the predictions of Isaiah made with reference to Hezekiah which were not in fact fulfilled in his reign.

[8] H. H. Rowley, *The Faith of Israel* (London, 1956), p. 192. See further, J. A. Motyer in *The New Bible Dictionary*, ed. J. D. Douglas (London, 1962), p. 814.

Such psalms, like the 'Messianic' prophecies referred to above, arise out of, and have a primary reference to, historical situations, but this does not diminish the fact that they have a true, intended, eschatological reference. 'The *Sitz im Leben* is not a kind of ceiling above which the thought of the pertinent Old Testament passages cannot rise, but is a springboard from which the thought leaps beyond the immediate occasion.'[9]

Thus the eschatological hopes of the Old Testament are not confined to passages which specifically mention 'the day of Yahweh', *etc.* Both in the prophets and in the psalms it is not only legitimate, but true to the intention of the author, to see in many passages, whose primary reference is to contemporary history, the hopes of that glorious future which was to be brought about by the decisive act of God, when the ideal would be realized.

But eschatology, even in the pre-exilic prophets, is not confined to this secondary application. From Amos to the Exile, and beyond, we find frequent explicit predictions of the 'day of Yahweh'.[10] Expressions such as 'in that day'[11] and 'the days are coming'[12] give further evidence of a continuing expectation of the day of Yahweh, a decisive time of judgment (on the nations, and on Israel herself) and restoration. While similar phrases sometimes refer to definite acts of judgment in the near future, this cannot be said of expressions like 'in the end of days',[13] nor of the pictures of the coming golden age such as occur in Isaiah 11:1–9 or Zephaniah 3:11–20; the universal character of the work of God so described demands an eschatological frame of reference. It may not be easy, or even desirable, to separate the historical from the eschatological; the immediate and the distant future are generally tantalizingly telescoped in a single perspective. But at many points there can be no doubt that what the prophet looked for was the end of the present order of things and a new beginning, brought about by a decisive act of God; and that is eschatology.[14]

[9] R. H. Gundry, *op. cit.*, p. 224.
[10] *E.g.* Am. 5:18–20; Is. 2:12–21; Zp. 1:7–18; Joel *passim.*
[11] *E.g.* Am. 8:3, 9; 9:11; Is. 4:2; 11:10–11; 19:16–25; Zp. 3:11.
[12] *E.g.* Am. 8:11; 9:13; Je. 23:5; 31:31; Ezk. 12:23.
[13] *E.g.* Ho. 3:5; Is. 2:2; Mi. 4:1; Ezk. 38:8, 16; *cf.* Dt. 4:30. See BDB, p. 31.
[14] See further, E. Jacob, *Theology of the Old Testament* (ET London, 1958), pp. 319–327; H. H. Rowley, *Faith*, pp. 177ff., esp. the firm distinction on

b. Messianism

The term המשיח ('the Messiah'; lit. 'the anointed') as a technical term for an eschatological saviour-figure came into use after Old Testament times. We shall, however, use the term 'Messianic' to single out from among the eschatological hopes of the Old Testament 'those prophecies that place a person in the limelight as the figure of salvation'.[15] This definition is, of course, an arbitrary one, and is not uncontested. There is a popular tendency to apply the term 'Messianic' to any eschatological hope of salvation.[16] But as the definition proposed conveniently draws a distinction within the field of eschatological expectation which is of importance in our study, we may usefully adopt it.[17]

Messianic expectation, thus defined, forms only a small part of the total eschatological hope of the Old Testament. Most of the predictions of eschatological judgment and blessing refer directly to the work of God and its results, without recourse to a personal mediator or agent. Nor, when a Messianic figure is in view, is there any uniform idea of his character.

The predominant conception of the Messiah is a kingly one. In the Old Testament the term משיח, while it may be used of other figures (the High Priest[18] and even, on one occasion, the Patriarchs[19]), is generally a description of the king, and the later technical use of המשיח in an eschatological sense derives from this usage. He is the projection of the ideal of kingship, very often conceived as a member of the family of David, or even a David *redivivus*.[20] The 'Branch' of Isaiah 11:1ff.[21] is explicitly a Davidic ruler, and the Messianic figures of Isaiah 9:6–7; 16:5; Micah 5:1–3 (EVV verses 2–4) are all described in Davidic terms. Whether the Messiah is conceived as human,

---

pp. 179–180 between passages with a historical and an eschatological reference.

[15] T. C. Vriezen, *An Outline of Old Testament Theology*² (ET Oxford, 1958), p. 353.

[16] *Cf.* J. Klausner, *op. cit.*, p. 9.

[17] For a similar delimitation of the term, see S. Mowinckel, *He That Cometh*, pp. 3–4. J. Klausner (*op. cit.*, p. 9), having adopted the wider use of the term, is compelled to distinguish between 'the Messianic expectation' and 'belief in the Messiah'. Such a confusing expedient is better avoided.

[18] Lv. 4:3, 5, 16; 6:15 (EVV v. 22).

[19] Ps. 105:15.

[20] *E.g.* Ho. 3:5; Je. 30:9; Ezk. 34:23–24.

[21] *Cf.* Je. 23:5–6.

though idealized, or, as in Isaiah 9:6–7, as no less than divine, the kingly ideal is the formative influence.

Other conceptions of an eschatological redeemer do, however, occur. Deuteronomy 18:15–19 points to a prophetic figure, and in Psalm 110:4 and Zechariah 6:12–13 we have glimpses of a priestly figure, though only in conjunction with the kingly idea. Other less easily categorized figures are found, some of which we shall have to examine below.[22] Finally we may note two figures whose individual character is disputed, the Servant of Yahweh and the Son of man. The corporate aspect of both these figures must be recognized, but so also must the fact that both are described in strongly individual terms. They are, therefore, at least *prima facie*, Messianic in terms of our definition.[23]

Our main concern will be with Jesus' use of these Messianic ideas. But it must be recognized that they are closely bound up with the other and more numerous eschatological hopes. The blessings and judgments expected are of essentially the same character in each case, the Messianic predictions being a development from the non-Messianic, with essentially the same content, but now focused in a person. We cannot, therefore, properly consider the Messianic predictions in isolation, even though our emphasis must be on these.

We consider first, then, Jesus' application to his own work of predictions of eschatological judgment and blessing which do not involve a personal Messiah. Then we shall consider in detail the few, but important, directly Messianic predictions employed, aiming to establish with which Messianic figures of the Old Testament Jesus identified himself, and the significance of his selection. Finally we shall add a group of predictions, both Messianic and non-Messianic, which in the Old Testament concern the work of God himself, and which Jesus apparently applies to his own work.

II. NON-MESSIANIC PREDICTIONS

In the eschatological expectations of the Old Testament the ideas of judgment and salvation are usually closely linked to-

[22] *E.g.* the 'stone' of Dn. 2 (pp. 98–99), and the three Messianic figures from Zc. 9–14 (pp. 103–110).

[23] See further, below, p. 110 n. 102, and Excursus 3, pp. 169–171.

gether. This, as we shall see, is true also of Jesus' view of his own work, and so is reflected in his use of these predictions. For convenience, however, we shall deal first with those predictions in which the idea of judgment is uppermost, and then with those more directly concerned with salvation.

a. Predictions of judgment

Jesus' belief that part of his work as predicted in the Old Testament was to be judgment is summed up in his words concerning the coming destruction of Jerusalem, 'These are days of vengeance, to fulfil all that is written' (Lk. 21:22). The Old Testament contains many threats of judgment on God's rebellious people, and especially on Jerusalem, and now, with the coming of Jesus, the day of vengeance has arrived.

In the words of Luke 21:22 the primary reference is probably not so much to unfulfilled predictions in the Old Testament as to those great judgments both predicted and accomplished on Israel and other nations, which Jesus saw as types of the coming judgment on Jerusalem.[24] But there are at least two predictions of judgment which Jesus applied to the fall of Jerusalem, which their context shows to have been intended to refer not to a specific historical event, but to an eschatological judgment. In using these predictions Jesus implies that the coming disaster will not only be like, or even greater than, those which occurred in Old Testament times; it will be the final judgment on the Jewish nation, that decisive act of God which will put an end to the present order, and usher in a new era of blessing for the new people of God.

Mark 13:19 (Mt. 24:21), alluding to Daniel 12:1. Despite considerable variation in the wording both between Mark and Matthew and also between the MT and the Greek versions, there is quite sufficient correspondence of thought and expression to establish the allusion. The vision of Daniel 11 covers in some historical detail the events of the Seleucid–Ptolemaic struggle of the second century BC. But in 11:40 we reach 'the time of the end', and by the beginning of chapter 12 the vision has lost its historical precision, and taken a clearly eschatolo-

[24] See above, pp. 71–74.

gical turn; the coming of Michael (12:1) apparently heralds the final judgment, and 12:2–3 depicts the resurrection and eternal bliss of the righteous. It is the time of judgment following the coming of Michael that is described in the words to which Jesus alludes. Thus Jesus describes the distress immediately prior to the fall of Jerusalem in strongly eschatological terms.

Matthew 24:30, alluding to Zechariah 12:12.[25] Jesus here looks forward to a fulfilment in AD 70 of Zechariah's vision of the mourning of Israel.[26] The whole of Zechariah 12–14 appears to have an eschatological reference, concerning God's final vindication and purification of his people; the constant use of 'on that day' suggests that the thought is of the day of Yahweh. This eschatological mourning of repentance will occur, according to Jesus, when they see his triumphant judgment on Jerusalem. But it will issue not, as in Zechariah 13:1, in the opportunity of spiritual restoration for the mourners (Israel), but in the gathering instead of the true people of God from all nations.[27] The Jewish nation mourns over its final judgment; it is the followers of Jesus who experience the salvation.

Mark 9:48, quoting Isaiah 66:24. Jesus' description of Gehenna is drawn from an apocalyptic passage of Isaiah, describing the final state of those who have rebelled against God, and set at the time when God will make a new heaven and a new earth. To Isaiah the vision is future; to Jesus it is a present reality, the state of those who rebel against God now. It is possible that Jesus is here simply using a convenient form of words from the Old Testament without reference to the eschatological context in which they occur,[28] but more probably this allusion is further evidence of his conviction that in his coming the eschatological judgment and blessing of God is already a reality.

[25] We have treated this allusion here as well as under the heading of Messianic prediction (pp. 106–107) because Jesus' explicit use of Zc. 12:10ff. is with reference to the mourning itself, not to the one who is its cause.

[26] For this interpretation see below, pp. 236–238.

[27] See below, pp. 238–239.

[28] The Jewish conception of hell drew much on these words. See J. Skinner, *The Book of the Prophet Isaiah*[2] (Cambridge, 1915–1917), vol. 2, pp. 255–256; H. B. Swete, *Mark*, p. 212.

Mark 9:12–13 (Mt. 17:11–12), alluding to Malachi 3:23–24 (EVV 4:5–6).

Matthew 11:10 (Lk. 7:27),[29] quoting Malachi 3:1.[30]

Matthew 11:14, alluding to Malachi 3:23 (EVV 4:5).

These three passages may be considered together, as in each Jesus identifies John the Baptist in terms of the predictions of Malachi 3:1, 23–24, of the sending of 'my messenger' and of Elijah before God's own coming to judgment. Malachi 3:1 introduces 'my messenger', who is to refine and purify the people before the coming of Yahweh.[31] Malachi 3:23–24 introduces the figure of Elijah *redivivus*, whose function is also to

[29] The presence of this quotation in Mk. 1:2 is very likely due to later interpolation; see M.-J. Lagrange, *Évangile selon Saint Marc*[4] (Paris, 1947), pp. 3–4; J. A. T. Robinson, *Twelve New Testament Studies*, p. 34. As it is not there attributed to Jesus, it in any case falls outside our scope.

[30] For the conflation with Ex. 23:20 see below, pp. 242–243.

[31] In Mal. 3:1 the speaker is Yahweh, who mentions three persons who are shortly to come. He will send מלאכי to prepare for his own coming; האדון, whom they are seeking, will come to his temple, ומלאך־הברית in whom they delight. The repetition of the noun suggests that מלאכי and מלאך־הברית describe the same person, distinguished from Yahweh, and sent to prepare for his coming. But both the grammar and the rhythm of the sentence throw האדון and מלאך־הברית together, apparently in apposition. This means that all three figures are in fact different descriptions of the same messenger of Yahweh, joined in typical Hebrew parallelism. The only objection to this exegesis is the term used for the second figure; the EVV, by translating האדון as 'the Lord', suggest an identification with Yahweh. (The fact that RV, RSV, and NEB print 'Lord' as opposed to the usual 'LORD' generally escapes notice, and the term 'the Lord', however printed, inevitably conveys 'God' to English ears.) But אדון need have no such meaning: it is commonly applied to men, meaning 'lord, master', and as a 'general recognition of superiority' (BDB, p. 11, with numerous examples; *cf.* below, p. 163), and האדון alone is never used as a title of Yahweh; it is applied to God only in Ex. 23:17; 34:23; Is. 1:24; 3:1; 10:16, 33; 19:4, always in conjunction with יהוה and usually with other titles (צבאות *etc.*) as well. האדון is thus a descriptive term added to recognized titles of God to heighten the sense of majesty, but not in itself implying divinity. The nearest parallels to this use of האדון alone which refer to God are אדון without article, in parallelism with אלוה (Ps. 114:7 only), and the occasional title אדון כל־הארץ. As there is, therefore, no close parallel to this use of the singular with the article, the context must decide its reference, and, as we have seen, the parallelism points to an identification of the three figures as the same messenger of Yahweh, who is thus described as 'the master, lord, mighty one'. If, however, this exegesis is not accepted,

purify the people, here specifically by effecting family reconciliation, before the terrible coming of Yahweh. Probably Elijah *redivivus* is intended to be identified with 'my messenger'.[32] Certainly Jesus is justified in applying both to John the Baptist, for their functions are the same.

Jesus, then, sees the ministry of John the Baptist predicted in the figure of 'my messenger'/Elijah, who was to be sent to prepare the way for the coming of Yahweh to judgment, the day of Yahweh. The very least this application can imply is that in the ministry of Jesus, for which John the Baptist prepared the way, the day of Yahweh has come;[33] as we shall argue below,[34] more is implied: Jesus is thus set in the very place of Yahweh. But for our present purposes the clear affirmation must be noted that the one who was to usher in the day of Yahweh's judgment has come, and so that day is now imminent or already present.

b. Predictions of salvation

'Salvation' is an umbrella term. We use it here to include all that the Old Testament prophets saw as the beneficent eschatological activity of God on behalf of his people. It is a varied picture, including material as well as spiritual and moral blessing, and in the teaching of Jesus several different aspects of that variety find an echo.

Mark 11:15–16 (Mt. 21:12; Lk. 19:45). Jesus' action in clearing the Temple of various kinds of traders is probably a conscious fulfilment of the prediction of Zechariah 14:21 that, in the eschatological purity of Jerusalem, 'there shall no longer be a trader in the house of the Lord of hosts on that day.'[35]

---

and האדון is taken to mean Yahweh, the passage still mentions only two persons, Yahweh and the messenger. There is no reason to introduce a third, Messianic figure. *Cf.* R. H. Fuller, *Foundations*, p. 48.

[32] *Cf., e.g.*, T. H. Robinson, *Prophecy and the Prophets in Ancient Israel*[2] (London, 1953), p. 209. That this identification is assumed in Mt. 11 is suggested by the fact that v. 14 follows closely on v. 10 without any explanation of the introduction of Elijah.

[33] So C. F. D. Moule, *The Birth of the New Testament* (London, 1962), p. 63. *Cf.* G. E. Ladd, *op. cit.*, p. 155.

[34] See p. 155.

[35] *Cf.* B. Lindars, *op. cit.*, p. 108 n. 3. Lindars' suggestion (*ibid.*, p. 108) that the incident is 'a dramatisation of Mal. 3.1' is unlikely since, as he

Thus by a literal fulfilment of the prediction Jesus claims that the eschatological age described in Zechariah 14, with its purification of worship, has arrived.[36]

Mark 11:17 (Mt. 21:13; Lk. 19:46), quoting Isaiah 56:7, a passage which has a primary reference to the return from the Exile, and the consequent blessings, but whose terminology suggests that the eschatological salvation is also in view, and which was in fact so interpreted in Jewish circles.[37]

The quotation in Mark includes the additional words 'for all the nations', and on this basis it is suggested that Jesus' concern is not with the propriety of trading in the Temple, but with the inclusion of the Gentiles in its worship.[38] Certainly this is the thrust of Isaiah 56: Gentiles who love and serve Yahweh will be accepted as worshippers in the Temple. But little in Mark, any more than in Matthew and Luke, supports this exegesis. Jesus' action is directed at those who were rendering the Temple unsuitable for worship, and there is no other reference by word or deed to the Gentiles. The contrast of verse 17 demands an emphasis on the 'house of prayer' in Isaiah 56:7: 'den of thieves' contrasts with 'house of prayer', not with Gentile participation. Matthew and Luke have omitted 'for all the nations', not because they failed to understand the main point, but because they *have* seen it, and omit details which might distract attention from it (as Matthew often does with details in the Marcan narrative).[39] Jesus' protest is directed primarily against the profanation of the Temple by turning it into a market. The fact that this occurred in the Court of the Gentiles, however, renders the additional words 'for all the nations' far from irrelevant.

Jesus' use of Isaiah 56:7, therefore, though not out of harmony with the original meaning, centres on what is only a

---

himself notices, 'although Mal. 3.1 is quoted more than once by the Synoptists, none of the accounts of the cleansing contain any hint of it,' and also because Jesus elsewhere applied Mal. 3:1 to John the Baptist, not himself.

[36] *Cf.* C. Roth, *NT* 4 (1960), pp. 174–181, who sees this prediction of Zechariah as the central cause of Jesus' 'Messianic gesture'.

[37] *Cf.* K. Stendahl, *op. cit.*, pp. 66–67, and references *ad loc.*

[38] So B. Lindars, *op. cit.*, pp. 107–108.

[39] *Cf.* K. Stendahl, *op. cit.*, p. 67; R. H. Gundry, *op. cit.*, p. 19.

subsidiary idea in the Old Testament context, and has only a minor place for the main thrust of the passage. One must accordingly be careful in drawing conclusions from the use of Isaiah 56. Since, however, the implications of the use of this passage, with its eschatological aspect, are in harmony with those of the other allusions here under consideration, we may properly suggest that the Old Testament context was not absent from Jesus' mind, especially as we have already seen cause to postulate an eschatological thrust in the incident itself, on the basis of Zechariah 14:21. Thus again Jesus is implicitly claiming that his action is bringing into reality the eschatological blessings predicted in the Old Testament.[40]

Mark 14:24 (Mt. 26:28; Lk. 22:20). In addition to the typological allusion to Exodus 24:8,[41] the phrase 'the new covenant' in the Lucan version is a clear allusion to Jeremiah 31:31. Even if this phrase were not part of Jesus' original words,[42] it is still hard to imagine that Jesus, in referring to the covenant of Exodus 24:8, and seeing it as re-enacted in his own death, did not have Jeremiah 31:31 in mind. The phrase 'for the forgiveness of sins' in the Matthean version may also be an echo of Jeremiah 31:34. The Old Testament passage looks forward to a time of spiritual renewal, when the law of God will be written on men's hearts, when they will know God, and their sins will be forgiven. The phrase 'the days are coming' confirms that this new covenant is seen in eschatological terms, the final answer to the problem of man's rebellion against God. This covenant, Jesus affirms, he has now come to inaugurate.

Matthew 6:8, a possible allusion to Isaiah 65:24. There is no verbal echo, but the thought is closely parallel. The passage in Isaiah describes the blessings of the new heaven and earth which

[40] E. Lohmeyer (*Das Evangelium des Markus*[3] (Göttingen, 1953), p. 237) sees the unhindered worship of the Gentiles as in itself of eschatological significance.

[41] See above, pp. 66–67.

[42] Lk. 22:19b–20 is relegated to the margin by RSV and NEB, as a later addition to the text (from 1 Cor. 11:25?). Recent studies have shown that it is most probably original: see E. E. Ellis, *The Gospel of Luke* (London, 1966), pp. 253–255, summarizing the extensive study by H. Schürmann. In more detail see J. Jeremias, *The Eucharistic Words of Jesus*[3] (ET London, 1966), pp. 138–159.

God will create, so that the implication of the allusion would be that those conditions are now already present in the experience of the disciples. The new heaven and earth have appeared.

Matthew 8:11–12 (Lk. 13:28–29). We have seen above[43] that the wording of this saying is drawn from descriptions of the deliverance of Israel, typologically applied to the Gentile church. But the thought behind the words reflects other currents in Old Testament thought, both that of the worship of Yahweh by the Gentiles in all the world (*e.g.* Is. 45:6; 59:19; Mal. 1:11, all of which, like Mt. 8:11, mention east and west), and that of the pilgrimage of the Gentiles to Jerusalem to worship Yahweh (*e.g.* Is. 2:2–3 = Mi. 4:1–2; Zc. 8:20–23). J. Jeremias has shown in detail that through much of the Old Testament ran an expectation of an 'eschatological pilgrimage of the Gentiles to the Mountain of God',[44] and believes that it was this idea that Jesus had in mind in this saying. He therefore sees Jesus' words as applying to 'the hour of the final judgement'.[45] What he does not go on to point out is that this coming of the Gentiles into the kingdom is, in the Lucan version, something which his hearers will *see*; it is imminent.[46] Jeremias believes that Jesus distinguished sharply between his own mission and the future eschatological act of God which would include the salvation of the Gentiles. We have already seen good reason to question this interpretation; as Jesus sees it, in his own ministry the eschaton of Old Testament prophecy has arrived. So the day for the gathering of the Gentiles into his kingdom is not far off, but is already beginning.

Matthew 11:5 (Lk. 7:22). Jesus' description of his ministry of healing and preaching is drawn from at least two Old Testament passages, Isaiah 35:5–6 and 61:1.[47] τυφλοὶ ἀναβλέπουσιν

[43] See above, p. 63.
[44] *Promise*, pp. 55–60.
[45] *Ibid.*, p. 56.
[46] *Cf.* Mk. 13:27 (Mt. 24:31), referring to the years following AD 70. See above, pp. 63–64.
[47] A further allusion to Is. 26:19 in the phrase 'the dead are raised up' and to Is. 29:18–19 in the blind, deaf and poor is not improbable. (So M.-J. Lagrange, *Évangile selon Saint Luc*[8] (Paris, 1948), p. 215.) As the aim of Jesus' reply is to establish that he is 'he who is to come' as predicted in the OT, an OT background to each phrase is likely.

('the blind receive their sight') and *πτωχοὶ εὐαγγελίζονται* ('the poor have good news preached to them') may be taken as direct verbal echoes of Isaiah 61:1. Isaiah 35:5–6 also contains the idea of restoration of sight, and contributes also those of the healing of the lame and the deaf. We shall consider Isaiah 61:1 below as a Messianic prediction; but in Isaiah 35 no Messianic figure is included. The chapter is an idyllic description of the return of God's ransomed people to Zion, in terms which clearly look beyond the historical event to its eschatological counterpart. Whether or not Isaiah intended his language to be taken literally, Jesus points to its literal fulfilment as evidence of his own status. In his ministry the blessings predicted as accompanying the eschatological acts of God are being realized. This, for John, should be sufficient evidence that he is 'he who is to come'. 'It is clear, by the simple application of the traditional terms to the present situation, that salvation has already begun.'[48]

Luke 19:10, alluding to Ezekiel 34:16, 22.[49] The context in Ezekiel is Yahweh's declaration that since his shepherds (the rulers) have failed to look after his sheep (the people), he himself will punish the shepherds and assume their function, seeking and saving the lost sheep. The point of departure is, therefore, a historical reference to a period of unsatisfactory rule. But the chapter goes on to speak, in apparently Messianic terms, of the setting up of a good ruler, David, while the blessings promised at the close of the chapter, after due allowance has been made for the requirements of the shepherd metaphor, are clearly reminiscent of Isaiah's predictions of eschatological bliss. The verses alluded to by Jesus, therefore, while not carrying the Messianic content of the later verses, fall in a context where the historical is mixed with the eschatological, where a historical act of deliverance leads to a view of the final and complete salvation. The implication is again that in the work of Jesus this saving act of God is being accomplished.

Luke 24:49, a possible allusion to Isaiah 32:15. The clause ἕως

[48] M.-J. Lagrange, *ibid. Cf.* G. E. Ladd, *op. cit.*, pp. 109–110.

[49] 'A clear allusion' according to A. J. B. Higgins, *Jesus and the Son of Man* (London, 1964), p. 77.

οὗ ἐνδύσησθε ἐξ ὕψους δύναμιν ('until you are clothed with power from on high'), with reference to the promised gift of the Holy Spirit (implicit here in Luke, and explicit in the parallel Acts 1:5–8), is verbally quite close to the MT עד־יערה עלינו רוח ממרום (LXX *ἕως ἂν ἐπέλθῃ ἐφ' ὑμᾶς πνεῦμα ἀφ' ὑψηλοῦ*), and it is not unlikely that Jesus should have in mind this Old Testament promise of a gift of the Spirit. Isaiah describes an ideal king, and a terrible desolation which will continue until the gift of the Spirit ushers in a new age of peace, prosperity and righteousness. It is, therefore, at least possible that Jesus here presents the coming of the Spirit, the sequel to his earthly ministry, as the beginning of this new age of blessing.

Not all of the above are clearly intentional allusions, but they provide sufficient warrant for stating that Jesus believed that in his ministry the eschatological hopes of the Old Testament, with their complementary elements of judgment and salvation, were being fulfilled. The variety of conceptions of this salvation found in the prophets is well represented in those passages which Jesus selects, ranging from the material level of physical healing to the more spiritual blessings of forgiveness of sins, the hearing of prayer, a renewed and purified worship, and the gift of the Spirit. And in this comprehensive salvation the Gentiles, as the Old Testament envisaged, have a share. The recorded allusions represent only a very small selection from among the eschatological hopes of the Old Testament, but they are enough to show that it was no chance remark with which Jesus began his ministry: 'The time is fulfilled, and the kingdom of God is at hand.'

III. SOME POSSIBLE MESSIANIC PREDICTIONS

That Jesus should have applied the specifically Messianic predictions of the Old Testament to himself is not surprising in view of his use of the more general eschatological hopes. Again the number of passages so used is not large, though the importance of some is attested by the frequency of their use. Only seven Messianic figures are used at all certainly, and a further two possible cases must be mentioned.[50] The seven are distribu-

[50] Two further suggested cases are the use of Ps. 22:2 (EVV 22:1) in

ted as follows: one in the Psalms, one in Daniel, two in Isaiah, and three in Zechariah. The two possible cases are in Daniel and Zechariah. These two must first be considered briefly.

a. The Stone

Luke 20:18 (?Mt. 21:44). The authenticity of this verse in Luke seems textually certain; in Matthew, as a 'Western non-interpolation', it is questionable. The allusion to Isaiah 8:14–15 in the first half of the verse is obvious, and will be treated below,[51] as it is not a Messianic passage in terms of our definition. The second half is very likely an allusion to another 'stone' passage, Daniel 2:34–35, 44–45. The verb λικμήσει ('crush') occurs in Thdt Daniel 2:44, and represents also the simile of Daniel 2:35, where the broken pieces of the statue are 'like the chaff of the summer threshing floors'.[52] The idea of a stone falling on a person and destroying him is closely parallel to the vision of Daniel 2, and an Old Testament allusion is to be expected after that in the first half of the verse.

The vision of Daniel 2 is closely parallel to that of Daniel 7, representing the triumph of the people of God over the successive pagan empires. For the beasts and the human figure of Daniel 7, Daniel 2 has the statue and the stone which shatters

---

Mk. 15:34 (Mt. 27:46) and that of Ps. 118:26 in Mt. 23:39 (Lk. 13:35). Both of these cases have been treated above as typological applications, rather than as appeals to Messianic prediction. In the case of Ps. 22, there is hardly any evidence for a *Messianic* interpretation of the psalm before Christians so used it after the death of Jesus. While Ps. 118:22 may have been eschatologically interpreted in late Judaism (see *e.g.* A. Plummer, *The Gospel according to S. Luke*[4] (Edinburgh, 1901), p. 462; A. H. McNeile, *Matthew*, p. 311), a Messianic understanding of v. 26 of that psalm is postulated solely on the basis of its use by the crowd at the entry to Jerusalem (Mk. 11:9 and parallels), and on the supposition that ὁ ἐρχόμενος (Mt. 11:3; Lk. 7:19) was a recognized Messianic title derived from this verse. J. Blenkinsopp (*JBL* 80 (1961), p. 58) bases this supposition on its use 'several times in Mark', but these 'several times' boil down in fact to the single citation of Ps. 118:26 in Mk. 11:9. (In Mk. 13:26; 14:62 ἐρχόμενον is an inevitable part of the citation of Dn. 7:13, and in Mk. 13:36 there is no trace of ἐρχόμενος!) A typological principle best accounts for Jesus' use of both Ps. 22:2 and Ps. 118:26, as it clearly accounts for his use of Ps. 118:22 (see above, pp. 58–59), and they are not therefore relevant to our present discussion.

[51] See pp. 152–153.

[52] *Cf.* J. M. Creed, *The Gospel according to St. Luke* (London, 1930), p. 247: 'The proper meaning of λικμᾶν is "to winnow chaff from grain" and then derivatively "to scatter as chaff", "to make to disappear."'

it. Since, as we shall see below, Jesus saw the human figure of Daniel 7 as a picture of his own work, it is not improbable that he took the stone of Daniel 2 in the same way.[53] The application would then be the same, that Jesus brings in the final and triumphant kingdom, which supersedes and destroys all who oppose it. The primary reference in the context is to the Jews.[54]

Not much can be based on this allusion. There are too many doubtful factors. (The allusion is not certain; the Old Testament passage is not certainly Messianic in terms of our definition; the verse in Luke may be seen as an editorial comment rather than a part of the discourse of Jesus.[55]) But it is possible that not only Daniel 7, but the parallel Daniel 2, was an influence on Jesus' conception of his mission, and that he saw the stone of Daniel 2 as a metaphor for himself as the one who was to bring in the kingdom of God.

b. The Branch

Mark 14:58 (Mt. 26:61. *Cf.* Mk. 15:29; Mt. 27:40). It is likely that these citations by Jesus' opponents of sayings alleged to have been uttered by him do represent some genuine utterance, since it is improbable that the Christians would otherwise have preserved such embarrassing charges. (They were, literally at least, unfulfilled predictions, and liable to cause misunderstanding and hostility in a Jewish milieu.) That Jesus predicted the destruction of the Temple we know from Mark 13:2 and Luke 19:44 (probably also from Mt. 23:38). But none of these sayings refers to a rebuilding. This is, however, found in John 2:19, set at the time of the cleansing of the Temple; the occasion is a likely one for such a saying, and for its hostile construction by the authorities, and this may well be the source of the charge.[56]

[53] That the reference of this verse is to himself, not to the church (so B. Lindars, *op. cit.*, p. 184), is indicated both by the context, and especially by the use of Is. 8:14–15, which could hardly have such a reference: see below, pp. 152–153.

[54] For the implications of this fact see below, pp. 146–147.

[55] Such a comment on Jesus' use of Ps. 118:22 is possible, and would account for the late insertion of the saying in Matthew. But the context does not indicate it, and such a running together of reported speech and comment is more typical of the Fourth than of the Third Gospel.

[56] The imperative λύσατε is changed in the charge to an indicative, thus

John interprets Jesus' saying as a prediction of his resurrection. But the metaphor chosen may well be an allusion to the expectation that the Messiah would restore the Temple, found in Tg Isaiah 53:5 ('He shall build the sanctuary that was polluted because of our transgressions'), and deriving from Zechariah 6:12–13: 'the man whose name is the Branch . . . he shall build the temple of the Lord.'[57] The implied Messianic claim would increase the significance of the use of this saying at the trial.

In Zechariah 6:11–13 the High Priest Joshua is symbolically crowned, and hailed as 'the Branch' (צמח, a Messianic title derived from Je. 23:5 = 33:15; *cf.* Is 4:2), and it is predicted that he will build the Temple, and bear royal office, supported by a priestly figure. Joshua is thus set up as a type of the coming Messiah,[58] and the prediction of building the Temple is a symbol, probably of the Messiah's creation of a true worshipping community.[59] Jesus' reference to rebuilding the Temple was also figurative, referring primarily to his resurrection, but perhaps also to the creation of his church which was to be accomplished through it.[60] At any rate, if, as seems likely, an allusion to Zechariah 6:12–13 lies behind the charge of Mark 14:58, it involves a claim to be the promised 'Branch', the Messiah.

IV. DAVID'S LORD

Psalm 110:1 occurs twice in the sayings of Jesus. Once it is as a formal quotation, on which an argument regarding the status

---

making Jesus the agent not only of the restoration (hardly a criminal act!) but of the destruction.

[57] *Cf.* B. Lindars, *op. cit.*, pp. 69–71, with other suggested allusions to Zc. 6:11–13 in Matthew.

[58] Zc. 3:8 makes it clear that the 'Branch' is a future figure, distinct from Joshua. The prediction of royal office with a priestly partner could hardly apply literally to Joshua, who was already High Priest. See further J. G. Baldwin, *VT* 14 (1964), pp. 94–97.

[59] Such a figurative interpretation is necessitated not only by the symbolic nature of the passage, but by the fact that Joshua was already engaged in encouraging the building of the Second Temple; it would be strange to predict that the Messiah would build a literal temple when one was already well on the way to completion.

[60] So C. K. Barrett, *The Gospel according to St. John* (London, 1955), pp. 167–168; and *cf.* above, p. 55 on the use of Ho. 6:2.

of the Messiah is based; the other use is in the combined allusion to Daniel 7:13 and Psalm 110:1 with which Jesus followed his confession of his Messiahship before the Sanhedrin. It seems probable, therefore, that this psalm contributed significantly to Jesus' idea of Messiahship.

a. The formal quotation

Mark 12:36 (Mt. 22:44; Lk. 20:42–43).[61] The argument of Jesus here is not that the Messiah is not David's son, but that he is more than David's son.[62] Mere physical descent alone does not constitute Messiahship; the Messiah is superior to any human king, David included.[63] The argument runs as follows: in Psalm 110 David designates the Messiah by the term אדוני ('my lord'); this term implies the superiority of the one so described; the Messiah is therefore superior to David. To call him David's son is to imply a descendant of David, occupying his political throne. The Messiah is more than this; he is greater

[61] The authenticity of this pericope as an argument by Jesus has been challenged, *e.g.*, by Bultmann (*History*, pp. 136–137, *etc.*). V. Taylor's answers to his arguments are convincing (*Mark*, p. 493), and are further reinforced by R. P. Gagg, *Theologische Zeitschrift* 7 (1951), pp. 20–22 and E. Lövestam, *Svensk Exegetisk Årsbok* 27 (1962), pp. 81–82. A saying which must have been at least puzzling, perhaps embarrassing, for those who proclaimed Jesus as Son of David is hardly likely to have been created and circulated by the Christian church. R. H. Fuller (*Foundations*, pp. 19, 111) rejects the saying because 'the use of the LXX is pivotal' to the argument, but does not explain this verdict. Presumably he refers to the double use of *κύριος*; but אדוני no less than *κύριος* carries the implication of superiority on which the argument rests.

[62] Against the view that this pericope *is* intended to deny the Davidic descent of the Messiah, see V. Taylor, *Mark*, p. 491; O. Cullmann, *Christology*, pp. 131–133; E. Lövestam, *loc. cit.*, pp. 72–73. The theory of R. P. Gagg (*loc. cit.*, pp. 18–30, adopted by C. E. B. Cranfield, *The Gospel according to St. Mark* (Cambridge, 1959), pp. 381–383), that the extant pericope is the end of an originally longer account of a trick question by the Pharisees, and thus represents an evasive counter-question with no intention of conveying Christological teaching, is really a counsel of despair, and should be considered only if more uncomplicated exegesis fails to produce a satisfactory explanation of the saying.

[63] For a fuller presentation of this interpretation see O. Cullmann, *Christology*, pp. 130–133; V. Taylor, *Mark*, pp. 491–493; C. F. D. Moule, *Birth*, pp. 64–65. E. Lövestam (*loc. cit.*) argues on similar lines, linking the use of Ps. 110 with the idea of the fulfilment of the promise to David in 2 Sa. 7.

than David, a position which no mere Israelite king could claim.

The argument may thus be seen to rest upon three premises, that the speaker in Psalm 110 is David, that the person addressed by Yahweh in verse 1 is the Messiah, and that the use of the term אדוני ('my lord') implies the superiority of the one so described.[64] Without any one of these premises the argument would be invalid. A discussion of their validity is undertaken in Excursus 2 below.[65]

There is not at this point any explicit claim that Jesus is himself the Messiah spoken of in the psalm; the point at issue is the status of the Messiah, not his identity. Mark 14:62, however, proves that Jesus did in fact apply this psalm to himself; and the title 'Son of David' had already been applied to Jesus by others more than once. It was not as a purely academic exercise that Jesus undertook to correct erroneous ideas of the nature of the Messiahship which they attributed to him.

His argument sets aside the political notions which clustered around the title 'Son of David' in favour of a superior conception. What that conception is he does not explicitly state, but the content of Psalm 110 indicates that it involves a close relation with God himself, and includes the office not only of king, but of priest (verse 4). It is a position of victory and dominion, but a victory and dominion conferred by the power of God. Thus in place of a political rule received by earthly heredity, Jesus sets a higher dominion at God's right hand, conferred by God himself. The similarity of this conception to that derived from the king of Zechariah 9:9, the Servant of Isaiah 53, and the Son of man of Daniel 7, will become apparent as we proceed. For the moment we may endorse the verdict of E. Lövestam: 'Jesus' question quite plainly involves an attack on every national-political interpretation of the promise to David.'[66]

[64] B. Lindars (*op. cit.*, p. 47) suggests that the argument depends on the exegesis of the phrase 'to sit at the right hand' as indicating the exaltation of Jesus, and uses this as evidence for the post-resurrection origin of the saying. We can see no basis for this suggestion in any of the Synoptic accounts; the wording as we have it bases the argument solely on the use of אדוני, not on the heavenly session.

[65] Pp. 163–169.

[66] *Loc. cit.*, p. 81.

b. The declaration before the Sanhedrin

Mark 14:62 (Mt. 26:64; Lk. 22:69). Combined with the allusion to Daniel 7:13 are the words 'sitting at the right hand of Power' ('of the power of God', Lk.),[67] a clear allusion to Psalm 110:1, 'Sit at my right hand'. This conflation confirms the close connection of thought we have just suggested between Psalm 110:1 and Daniel 7 (as well as Zc. 9:9–10 and Is. 53), in that both envisage a Messiah whose exaltation and domination is the gift of God, not won by his own power. The context confirms this further; Jesus is on trial, apparently defeated and powerless; he appeals not to his own miraculous power, but to his imminent vindication by God.[68]

Confronted with the question whether he is in fact the Messiah, Jesus accepts the title, but immediately reinterprets it, as he had done in Mark 12:35–37, in terms of Daniel 7:13 and Psalm 110:1. This is consistently Jesus' reaction to the currently accepted implications of the titles 'Messiah' and 'Son of David'.[69] We have no case in the Synoptic Gospels of his accepting either without such reinterpretation, in terms of either Daniel 7:13, Isaiah 53, Zechariah 9:9 or Psalm 110:1.

The type of Messiahship which Jesus saw in Psalm 110:1, therefore, and which he saw as his own, was one in contrast with any merely political ideal. The Messianic dominion was not to be won by his own power, but would be conferred on him by God, and would be exercised in a realm higher than that of a national kingship, at the right hand of God. It carried also a priestly function, and it would last for ever.

V. THREE FIGURES FROM ZECHARIAH 9–14

It is commonly recognized that Zechariah 9–14 formed an important background both for Jesus' thought and words especially at the time of the passion, and also for the Evangelists'

[67] For δύναμις as a typical 'targumizing' paraphrase for God, see G. Dalman, *The Words of Jesus* (ET Edinburgh, 1902), pp. 200–201.

[68] For the exegesis of this verse, and the significance of the use of Dn. 7:13, see below, pp. 140–142.

[69] *Cf.* Mk. 8:29–31, and the treatment of these and other such passages by O. Cullmann, *Christology*, pp. 117–125. R. H. Fuller's attack on this position (*Foundations*, pp. 109–111) depends on a radical criticism which rejects all the relevant sayings.

presentation of the narrative.[70] This section introduces four figures which may be taken as Messianic: the king riding on an ass (9:9–10), the good shepherd (11:4–14), the one 'whom they have pierced' (12:10), and the smitten shepherd (13:7). P. Lamarche, in a detailed study of Zechariah 9–14,[71] has attempted to demonstrate the unity of these chapters by tracing an elaborate chiastic structure in their subject-matter. In his scheme, the passages containing these four figures (9:9–10; 11:4–17; 12:10–13:1; 13:7–9) are thrown together as structurally parallel, constituting together one of the four themes on which the chiastic structure is based.[72] Thus the four passages are seen as four aspects of a single Messianic conception, 'the Shepherd-King', presenting successive phases of his coming and the reaction of the people. It is a conception built up through reflection on the figure of the Servant of Yahweh in Isaiah, and therefore concentrating on the problem of the rejection, suffering and death of the Messiah.[73]

Lamarche's unified picture of a Shepherd-King,[74] whether or not we approve the suggestion of a chiastic structure, seems plausible in view of the use of the shepherd metaphor for rulers in the Old Testament.[75] The basic consistency of the various figures in Zechariah 9–14 thus united will appear in our following discussion, and will lend weight to at least this part of Lamarche's theory. We may, therefore, cautiously accept it as the basis for our discussion of Jesus' use of these passages.

Jesus refers clearly to no less than three of the four passages concerned.[76] Considering the small number of Messianic

[70] See esp. F. F. Bruce, 'The Book of Zechariah and the Passion Narrative', *BJRL* 43 (1960/1), pp. 336–353, and *idem*, *This is That* (Exeter, 1968), pp. 101–114. Also B. Lindars, *op. cit.*, pp. 110–134; C. F. Evans, *JTS* 5 (1954), pp. 5–8.

[71] *Zacharie IX–XIV:* Structure Littéraire et Messianisme (Paris, 1961).

[72] *Ibid.*, pp. 110–115.

[73] On pp. 118–123 Lamarche discusses the identity of 'the Shepherd-King', and concludes that the figure is built round a recent or contemporary personage (perhaps Zerubbabel), who is seen as a figure of the coming Messiah.

[74] F. F. Bruce (*BJRL* 43 (1960/1), pp. 342–349) traces this same figure both in Zc. 9–14 and in Jesus' thought during the closing phases of his ministry.

[75] *E.g.* Je. 23; Ezk. 34.

[76] For possible allusions to the fourth (11:4–14) *cf.* F. F. Bruce, *BJRL* 43 (1960/1), p. 346.

passages to which he alludes, this concentration is remarkable, and further strengthens Lamarche's view of the unity and the significance of the conception of the Shepherd-King. We now consider these three references in detail.

a. The King

Mark 11:1ff. (Mt. 21:1ff.; Lk. 19:29ff.). Jesus' entry to Jerusalem is carefully staged, and equally carefully recorded, even by Mark and Luke who do not insert an explicit quotation,[77] in such a way as to make the reference to Zechariah 9:9 quite unmistakable. That this intention goes back to Jesus himself seems clear; the allusion derives not merely from the wording of the narratives, but from the deliberately significant nature of the acts themselves.[78]

The king, for whose coming to Jerusalem Zechariah 9:9–10 hopes, is described thus: צדיק ונושע הוא עני ורכב על־חמור (LXX *δίκαιος καὶ σῴζων αὐτός, πραῢς καὶ ἐπιβεβηκὼς ἐπὶ ὑποζύγιον*; RSV 'Triumphant and victorious is he, humble and riding on an ass'). The LXX gives a wrong impression of the first phrase. *δίκαιος* misses the note of deliverance often inherent in צדיק, which in this context is best translated 'vindicated'.[79] This passive idea is explicit in the following נושע, which is Niphal, and therefore means 'saved'; if it can properly be translated 'victorious', it is only in the sense of one who has been given the victory by another's power.[80] Thus there is no contrast with the lowliness depicted in the following phrase. The picture is of a humble and gentle king, who, like the Servant of Yahweh,[81] is

[77] *Cf.* J. Blenkinsopp, *JBL* 80 (1961), pp. 55–56; R. H. Fuller, *Foundations*, p. 199 n. 24.

[78] H. P. Kingdon (*Studia Evangelica III*, Texte und Untersuchungen 88 (Berlin, 1964), p. 83) refers to it as 'His deliberate symbolically-acted reference to Zechariah 9, 9.' *Cf.* V. Taylor, *Mark*, p. 452. C. E. B. Cranfield (*Mark*, pp. 352–354) recognizes Jesus' intention to point to Zc. 9:9, but denies that it was intended as a public demonstration. R. H. Fuller (*Foundations*, p. 114) succeeds in denying that Jesus intended any allusion by treating most of the story as unhistorical, but gives no alternative interpretation of the riding on an ass, which he retains.

[79] *Cf.* H. G. Mitchell, in *Haggai, Zechariah, Malachi and Jonah* (*ICC*, Edinburgh, 1912), p. 273; P. R. Ackroyd in *Peake's Commentary on the Bible* (London, 1962), p. 652. The latter renders 'declared right, acquitted'.

[80] *Cf.* BDB, p. 446, and H. G. Mitchell and P. R. Ackroyd, *locis cit.*; more fully, P. Lamarche, *op. cit.*, p. 43.

[81] *Cf.* H. G. Mitchell, *ibid.*; P. Lamarche, *op. cit.*, p. 44.

ctorious only because God has vindicated and delivered him. nd he comes to bring not war and violence, but peace and rosperity.[82]

Among the many specifically royal Messianic hopes of the Old Testament (this, as we have seen, was the dominant note of Old Testament Messianism), Jesus applies only two to himself, Psalm 110:1 and Zechariah 9:9. This in itself is sufficiently remarkable, but still more remarkable is the fact that the first is cited specifically in order to contradict any purely political notion of Messiahship, and is applied in a way which emphasizes this point, and the second is unique in the Old Testament in the character of the kingship it describes, a character which is closer to that of the Servant of Yahweh than to the dominant hope of a Davidic deliverer of Israel and conqueror of hostile nations.[83] The least majestic and powerful of Old Testament hopes of a royal Messiah is the only one applied by Jesus to himself without qualification. The significance of this fact, and its coherence with the other figures selected, will appear as we proceed.

b. The Martyr

Matthew 24:30. The allusion to Zechariah 12:12 has already occupied our attention.[84] As we have seen, the explicit allusion is to the mourning of Israel, which Jesus says will occur in AD 70, when the Jews see his act of judgment on their capital and nation. Such an allusion, however, could hardly be made without reference to what in Zechariah 12 is the cause of their mourning: 'they shall look on me whom they have pierced'. It may be that 'they will see' in Matthew 24:30 is an echo of this clause, in which case Jesus would be identifying himself not only as the Son of man coming on the clouds of heaven, but also as the one whom they 'pierced'. In view of his

[82] *Cf.* C. F. D. Moule, *The Gospel according to Mark* (Cambridge, 1965), p. 87. The suggestion of D. R. Jones (*VT* 12 (1962), pp. 256–258), that the coming of the king is here modelled on David's humble and peaceful return to Jerusalem after the rebellion of Absalom, merits consideration. The fact that David's route was over the Mount of Olives (*cf.* 2 Sa. 15:30), and his transport probably an ass (2 Sa. 16:1–2), would lend further point to Jesus' re-enactment of the scene.

[83] For Jewish embarrassment with so humble a Messianic figure see San. 98a, and the comments of J. Blenkinsopp, *loc. cit.*, p. 60.

[84] See above, p. 90. *Cf.* below, pp. 236–238.

expectation of a violent death, and his use of the parallel passage Zechariah 13:7 to explain it,[85] such an identification seems in any case to be probable. The cause of the Jewish mourning at the destruction of Jerusalem is, then, the realization that the one whom they have rejected and killed has been given the dominion of the Son of man, and is now their judge.

Whatever the explanation of the strange first person אלי,[86] the one pierced is clearly connected with the Messianic figures of 11:4–14 and 13:7; in the former passage the subject is the rejection of the good shepherd by the people, and in the latter his smiting by the sword of God. If we may follow Lamarche's scheme, these passages predict the hostile reaction of Israel to the Messianic king of 9:9–10, involving not only contemptuous rejection, but (whether figuratively or literally) his murder. It is only after they have murdered him that the memory of his martyrdom will cause their repentance, and thus, after thorough purification, their final salvation. It seems, then, that in this martyrdom with its issue in the salvation of God's people Jesus saw a prediction of his own fate.

c. The Shepherd

Mark 14:27 (Mt. 26:31),[87] quoting Zechariah 13:7. The textual phenomena of the quotation are examined below.[88] The indicative πατάξω ('I will strike'), which differs from the

[85] See below, pp. 107–109.

[86] The correctness of the reading is not important at this point. See below, p. 153.

[87] B. Lindars (*op. cit.*, pp. 129–130) argues that this is not an authentic quotation by Jesus, on the grounds that to omit verses 27b–28 eases the sequence of thought, Peter's reply following immediately on Jesus' warning. However, the form of Jesus' saying (warning, with its scriptural confirmation, balanced by encouragement) is not in itself improbable, and the fact that Peter's reply does not interrupt it proves nothing. The omission of verse 28 from the Fayyum Fragment adds little weight, as this fragment is not an exact Gospel text, and in any case *does* include the quotation in 27b. (For the text see F. J. Foakes Jackson and K. Lake, *The Beginnings of Christianity: Part 1, The Acts of the Apostles* (London 1920–1933), vol. 5, p. 12; see also J. de Waard, *A Comparative Study of the Old Testament Text in the Dead Sea Scrolls and in the New Testament* (Leiden, 1965), p. 38 n. 3). Moreover, the quotation agrees with many uses by Jesus of the shepherd motif from the OT (see below, p. 208), and also with his frequent use of Zc. 9–14 during the passion.

[88] See below, pp. 241, 246.

imperative of all versions of the Old Testament, is a necessary grammatical adaptation to the New Testament context, caused by the abbrevation of the quotation to exclude the mention of the sword of Yahweh, which would render the imperative meaningless. The one who strikes is in either case Yahweh himself, though the New Testament indicative may perhaps emphasize the divine initiative.

Zechariah 13:7–9 appears to stand very much on its own. Many commentators would therefore transfer it to the end of chapter 11, where it would follow and complete the description of the 'worthless shepherd' of 11:15–17 and his punishment by the sword.[89] In a book which is certainly not marked by structural simplicity and logical progression,[90] this is a hazardous expedient. The decisive objection to this transposition is the utterly different character of the shepherds of 11:15–17 and 13:7–9. The former is אולי ('foolish', with the implication of moral perversity), and behaves carelessly and irresponsibly, while the latter is described by Yahweh as רעי . . . גבר עמיתי ('my shepherd, the man that is my fellow', RV), implying a close relationship with Yahweh.[91] An arbitrary rearrangement of the text which involves the identification of such different characters is hardly compelling.

A more satisfactory exegesis of Zechariah 13:7 is to take it where it stands, as describing a Messianic personage. The terminology strongly suggests this exegesis,[92] and it is strengthened by the close correspondence with 12:10, for in both passages the wounding of a figure closely associated with Yahweh leads, through mourning or refining, to salvation.[93]

Jesus' application of the passage is explicit. He is this Messianic shepherd,[94] and as such he is to be smitten. His

[89] Thus H. G. Mitchell (*op. cit.*, pp. 219, 235, 253ff., 314ff.) assumes this transposition, and interprets the whole as a diatribe against the king of Egypt. NEB has incorporated the transposition in its text.

[90] *Cf.* the recurrence of the sheep-shepherd motif in 9:16; 10:2–3; 10:8–10; 11:4–17; 13:7–9.

[91] See further, below, p. 154.

[92] See in detail P. Lamarche, *op. cit.*, pp. 92–93. Also P. R. Ackroyd, *loc. cit.*, pp. 654–655.

[93] *Cf.* P. Lamarche, *op. cit.*, pp. 107–108. For a defence of the position of the passage in the train of thought of Zc. 12–14 see T. T. Perowne, *Haggai and Zechariah* (Cambridge, 1888), pp. 138–139.

[94] There is little to be said for the theory of B. Lindars (*op. cit.*, p. 129) that if the text is correct Jesus must be the *subject* of πατάξω, and the shepherd

Messianic work is to be accomplished through suffering, for only so can the predicted salvation come.[95]

In at least three of the four Messianic passages of Zechariah 9–14 isolated by Lamarche, Jesus saw predictions of his own status and work. They present a unified picture, of the lowly king, rejected and killed by the people to whom he comes, whose martyrdom is the cause of their repentance and salvation. The correspondence of this figure with the actual mission of Jesus is striking, and it is clear that he expected it to be so. In alluding to these passages of Zechariah he made clear both to his disciples and to the crowds the sort of Messianic work he envisaged himself as accomplishing. It was not to be one of triumphant and majestic sovereignty, bringing political deliverance for the Jews, but one of lowliness, suffering and death. If he was their king, it was in the character of the lowly and rejected Shepherd-King. The many Old Testament passages which speak of the Messiah's glory and triumph are largely passed over, and his emphasis falls, as we shall see, almost exclusively on Zechariah 9–14, Isaiah 53, and Daniel 7, which are the only three passages in the Old Testament where it can plausibly be claimed that the suffering of the Messiah is predicted.[96] This can hardly be accidental.

The close relationship between the Messianic passages of Zechariah 9–14 and the Servant Songs of Isaiah is of special interest. Lamarche concludes, after a lengthy study of this subject, that while verbal echoes and similarities of imagery are not impressive,[97] the concepts involved in the two prophecies are very closely related, the four passages in Zechariah 9–14 being based on the four Servant Songs, not by slavish imitation, but because 'it is the same prophetic current, foretelling a humble and suffering Messiah, which runs through these two

---

must be Peter. The following mention of Jesus' resurrection can only make sense if his death, not Peter's, has just been mentioned. The fact that one first person indicative is in reported speech (*i.e.* the quotation) while the other is in *oratio recta* makes a confusion of their subjects impossible.

[95] For the implications with regard to the position of the disciples see above, p. 65.

[96] We shall argue below (pp. 128–130, 146) that this interpretation of Dn. 7 is questionable.

[97] *Op. cit.*, pp. 138–139.

writings'.[98] And these two prophetic figures together furnished a large proportion of the Messianic quotations applied by Jesus to himself.

VI. THE SERVANT OF YAHWEH AND THE ANOINTED DELIVERER[99]

In 1948 I. Engnell could speak of 'the indisputable role that the 'Ebed Yahweh figure and its ideological world played for Jesus and his messianic interpretation of himself',[100] and C. R. North could claim that 'It is almost universally admitted that Jesus saw His way by the light that Isaiah liii shed upon His predestined path'.[101] Today this confident position is less securely held; it has been the object of several strong attacks, and must be justified rather than assumed.

We shall, accordingly, first consider these attacks, and the general question of Jesus' use of the Servant figure, and then proceed to a detailed study of the individual passages and ideas where this use has been postulated, before attempting to summarize the significance of the Servant figure in Jesus' thought.

Our inclusion of this subject at this point depends on the belief that it is correct to speak of 'a Servant figure' in Isaiah 42ff., and that this figure is Messianic in terms of our definition. Neither point is without controversy, but both command a sufficiently wide assent to justify our assuming them with no more than a reference to fuller discussions elsewhere.[102]

[98] *Ibid.*, pp. 145–147.

[99] This section of the original thesis formed the basis of a Tyndale Lecture, entitled 'The Servant of the Lord in the Teaching of Jesus', delivered in July 1967, and printed, with fuller documentation than is possible in the present publication, in the *Tyndale Bulletin* 19 (1968), pp. 26–52.

[100] *BJRL* 31 (1948), p. 54.

[101] *The Suffering Servant in Deutero-Isaiah* (Oxford, 1948), p. 218.

[102] The best recent discussion of both points is W. Zimmerli and J. Jeremias, *The Servant of God* (revised edn. London, 1965), which is an ET of their article *Παῖς Θεοῦ* in *TWNT*, the revised edition being printed in *TDNT* V, pp. 654–717. (References in the present work are to the 1965 publication.) M. D. Hooker has argued against a 'Servant figure' as such in Isaiah (*Jesus and the Servant* (London, 1959), esp. pp. 156–158). Her contention that it is indefensible to separate off Duhm's 'Servant Songs' as a prophetic work independent of their context in the book of Isaiah is widely accepted, but few would therefore deny that, within the flow of thought of Is. 40–55, a 'Servant figure' emerges. The point of dispute is

A study of Jesus' use of the figure of the Lord's Anointed in Isaiah 61:1–3 is included in this section, since the two figures, though not to be identified, are closely connected.

a. General considerations

The modern attack on the view that the Suffering Servant was a major influence on Jesus' self-estimation is traced by M. D. Hooker to the work of F. J. Foakes Jackson and K. Lake.[103] Later repeated by a few scholars,[104] it has recently received a new lease of life, notably (in this country) at the

whether this figure should be regarded as an individual (so esp. W. Zimmerli, *op. cit.*), or as purely collective, a personification of Israel. C. R. North (*Servant*, pp. 6–116) and H. H. Rowley (*The Servant of the Lord* (London, 1952), pp. 4–48) survey the various interpretations offered. *Cf.* more briefly but more recently W. D. Davies, *Sermon*, pp. 131–133. There is now a wide agreement that the solution lies in an idea akin to that of 'corporate personality', of an individual who sums up in himself the character and destiny of the community he represents, the individual character of this figure becoming progressively clearer until in chapter 53 he stands over against the community of Israel as the one who suffers *in their place*. 'What began as a personification (has) become a person' (Rowley, *Servant*, p. 51). (*Cf.* our discussion in the last chapter of Jesus' view of himself as summing up the status and destiny of Israel, and thus bringing in the eschatological salvation for which Israel looked; and below, pp. 169–171 on the Son of man figure.) Thus while a purely individual Messianic interpretation fails to recognize the simple fact that the Servant *is* Israel, we may nonetheless fairly see the Servant, and believe that Jesus saw him, as a Messianic figure. That this was the dominant interpretation within Palestinian (though not Hellenistic) Judaism is demonstrated by Zimmerli and Jeremias (*Servant*, pp. 37–79) with a wealth of evidence; if not every example is convincing, the thesis as a whole is supported by a much more thorough examination of the evidence than the tendentious and incomplete survey by M. D. Hooker (*Servant*, pp. 53–58), reaching the opposite conclusion. *Cf.* also J. Jeremias in *Aux Sources de la Tradition Chrétienne*: Mélanges offerts à M. Goguel (Neuchatel, 1950), pp. 113–119. Other useful discussions of the Jewish interpretation are those by W. D. Davies, *Paul and Rabbinic Judaism*[2] (London, 1955), pp. 274–283; O. Cullmann, *Christology*, pp. 55–60. While Jewish exegetes often fought shy of the implication of Messianic *suffering* (this being the point brought out in Hooker's treatment, and in R. H. Fuller, *Foundations*, pp. 43–46), this did not lead them to deny the Messianic character of the Servant as such (see esp. Tg Jon on Is. 53); this in itself is testimony to the strength of the Messianic interpretation.

[103] *Op. cit.*, vol. 1, pp. 383–392.

[104] Hooker (*Servant*, pp. 3–5) mentions F. C. Burkitt, H. J. Cadbury, W. Bousset, and R. Bultmann. We may add also C. T. Craig, *Journal of Religion* 24 (1944), pp. 240–245.

hands of C. F. D. Moule,[105] C. K. Barrett,[106] and, most fully, M. D. Hooker.[107]

The presupposition underlying the arguments of these scholars (which we have summarized elsewhere[108]) is that mere verbal allusion is not sufficient to establish that Jesus interpreted his mission as that of the Servant; what is required is deliberate quotation with a clear intention to provide a theological explanation of his approaching death in redemptive terms.[109] On this basis, and by means of a piecemeal examination of the evidence, they are able to conclude that Daniel 7 and not Isaiah 53 was the source of Jesus' expectation of his suffering and death.

Against this presupposition, the defenders of the traditional view stress the danger of regarding the New Testament allusions as mere 'proof-texts' without regard for the context, and of restricting attention to the formal quotations.[110] H. E. W. Turner[111] goes a stage further, and believes that even if no word of Jesus referring to the Servant were extant, the record of his life and character would compel us to believe that he saw his mission in that light.

But such a debate cannot be conducted in general terms. We propose, therefore, to examine in some detail the supposed allusions to the Servant idea by Jesus, in order to determine

[105] 'From Defendant to Judge – and Deliverer', *Studiorum Novi Testamenti Societas Bulletin* 3 (1952), pp. 40–53, now reprinted in his *The Phenomenon of the New Testament* (London, 1967), pp. 82–99; references are to the latter publication. *Cf.* also his *Birth*, pp. 81–83.

[106] 'The Background of Mark 10:45' in *New Testament Essays*: studies in memory of T. W. Manson, ed. A. J. B. Higgins (Manchester, 1959), pp. 1–18.

[107] *Jesus and the Servant* (1959). *Cf.* also J. Knox, *The Death of Christ* (London, 1959), pp. 106–109; R. H. Fuller, *Foundations*, pp. 115–119.

[108] *Tyndale Bulletin* 19 (1968), pp. 27–28.

[109] The following words of Hooker (*Servant*, p. 155) make the point explicit: 'In the absence of any passage in the primitive tradition which clearly applies Isa. 53 to the *meaning* of Christ's death, and not merely the *fact* of that event, it is impossible to accept linguistic similarity as evidence that any connection was intended *doctrinally* with the Servant concept.' *Cf.* Moule's search (*Phenomenon*, p. 96) for allusions 'to the *redemptive* work of the Servant' (our italics), and passing over of other suggested allusions to the Servant, even to his suffering if the redemptive aspect is not explicit.

[110] So esp. H. W. Wolff, *Jesaja 53 in Urchristentum*[2] (Berlin, 1950). *Cf.* J. Jeremias, *Servant*, p. 88 and n. 392a. For the same emphasis with regard to the OT allusions in general see R. H. Gundry, *op. cit.*, pp. 2–5.

[111] *Jesus, Master and Lord*[2] (London, 1954), pp. 205–209.

both whether any such allusion is intended and also whether there is any indication that this allusion is intended to convey a conscious self-identification of Jesus with the Servant. It must be admitted that our presuppositions are decidedly on the side of the traditional view. We find it hard to believe that allusions to so strikingly appropriate a figure in the Old Testament were merely by chance, or that the appropriateness of the figure escaped Jesus. To the Christian church the relevance of the Servant of Yahweh to the mission of Jesus has always been obvious; why should it be less obvious to him? 'The supreme exemplification of the principle of divinely appointed suffering is more likely to have provided the Biblical key to our Lord's understanding of his impending death than the later alternatives which have been suggested as substitutes.'[112] This position at least has the merit that it is obvious.

We believe, however, that we have more to work on than mere *a priori* assumption. We turn accordingly to an examination of the individual allusions.

The question of authenticity must be briefly mentioned. While the scholars mentioned above direct their attacks at the significance rather than the authenticity of the allusions, others have suggested that these reflect the understanding of Jesus' death in the early church. In reply, V. Taylor concludes a valuable discussion with the view that 'the Servant Christology was at its height . . . in the period AD 30–50, and in the earlier of the two decades more than in the later'.[113] He goes on to trace it to Jesus himself. His arguments, based on a theory of theological development, are reinforced on literary grounds by B. Lindars,[114] with the argument that the fact that the allusions are so deeply embedded in the work of all the principal New Testament writers indicates the early origin of the concept. Further, 'The wide variety of non-Septuagintal phrases indicates that the biblical work has been done at the earliest possible period, very probably by Jesus himself. The results have entered into normal Christian speech, and there is no need to adduce the specific text.' We see here the danger of the approach

[112] H. E. W. Turner, *Historicity*, p. 86.
[113] *NTS* 1 (1954/5), p. 163.
[114] *Op. cit.*, pp. 77–79. *Cf.* V. Taylor, *Jesus and His Sacrifice* (London, 1937), pp. 47–48.

which demands formal quotations before it will admit the influence of the concept. Such allusions are in fact stronger evidence of its influence; they show that it is assumed and accepted.

We deal, first, with the one formal quotation of Isaiah 53 by Jesus; secondly with two allusions which are so clear as to be, in our view, indisputable; thirdly with three suggested allusions, of varying degrees of probability and significance; and fourthly with the numerous predictions of his suffering which, while not verbal allusions, are seen by many as derived from Isaiah 53. It will be noted that virtually all the allusions considered are to Isaiah 52:13–53:12; there are possible allusions to Isaiah 42, but none to the second and third 'Servant Songs'. Thus it is to the one passage which above all presents the Servant as an individual figure, and in which his role of vicarious suffering is central, that Jesus' references, almost without exception, are made.[115] If these are found to be intentional allusions, it will be hard to deny that this figure played a central role in forming Jesus' view of his mission, for there is no other Old Testament passage except, as we shall see, Daniel 7 to which such frequent allusion can be found.

b. The one formal quotation

Luke 22:37. καὶ μετὰ ἀνόμων ἐλογίσθη ('and he was reckoned with transgressors'), quoting Isaiah 53:12 ואת־פשעים נמנה (LXX καὶ ἐν τοῖς ἀνόμοις ἐλογίσθη).

Jackson and Lake[116] assume without argument that this quotation is the work of Luke, and Hooker[117] writes, 'Unfortunately it occurs in a very obscure passage, of which both the meaning and genuineness are extremely doubtful', but does not explain the statement. Actual arguments against its authenticity are few. J. M. Creed[118] suspects the passage Luke 22:35–38 as being obscure and clumsily constructed, and also because 'it is unlikely that Jesus seriously entertained the thought of

[115] This means that our argument does not depend on the assumption, rightly questioned, *e.g.*, by Hooker (*Servant*, pp. 25–30, 61, 155–158), that the four 'Servant Songs' isolated by Duhm were regarded as a distinct group in Jesus' day. Our concern is with the single key passage, Is. 52:13–53:12.

[116] *Op. cit.*, vol. 1, p. 390.

[117] *Servant*, p. 86.

[118] *Luke*, p. 270.

armed resistance'. It is, however, still more unlikely that any early Christian would attribute to him a thought so out of character and so embarrassing to Christian apologetics; the words of verse 36 are best explained as a metaphorical warning of dangerous times ahead.[119] Nor is it clear why the obscurity of a saying should mark it as unauthentic. V. Taylor[120] has demonstrated clearly the appropriateness of the quotation in Jesus' situation on the night before the crucifixion, and J. Jeremias[121] sees the quotation as indispensable to the context, where it stands 'between the two quite obviously ancient words about the swords'. The non-LXX character of the quotation further suggests a Semitic origin.[122] In the absence, therefore, of arguments to the contrary, this quotation may be taken as authentic.

Does this quotation warrant us in postulating a belief of Jesus that he was fulfilling the redemptive work of the Servant? H. J. Cadbury[123] points out that Luke, 'the one time that he does quote Isaiah liii. almost unbelievably escapes all the vicarious phrases with which that passage abounds', and draws the conclusion that Luke 22:37 is no indication of a use of Isaiah 53 to explain Jesus' death in terms of vicarious suffering. Two factors, however, tell against this conclusion. The first is the context: that Jesus on the eve of his death should quote from Isaiah 53 at all is surely significant, and indicates that he saw his death in the light of that chapter; that he should quote the phrase 'was numbered with the transgressors', far from indicating that vicarious suffering was absent from his mind, shows that he was preoccupied with the fact that he, who least deserved it, was to be punished as a wrong-doer. There may be the further idea of his identification with sinful mankind for their redemption. 'This thought is not explicit in His words, but it is a natural reflection in the mind of one who had pondered the Servant-conception and who quotes a passage immediately followed by the words: "yet he bare the sin of many, and made intercession for the transgressors" (Isa. liii. 12).'[124] The second

[119] *Cf.* F. C. Burkitt, *The Gospel History and its Transmission* (Edinburgh, 1906), pp. 140–142.

[120] *Sacrifice*, pp. 191–194.

[121] *Servant*, p. 105.

[122] See below, p. 244.

[123] In F. J. Foakes Jackson and K. Lake, *op. cit.*, vol. 5, p. 366.

[124] V. Taylor, *Sacrifice*, p. 194.

factor is the formula with which Jesus introduces the quotation: 'This scripture must be fulfilled in me . . . for what is written about me has its fulfilment.' This, one of the strongest fulfilment-formulae ever uttered by Jesus, is hardly the way to introduce a casual catch-phrase. If Jesus saw these words as destined to be fulfilled in him, and as written about him, it is hard to avoid the conclusion that he identified himself with the one of whom they were written, the Servant of Yahweh.

We conclude, therefore, that Jesus saw the events of Good Friday as the destined fulfilment of the suffering of the Servant depicted in Isaiah 53, and that his thoughts turned especially to the impending imputation of guilt to one who did not deserve it. This is not far from saying that he was preoccupied with the thought of vicarious suffering, and that this thought derived from Isaiah 53.

c. *The two clear allusions*

(i) *Mark 10:45* (Mt. 20:28). The debate on the authenticity of this saying is usefully summarized by H. E. Tödt,[125] who himself separates off the second part of the verse as a Palestinian gloss[126] on Jesus' saying about service, which ends at verse 45a. His reasons[127] are essentially the same as those advanced by the earlier scholars who rejected this verse (*e.g.* Wellhausen, J. Weiss, Wrede, and Rashdall), viz. (1) that it introduces a concept alien to Jesus' thought, (2) that its absence in the Lucan parallel (22:27) proves its dispensability, and (3) that its content is inconsistent with the preceding discourse, a *μετάβασις εἰς ἀλλὸ γένος*.[128] These arguments must be briefly considered.

1. Tödt has wisely dropped the contention of earlier critics that these words were a distillation of Pauline theology;[129] as A. Richardson points out, the word *λύτρον* is not Pauline.[130]

[125] *Op. cit.*, pp. 135–136.

[126] That it is at least Palestinian is proved by the linguistic features; see J. Jeremias, *Servant*, p. 90, and in detail his *Eucharistic Words*, pp. 179–182. *Cf.* H. E. Tödt, *op. cit.*, pp. 202–203, 205.

[127] *Op. cit.*, pp. 206–207.

[128] So J. Wellhausen, *Das Evangelium Marci* (Berlin, 1903), p. 91.

[129] See *e.g.* H. Rashdall, *The Idea of Atonement in Christian Theology* (London, 1919), pp. 50–51.

[130] *Introduction*, p. 220. *Cf.* R. H. Fuller, *The Mission and Achievement of Jesus* (London, 1954), p. 57. For Fuller's later views see below, p. 122 n. 160.

But Tödt contends that the idea of a vicarious death occurs nowhere else in the Synoptic Son of man sayings. It does, however, appear certainly in Mark 14:24, and is implied, as we have seen, in Luke 22:37. In any case, it would be an indefensible criterion of authenticity which rejected a saying simply because it had no parallel. Moreover, the enigmatic and reserved character of the saying is not what one would expect in a deliberate distillation of the theology of the apostolic church.[131]

2. While we may grant that the discourse would not be noticeably incomplete if it lacked the last eight words, it must be observed that Luke 22:25–27 is anything but a close parallel to the present passage, and must, as Tödt himself recognizes,[132] be regarded as 'later and secondary',[133] if not a separate tradition. It cannot, therefore, be used to control the content of the Marcan passage.

3. It is true that the preceding words have not been concerned with a vicarious death, but with the true nature of Christian leadership, which is characterized as service; Jesus appeals for a revolution in the disciples' idea of what constitutes greatness, and appeals to his own example. That he should go on, however, to reinforce his appeal by the concrete example of his approaching death is by no means inconsistent. Mark 10:32–34, 38 show that the passion was already in his mind, and it furnished an excellent illustration of his point: the world saw greatness in lording it over others, but his type of greatness was in a service which to the world was humiliation; this paradoxical greatness was to be supremely exemplified in that his great work of redemption was to be accomplished through his death, which was thus itself an act of service. This is not a change of subject, but a topical illustration.[134]

In our study of the possible parallels between this saying and Isaiah 53, we shall not attempt to deal separately with parallels in word and in thought. C. K. Barrett's attempt to do this results in his virtually ignoring the latter, since in some

[131] So V. Taylor, *Sacrifice*, p. 105. [132] *Op. cit.*, pp. 202–203.

[133] So R. H. Fuller, *Mission*, p. 57.

[134] The logic of the sentence does not demand, as Tödt alleges (p. 207), that Jesus is calling the disciples to give *their* lives as a ransom for many. It is a specific (and unrepeatable) illustration of the general ideal of self-denying service.

cases the verbal parallel alone is not impressive, and acquires significance only when the underlying thought is considered.[135] We shall, therefore, use the verbal echoes as springboards for a consideration of the parallel ideas.

διακονῆσαι ('to serve'). Jeremias' dogmatic statement[136] that '*διακονῆσαι* is an allusion to the servant' is hardly self-evident. *διακονεῖν* and its cognates never translate עבד and its cognates in the LXX, so that '*linguistically*, *διακονεῖν* does not recall Isa. 53, or any of the Servant passages'.[137] It is, however, not unlikely that the Aramaic word used by Jesus was a more direct echo of Isaiah 53, for *διακονεῖν* does not, in the New Testament, as Hooker alleges,[138] always, or even usually, denote specifically domestic service.[139] That this cannot be its meaning in Mark 10:45 is indicated both by the fact that what is there in view is supposed superiority and inferiority, the latter being denoted by *διακονῆσαι*, and by the fact that in the preceding verse *διάκονος* and *δοῦλος* occur in parallelism. *διακονεῖν* is thus not to be clearly distinguished in meaning from *δουλεύειν*, and may well translate an Aramaic term which echoed עבד. The parallel may not be formally exact, in that the Servant in Isaiah 53 is the Servant of Yahweh, while Mark 10:45 is concerned with service to men; but in fact the Servant in Isaiah 53 *did* benefit men by his suffering, and Jesus *did* accept his suffering in obedience to God.[140] A linguistic connection cannot be proved, but there is a close connection in thought.

δοῦναι τὴν ψυχὴν αὐτοῦ ('to give his life'). Jeremias[141] regards this, and parallel expressions in the New Testament, as 'mere

[135] That it is the latter rather than the former which determines the existence of an intentional allusion is well stated by A. J. B. Higgins, *op. cit.*, p. 42. His detailed treatment of Mk. 10:45 (*ibid.*, pp. 41–47) follows similar lines to those here proposed. *Cf.*, much more briefly, F. Hahn, *The Titles of Jesus in Christology* (ET London, 1969), pp. 56–57.

[136] *Servant*, p. 100.

[137] C. K. Barrett, *loc. cit.*, p. 4.

[138] *Servant*, p. 74.

[139] This primary sense is less frequent than a general sense of service to others. Domestic service cannot be intended in Jn. 12:26; 1 Pet. 1:12; 4:10. See AG, p. 183 for other examples.

[140] Hooker's contrast (*Servant*, p. 75) between the abject and enforced suffering of the Servant and the willing service of Mk. 10:45 is forced. Both Jesus and the Servant suffered according to the will of God (*cf.* Is. 53:4, 6, 10).

[141] *Servant*, p. 96.

translation variants of שים נפשו (Isa. 53.10 Heb. text) or מסר נפשיה (Isa. 53.12 *Targ.*).' The phrase in verse 10, תשים אשם נפשו is certainly not far removed from Jesus' words,[142] and the parallel between אשם and *λύτρον* shortly to be examined makes the echo of verse 10 in Jesus' words very compelling. Barrett, however, does not notice this parallel, but confines his attention to the echo in verse 12, where he stresses that the Hebrew expression הערה למות נפשו ('he poured out his soul to death') is unique in the Old Testament, and that 'the word *lammaweth* is generally excised by editors on metrical grounds'.[143] The latter point is clearly irrelevant for our purpose, since there is no evidence for the absence of למות in any ancient text; it must have been there in Jesus' day. The uniqueness of the expression is also scarcely relevant, as both Tg and LXX are quite clear as to the meaning of the Hebrew metaphor, which they render prosaically in exactly the sense of these words of Jesus.[144] Barrett concludes that 'It cannot be claimed that *δοῦναι τὴν ψυχήν* had a background of its own other than Isa. 53; but neither can it be said that it points unambiguously to that chapter'. Even if this allusion stood alone, this would be an understatement, when the parallel with 53:10 is taken into consideration. But in fact it stands in close relation with parallels to several other phrases in Isaiah 53. And the thought behind Jesus' words, of a voluntary giving up of life, is of course essential to Isaiah 53:12, and to the whole of that chapter.

λύτρον ἀντί ('a ransom for'). '*λύτρον* must be a free translation of אשם (in the common meaning of "compensation").'[145] However, *λύτρον* does not occur in the LXX of Isaiah 53, and never translates אשם in the LXX, but generally the roots גאל and פדה. Barrett[146] and Hooker[147] therefore argue that there is an essential difference in meaning, אשם being concerned with guilt and expiation, *λύτρον* with equivalence and compensation, a buying off by means of a price equivalent to that

[142] The Vg rendering, *si posuerit pro peccato animam suam*, adopted by RSV, makes the parallel much closer, the third person verb making the action reflexive, as it is in Mark. The LXX (*ἐὰν δῶτε περὶ ἁμαρτίας, ἡ ψυχὴ ἡμῶν ὄψεται* . . .) has apparently misunderstood the Hebrew.

[143] *Loc. cit.*, pp. 4–5.

[144] See below, p. 244 n. 18 for details.

[145] J. Jeremias, *Servant*, p. 100.

[146] *Loc. cit.*, pp. 5–7.

[147] *Servant*, pp. 76–78.

which is redeemed (though it is more commonly used metaphorically with the stress on the fact rather than the price of redemption). *λύτρον* is, therefore, an allusion to the idea of redemption in Deutero-Isaiah in general, not to the Servant, of whose work גאל and פדה are not used.

This conclusion is open to two objections. Firstly, the meaning of substitution is not absent from אשם: while in Numbers 5:7, 8 it is a restitution to the one wronged (though, presumably, except in cases of actual theft, the restitution of an *equivalent*), in other cases it signifies the sacrifice presented to make atonement for the sinner; he is guilty (אשם), but the presentation of an אשם in his place removes his guilt.[148] This is hardly distinguishable from the substitution of an equivalent, or, therefore, from the meaning of *λύτρον*. So in Isaiah 53:10, 'the Messianic servant offers himself as an אשם in compensation for the sins of the people, interposing for them as their substitute.'[149] *λύτρον*, or whatever Aramaic word lies behind it, is therefore not far from equivalent to אשם.[150] Secondly, Isaiah 53 as a whole presents the work of the Servant as one of substitution, in that in his suffering and death he bears the sins of the people, resulting in their healing; God places their sins on him, and bruises him for their iniquities. This idea of substitution is admitted to be central to *λύτρον*, and is even more obvious in *ἀντί*.[151] Even if no linguistic echo were established, *δοῦναι τὴν ψυχὴν αὐτοῦ λύτρον ἀντὶ πολλῶν* is a perfect summary of the central theme of Isaiah 53, that of a vicarious and redeeming death.

πολλῶν ('many'). This is probably the most commonly noticed allusion to Isaiah 53 in Mark 10:45. רבים is used in Isaiah 53:11, 12 to describe the beneficiaries of the Servant's sacrifice (LXX *πολλοῖς, πολλῶν*).[152] Jeremias describes it as 'a

[148] See esp. Lv. 5:17–19; the אשם is in this passage distinguished from the restitution of verses 16 and 23–24 (EVV 6:4–5), which is expressed by the verbs שלח and השיב.

[149] BDB, p. 80; and see the full treatment, *ibid.*, pp. 79–80.

[150] 'A perfectly adequate rendering' according to R. H. Fuller (*Mission*, p. 57). *Cf.* A. J. B. Higgins, *op. cit.*, pp. 45–46.

[151] V. Taylor (*Sacrifice*, pp. 103–104) argues for the regular meaning 'instead of', 'in the place of'. For a full discussion see R. E. Davies, *Tyndale Bulletin* 21 (1970), pp. 72–81.

[152] *Cf.* also 52:14. In 53:12 it is also used to designate those among whom the Servant is given an inheritance (or those given to him as an

veritable keyword in Isa. 53'.[153] Most scholars take it for granted that its occurrence in Mark 10:45 is a deliberate echo of Isaiah 53; it is hardly the word that one would expect unless it had some such purpose. The other allusions to Isaiah 53 in this verse suggest that this too is a feature drawn from that chapter, where it is no less peculiar, and rendered conspicuous and memorable by its repetition.

The cumulative effect of these parallels in word and thought between Mark 10:45 and Isaiah 53 is sufficient to demand a deliberate allusion by Jesus to the role of the Servant as his own. Even those who deny the influence of Isaiah 53 in Jesus' teaching commonly recognize this, and can only evade its significance by challenging the authenticity of the verse.[154] It is hard to understand why Barrett goes to such lengths to undermine the individual constituents of this case (without considering the cumulative effect of the whole, or even the essential parallels of thought underlying the two passages), in order to establish a dependence instead on Daniel 7, with which the only apparent connection is the use of the term 'Son of man', a title which, as we shall see,[155] is used in such a wide variety of contexts as to belie the suggestion that it must always involve a specific allusion to Daniel 7.

The fact that the allusion occurs almost incidentally, as an illustration of the true nature of greatness, far from indicating that the redemptive role of the Servant was not in mind (for it is specifically the redemptive aspects of Isaiah 53 to which Jesus alludes), is in fact evidence of how deeply his assumption of that role had penetrated into Jesus' thinking, so that it emerges even in an incidental illustration. 'It is as if Jesus said, "The Son of Man came to fulfil the task of the *ebed Yahweh*".'[156]

(ii) *Mark 14:24* (Mt. 26:28; Lk. 22:20). A full discussion of the authenticity of this saying is hardly necessary; most

---

inheritance, according to C. R. North, *The Second Isaiah* (Oxford, 1964), pp. 245–246).

[153] *Servant*, p. 95.

[154] *E.g.* H. Rashdall, *op. cit.*, p. 32, even though he denies every other use of Is. 53 by Jesus (*ibid.*, pp. 51–52).

[155] See esp. below, pp. 136–138.

[156] O. Cullmann, *Christology*, p. 65.

scholars accept that these or very similar words were spoken by Jesus at the Last Supper.[157]

The phrase 'the blood of the covenant' is, as we have seen,[158] a typological reference to Exodus 24:8. However, the Servant is twice referred to as a covenant to the people.[159] O. Cullmann goes so far as to rank the re-establishment of the covenant as one of the two 'essential characteristics' of the Servant.[160] There are, of course, many other Old Testament references to the covenant, and this alone could not constitute an allusion to the Servant theme, but it does not stand alone. The following words are *τὸ ἐκχυννόμενον ὑπὲρ πολλῶν* ('which is poured out for many'; Mt. *τὸ περὶ πολλῶν ἐκχυννόμενον*).

The word *ἐκχυννόμενον* is reminiscent of Isaiah 53:12 הערה, 'he poured out his soul'.[161] But whereas in Isaiah 53 הערה is a strange and rather mysterious metaphor, in Mark 14:24 *ἐκχυννόμενον* is the natural word for the shedding of blood, and need not in itself demand an Old Testament background. Like the reference to the covenant, its allusion to the Servant idea is only clearly established by its conjunction with the more obviously allusive phrase *ὑπὲρ (περὶ) πολλῶν*.

ὑπὲρ πολλῶν is as strange an expression for Jesus to use here as was *ἀντὶ πολλῶν* in Mark 10:45, and the allusion to Isaiah 53 is as widely recognized here as there. In fact the two references reinforce each other.[162] While *ὑπέρ* (and still more the Matthean *περί*) is not so clearly substitutionary as *ἀντί*, it is a very appropriate word for the vicarious death of the Servant. So not only the word *πολλῶν*, but the whole idea of 'dying on behalf of' which is central to Mark 14:24, renders an allusion to the Servant theme virtually certain.

[157] For discussion of this point see esp. V. Taylor, *Sacrifice*, pp. 125–136; J. Jeremias, *Eucharistic Words*, pp. 168–173, 178–182, 186–203.

[158] See above, p. 66.

[159] Is. 42:6; 49:8. Both passages fall just outside Duhm's 'Servant Songs', but many scholars regard them as continuing the Servant theme.

[160] *Christology*, p. 55. *Cf.* R. H. Fuller, *Mission*, p. 73; in *Foundations*, pp. 118, 153–154 Fuller has not altered his belief that Mk. 10:45 and 14:24 refer to Is. 53, but now, following Tödt, questions their authenticity.

[161] See below, p. 244 n. 18 for the objection that הערה means 'laid bare'.

[162] H. E. Tödt (*op. cit.*, p. 205 n. 1) speaks of 'the parallel way of speaking in 10.45b and 14.24b which we consider to be the decisive argument for the latter passage's referring to Isa. 53'. J. Jeremias (*Eucharistic Words*, pp. 226–231) assumes the allusion to be self-evident. *Cf.* F. Hahn, *op. cit.*, p. 59.

The connection of these words with the covenant idea is significant. In Isaiah 42–53 Yahweh makes his Servant a covenant to the people, and this involves his vicarious death for their redemption.[163] Jesus' words at the Last Supper, whose primary purpose is to explain to the disciples how his coming death is to benefit them, are drawn not only from Exodus 24:8 (and probably Jeremiah 31:31), but also from Isaiah 53. His work is to re-establish the broken covenant, but this can be done only by fulfilling the role of the Servant in his vicarious death. To make this point Jesus chooses words from Isaiah 53 which are as deeply imbued as any with the redemptive significance of that death, in that they highlight its vicarious nature.

Thus here, if anywhere, we have a deliberate theological explanation by Jesus of the necessity for his death, and it is not only drawn from Isaiah 53, but specifically refers to the vicarious and redemptive suffering which is the central theme of that chapter.[164]

d. Three possible allusions

(i) *Mark 9:12.* We shall consider Jesus' predictions of his suffering in general terms in our next section. This particular saying must, however, be singled out because, in addition to the similarity of the thought to that of Isaiah 53, the word ἐξουδενηθῇ ('be treated with contempt') is frequently regarded as a verbal allusion to Isaiah 53:3 נִבְזֶה. ἐξουδενεῖν, though not used in this verse by the LXX, was a standard translation of בזה,[165] and its occurrence in Mark 9:12 may well represent an Aramaic word which alluded to Isaiah 53:3, where בזה occurs twice.[166] This could not be advanced as even a possible

[163] G. Dalman (*Jesus-Jeshua* (ET London, 1929), p. 170) points out that here only in the OT is there a relationship between the covenant and the death of its mediator.

[164] Even C. F. D. Moule (*Phenomenon*, p. 96), while denying a *verbal* parallel, admits that these words are 'close in *theme* to that chapter'.

[165] For details of the various Greek translations of this and other occurrences of בזה see C. E. B. Cranfield, *Mark*, p. 298.

[166] The allusion is, according to B. Lindars (*op. cit.*, p. 81), 'generally recognised'. *Cf.* C. H. Dodd, *Scriptures*, pp. 92–93, and for a full discussion, R. Otto, *The Kingdom of God and the Son of Man* (ET[2] London and Redhill, 1943), pp. 249–251. H. E. Tödt (*op. cit.*, pp. 162–169), followed by R. H. Fuller (*Foundations*, p. 118), regards Mk. 9:12 as an allusion to Ps. 118:22, not to Is. 53:3, on the basis of the suggestion of W. Michaelis (*TDNT* V,

allusion if the context did not support it. But in fact the context, a declaration by Jesus that Scripture foretells his suffering and rejection, might well lead us to assume the influence of Isaiah 53 even without such a verbal hint. Our discussion of such predictions will show good reason for tracing Jesus' scriptural authority for them to Isaiah 53; this verse merely adds a verbal confirmation to that argument. Here, then, in a deliberate statement of the appointed pattern of his mission, Jesus refers to the suffering and rejection of the Servant.

(ii) *Matthew 3:15*. Jesus' enigmatic saying, 'Thus it is fitting for us to fulfil all righteousness', in defence of the propriety of his being baptized by John, is closely followed by what is almost universally recognized as an allusion to Isaiah 42:1 by the heavenly voice, which thus stamps his mission as that of the Servant.[167] This connection makes it conceivable that Jesus' cryptic explanation also implies a reference to the Servant. While some scholars see here a general reference to Jesus' identification of himself with sinful men for their redemption,[168] others have tied the allusion down to the figure of the Servant.[169] The particular point of reference would be Isaiah 53:11, 'By his knowledge shall the righteous one, my servant, make many

---

pp. 914–915) that *ἐξουθενεῖν* was a current translation of מאס in Ps. 118:22. Since, however, this version of Ps. 118:22 occurs only in Acts 4:11, whereas Mark elsewhere (12:10) follows the LXX version *ἀπεδοκίμασαν* (so also 1 Pet. 2:7), and there is nothing else in Mk. 9:12 to suggest Ps. 118:22, this theory has little weight.

[167] Mk. 1:11 and parallels. This allusion, not being attributed to Jesus himself, is outside our scope. M. D. Hooker (*Servant*, pp. 70–73) disputes the allusion on the grounds of its disagreement with the LXX version of Is. 42:1. It is, however, gratuitous to assume that the saying originated in Greek; and in any case Mt. 12:18 is evidence of a recognized Greek translation divergent from the LXX and very close to Mk. 1:11. See further, the full discussion by I. H. Marshall, *NTS* 15 (1968/9), pp. 326–336.

[168] See, *e.g.*, G. Barth in G. Bornkamm, G. Barth, and H. J. Held, *Tradition and Interpretation in Matthew* (ET London, 1963), pp. 138–141, following G. Bornkamm. H. Ljungman, in his massive treatment of this verse, *Das Gesetz Erfüllen* (*Lunds Universitets Årsskrift*, NF Avd 1, Bd 50, Nr 6, Lund 1954), notices the suggested connection with Is. 53 (*ibid.*, pp. 101–102), but concludes that the saying refers to Jesus' death and its beneficial effects, without any single OT allusion.

[169] So O. Cullmann, *Baptism in the New Testament* (ET London, 1950), pp. 16–19; J. A. T. Robinson, *SJT* 6 (1953), p. 261; J. Schniewind, *Das Evangelium nach Matthäus*[8] (Göttingen, 1956), p. 27; and most fully, J. Denney, *The Death of Christ* (new edn. London, 1951), pp. 21–23.

to be accounted righteous,' the central term *δικαιοσύνην* echoing the repeated יצדיק צדיק of that verse. The allusion on its own is not sufficiently clear to be made the basis for any theory; but at least we may be sure that Jesus, at the time of his baptism, was confronted with a delineation of his mission in terms of Isaiah 42:1. It is reasonable to infer that the figure of the Servant thereafter influenced his self-estimation.

(iii) *Luke 11:22*. An echo of Isaiah 53:12 את־עצומים יחלק שלל (LXX *τῶν ἰσχυρῶν μεριεῖ σκῦλα*) is seen by some commentators in the *ἰσχυρότερος* who *τὰ σκῦλα αὐτοῦ* (*τοῦ ἰσχυροῦ*) *διαδίδωσιν* ('one stronger than he . . . divides his (the strong man's) spoil'). K. H. Rengstorf[170] expounds the verse in terms of Jesus' conquest of the devil by his death as the Servant, and B. Lindars[171] adds his celebration of his victory by 'dividing the spoils *of* the strong'. However, the context in Luke says nothing of the suffering or death of Jesus. There is thus no clear conceptual parallel, and the verbal resemblance is not impressive.[172] Nothing can be deduced from this verse.

e. The predictions of suffering

It can hardly be disputed that Jesus did in some way predict his coming suffering and death. The circumstances of his life and ministry, and the consistent opposition of the authorities, must alone have made it a clear probability;[173] but in any case the predictions are too numerous and too varied to be lightly discounted, and many display clear signs of their authenticity in both their language and their content.[174]

In addition to the three formal announcements of the passion in Mark 8:31; 9:31; 10:33–34 and parallels, the following passages all show Jesus' consciousness that it was inevitable: Mark 2:20; 9:12; 10:38; 12:1ff.; 14:8, 21, 22–23, 25, 49;

[170] *Das Evangelium nach Lukas*[8] (Göttingen, 1958), p. 149.

[171] *Op. cit.*, pp. 84–85.

[172] The words are common ones, and the action of dividing spoil is a regular accompaniment of victory (Gn. 49:27; Ex. 15:9; Jos. 22:8; Jdg. 5:30; 1 Sa. 30:22–26, *etc.*); besides, the 'strong' are the *recipients* of the spoil in the Hebrew. Lindars' appeal (*op. cit.*, p. 85 n. 1) to the LXX is hardly convincing in a passage where the LXX is not conspicuous for its fidelity to the Hebrew.

[173] This point is developed at length by J. Jeremias, *Servant*, pp. 101–103.

[174] See J. Jeremias, *ibid.*, pp. 103–106 for details.

Matthew 26:54; Luke 9:31; 12:50; 13:32–33; 17:25. These are all general predictions without reference to any one Old Testament passage.[175] Some are simply predictions, but in others the statement is not simply that he will suffer, but that he *must* suffer (δεῖ in Mk. 8:31; Mt. 26:54; Lk. 13:33; 17:25; *cf.* 'as it has been determined', Lk. 22:22). If we ask why it is necessary, the answer is frequently forthcoming: 'it is written'.[176] Thus we find the simple 'it is written' (Mk. 9:12; 14:21), the epigrammatic 'But that the scriptures may be fulfilled' (Mk. 14:49), and the more formal and emphatic assertions of Matthew 26:54 and Luke 18:31.[177] But in none of these cases is a specific Old Testament passage mentioned.

Some have attempted to discover the passage in mind by a study of the actual wording of the predictions. Echoes of Isaiah 53 have been traced not only in the ἐξουδενηθῇ of Mark 9:12, but in the use of παραδίδοσθαι ('be delivered') in the formal predictions of Mark 9:31; 10:33 and parallels, and in Mark 14:21.[178] Of the two uses of παρεδόθη in LXX Isaiah 53:12 the first is a paraphrase (MT הערה), and the second a mistranslation (MT יפגיע), so that there is certainly no allusion to the Hebrew.[179] Nor is an allusion to the LXX likely, since in Mark 9:31; 10:33; 14:21 παραδίδοσθαι means 'to be betrayed, handed over (to his enemies)', a quite natural meaning, and different from that in Isaiah 53:12, where in each case it means 'to be given up (to death)'. A further suggested allusion to Isaiah 53:5 in the word μαστιγώσουσιν ('they will scourge him') (Mk. 10:34)[180] cannot be accepted, for while the idea is clearly the same, there is no *verbal* similarity to either MT חברתו or LXX μώλωπι. The only probable *verbal* allusion to any Old Testa-

[175] Passages which have a specific OT reference (*e.g.* Mk. 10:45; 14:24; 14:27) have already been considered.

[176] *Cf.* H. E. Tödt, *op. cit.*, p. 191: 'The reason for the "must" of the Son of Man's suffering is God's will as revealed in *Scripture*.' See the full discussion, *ibid.*, pp. 188–193.

[177] *Cf.* also Jesus' strong emphasis on the scriptural necessity of his suffering after the event: Lk. 24:25–27, 44–46.

[178] *E.g.* B. Lindars, *op. cit.*, pp. 80–81; *contra* H. E. Tödt, *op. cit.*, pp. 159–161.

[179] Or to the Aramaic, at least as represented by Tg Jon. Jeremias sees an echo of Tg Is. 53:5b אתמסר (*Servant*, p. 99) but the subject in the Tg is the sanctuary, not the Servant.

[180] So B. Lindars, *op. cit.*, p. 81.

ment passage in these predictions is ἐξουδενηθῇ in Mark 9:12.

Yet there is a strong consensus of opinion that the major, if not the only, Old Testament source of these predictions was Isaiah 53. The reason for this lies not only, or even primarily, in the allusions to Isaiah 53 in Mark 9:12; 10:45; 14:24; Luke 22:37, but also in the close correspondence in *content*, even if not in words, between Jesus' predictions of mocking, suffering and death, and the picture in Isaiah 53. Even M. D. Hooker, whose aim is to minimize the influence of Isaiah 53 on the teaching of Jesus, admits this.[181]

But, granted that Isaiah 53 was an influence in forming Jesus' conviction that he must suffer, were there not other, perhaps weightier, influences? Hooker writes: 'The portrait of Isa. 52–3, however, is only one element in the whole pattern of suffering and exaltation which marks all Deutero-Isaiah's thought, and which runs through Jewish literature, from ritual psalms to apocalyptic visions.'[182] It is, of course, true that 'suffering and exaltation' play a large part in the Old Testament, and indeed in the history of Israel. But what is required to explain Jesus' expectation of his own suffering is prediction of the suffering of the Messiah, and here the field is much more restricted. Certainly parts of Zechariah 9–14, as we have seen, furnished him with grounds for this conviction, and we have seen also that in at least some of the psalms he saw his own suffering foreshadowed.[183] A case has also been made, though, as we shall see shortly, hardly convincingly, for a prediction of Messianic suffering in Daniel 7. But not one of these passages, or any other which might be adduced, so clearly stresses suffering as the essential mission of the Messiah as does Isaiah 53; nowhere else is suffering of such central importance, or so strikingly presented. Isaiah 53, poetic as it is, gives a systematic exposition of the nature, necessity and purpose of the suffering of the Messiah, which is true of no other passage in the Old Testament. When we add to this the close correspondence between Jesus' predictions of his suffering and the pattern laid down in Isaiah 53, we must, on the ground of these general

[181] *Servant*, p. 95: 'As a general summary, however, the predictions do correspond broadly with the picture of Isa. 53.'

[182] *Ibid.*, p. 162.

[183] See above, pp. 56–58. For other psalms which might be sources for this idea see B. Lindars, *op. cit.*, p. 88 and the following discussion.

predictions alone, regard Isaiah 53 as the major source of Jesus' conviction that he, as Messiah, must suffer. The several clear cases of his use of Isaiah 53 in just this way which we have considered above give to this conclusion at least a very high degree of probability.

We have, however, mentioned above that those who minimize the role of Isaiah 53 in the thinking of Jesus find the source of his expectation of suffering instead in Daniel 7. In many of the predictions of suffering Jesus uses the term 'the Son of man', and says that it is written that 'the Son of man' must suffer.[184] Since this title is agreed to be derived mainly, if not solely, from Daniel 7:13, it is argued that Daniel 7 is also the source of the prediction of suffering. The fullest exposition of this view is by C. K. Barrett.[185] After outlining the development of the idea of vicarious suffering in post-Old Testament times,[186] he returns to Daniel 7, and argues for the same idea there. Observing that in Daniel 7 the 'saints of the Most High' had been subjected to oppression before the appearance of the Son of man (Dn. 7:21, 25), and that the Son of man represents them, he transfers their suffering and martyrdom to the Son of man;[187] as, therefore, his capacity is a representative one, his suffering is on their behalf: 'he gives his life as *λύτρον ἀντὶ πολλῶν*.'[188]

At least three serious objections may be raised against Barrett's theory, the cumulative effect of which is surely fatal.

1. In Daniel 7 the Son of man is a figure for the saints not in their suffering, but in their vindication and power.[189] It is neither stated nor implied that the Son of man suffers; he is throughout a victorious person, and it was as such that both

[184] Mk. 8:31; 9:12; 9:31; 10:33; 10:45; 14:21; Lk. 17:24–25.

[185] *Loc. cit.*, pp. 8–15.

[186] Barrett quotes 2 Macc. 7:37–38; 4 Macc. 6:27ff.; 17:22; 18:4 (which speak of the vicarious effect of the deaths of the martyrs), and certain rabbinic parallels.

[187] *Cf.* C. F. D. Moule, *Phenomenon*, p. 89 on Dn. 7:21–22: ' "The Son of Man" already means "the representative of God's chosen people, destined through suffering to be exalted".' *Cf.* also W. D. Davies, *Paul*, p. 280 n. 1.

[188] *Loc. cit.*, p. 14.

[189] *Cf.* H. H. Rowley, *Servant*, p. 62 n. 2; W. Manson, *Jesus the Messiah* (London, 1943), pp. 7–8; J. W. Doeve, *op. cit.*, p. 131. *Contra* most fully M. D. Hooker, *The Son of Man in Mark* (London, 1967), pp. 27–30.

Jewish apocalyptic and the rabbinic writers unanimously regarded him.[190]

2. Nowhere in Daniel 7 is it suggested that the Son of man acts *on behalf of* the people. He is never set over against them as an individual against a community. He *is* the people, represented in a visionary form. His triumph is their triumph. Even if the previous objection were overruled, and it were granted that it is legitimate to speak of his suffering, it would simply be a visionary presentation of *their* suffering. But he could not be said to suffer *in their place*. He is not a separate figure with a separate history; his experiences are theirs. Thus the very identity between the saints and the Son of man, which is used to justify the ascription of suffering to the latter, inevitably rules out the idea of *vicarious* suffering. Whatever may have been evolved in later apocalyptic or rabbinic thought, Daniel 7 has no place for this idea.[191]

3. The actual allusions to Daniel 7 by Jesus[192] run directly counter to Barrett's theory at two points: (i) Jesus in fact makes no allusion to an idea of suffering in Daniel 7. His allusions are exclusively to verses 13–14, the picture of the triumphant exaltation of the Son of man; there is no allusion to the suffering and oppression of the saints, still less to any such suffering of the Son of man.[193] (ii) Jesus applies Daniel 7 consistently to the period *after* his resurrection, and never to his earthly life and work.[194] The suggestion that Jesus' predictions of his earthly suffering and death were derived from Daniel 7 thus stands in striking contrast with his actual application of that chapter consistently to the glory and power which succeeded his resurrection.

To these three objections must be added the sheer improbability of the view that it was from Daniel 7, where the very

[190] For the apocalyptic literature see S. Mowinckel, *He That Cometh*, pp. 410–415; for the rabbinic use see below, p. 188.

[191] Note also that there is nothing redemptive about the suffering of the saints in Dn. 7: see A. Gelston, *SJT* 22 (1969), p. 191 n. 1.

[192] That the title 'Son of man' does not in itself constitute such an allusion is argued below, pp. 136–138.

[193] See pp. 139–144. This is true also of all early Christian interpretation: see below, p. 215.

[194] See pp. 145–146. The application of the 'coming of the Son of man' in Mk. 8:38 and Mt. 10:23 to the transfiguration or to some other episode in the life of Jesus owes more to apologetic than to exegetical considerations.

idea of Messianic suffering has only in recent years been detected, that Jesus derived his conviction that he must suffer, and not from Isaiah 53, which presents the vicarious suffering of the Servant of Yahweh so clearly and vividly that Christian exegesis from the days of the New Testament has agreed in interpreting it as a prediction of the suffering of Jesus. When further we observe that Jesus did in fact use Isaiah 53 with reference to his passion in Luke 22:37; Mark 10:45; 14:24 (in the last two cases with a primary reference to the idea of *vicarious* suffering), and possibly alluded to it also in Mark 9:12 and Matthew 3:15 (and *cf.* the inevitable effect of the pronouncement of Mk. 1:11 on his subsequent thinking), it seems little short of perverse to look for a source of Jesus' passion-predictions in a passage where suffering is not predicated of the Son of man, and to discount the clearest statement in the Old Testament that the Messiah must suffer.

f. Conclusions on the Servant

The opponents of the view that Jesus interpreted his mission largely as that of the Servant ask us to show four things: 1. that he referred to this figure at all; 2. that these allusions were intended to convey that he was the Servant, and were not mere stock phrases, repeated without regard to their context; 3. that he referred in particular to the suffering, which was the distinctive mark of the Servant; 4. that he saw this suffering, as Isaiah 53 depicts it, as vicarious and redemptive.[195] These four points may now be dealt with.

1. We have in fact found more frequent references to the Servant figure than to any other Old Testament figure except, as we shall see, the Son of man of Daniel 7. They consist of one formal quotation, two clear allusions, two other possible verbal allusions, and a whole series of predictions of which Isaiah 53 is the most probable source. When we add that Jesus' ministry was inaugurated by a heavenly voice which identified him as the Servant, it is hard to believe that this conception was not a major constituent in his view of his mission.

2. That these were not ill-considered catch-phrases is indicated by the formula of Luke 22:37, with its affirmation that

[195] *Cf.* our summary of the arguments, *Tyndale Bulletin* 19 (1968), pp. 27–28.

Isaiah 53:12 was written about him, and that he must fulfil it, and by the similar formulae introducing several of the predictions of his suffering, to the effect that these things *must* happen to him. There is no suggestion that these are general duties or experiences of all true servants of God; he, and he alone, must suffer, because it is written of *him*. Even where there is no formula, the sense of purpose is marked: 'the Son of man *came to* serve and to give his life.' The suggestion is that the Servant figure provided a 'blue-print' for his ministry, which he must follow. It is significant that an allusion to the Servant concept is found embedded in one of the most solemn of Jesus' sayings, the Words of Institution at the Last Supper, hardly an occasion for thoughtless catch-phrases; Jesus is not likely to have founded the central act of worship of the Christian community on an Old Testament allusion which he did not mean to be taken seriously.

3. It would, of course, have been very difficult for Jesus to see his mission as that of the Servant and yet to ignore the suffering which is the most prominent and revolutionary aspect of that figure. In fact every reference to the Servant which we have noted, with one exception, is in a context of the suffering of Jesus, either in a direct prediction of his suffering and death, or, in the case of Luke 22:37, in a reference to an aspect of that suffering which goes to the roots of its Old Testament significance, and spoken at a time when suffering filled the horizon. The one exception is Matthew 3:15, and even here the identification with sinners 'to fulfil all righteousness' may be expected to involve suffering. All the specific references (with the exception of the voice from heaven in Mk. 1:11) are to Isaiah 53, the passage where the suffering of the Servant comes to the fore, and are to parts of that chapter where suffering and death are emphasized (especially verses 10 and 12).[196]

4. The theological significance of the suffering of the Servant is not explicit in every allusion by Jesus; many are simple predictions of the fact that he must suffer. The three clearest references to the Servant, however, all go beyond the mere fact

[196] This fact contrasts strongly with Jesus' use of Dn. 7, where there is *no* explicit allusion to suffering. Thus while Is. 53 meets this criterion set up by M. D. Hooker and others for the source of Jesus' conviction that he must suffer, Dn. 7 fails to meet it.

of suffering, to its redemptive significance. Luke 22:37 was not, it is true, spoken in a context of theological explanation; but the words chosen emphasize that identification of the Sinless with sinners which was the essence of the Servant's substitutionary suffering, and the fact that this suffering was then so imminent suggests that Jesus was not unaware of the theological implication of the words.[197] (There is probably a similar implication in Mt. 3:15, with its mention of identification with sinners as a means to 'righteousness'.) Mark 10:45 is unambiguously redemptive in tone: 'a ransom for many' is an allusion to, and summary of, the part of Isaiah 53 which most explicitly portrays the Servant as dying in the place of sinners to achieve their salvation.[198] Further, the point of the phrase in its context is to provide an illustration of true service; Jesus' death is therefore viewed here not simply in itself, but in the light of the benefit it brings to others. Finally, there is no need to repeat here what we said above[199] about the theological significance of Mark 14:24: it is for their benefit that his blood is to be shed. Thus, even if we accept the contention that a theological purpose or understanding can be assumed only where it is explicit in the words of Jesus, the sayings considered provide us with sufficient evidence. We would, however, question the assumption that it would be possible for Jesus consciously to accept the role of the Servant, and yet to be unaware of the teaching of Isaiah 53 on the meaning of the Servant's suffering. To accept the role of the Servant is *ipso facto* to accept a vocation of suffering for the redemption of others, and this Jesus did.

We conclude, therefore, that Jesus saw his mission as that of the Servant of Yahweh, that he predicted that in fulfilment of that role he must suffer and die, and that he regarded his suffering and death as, like that of the Servant, vicarious and redemptive.

g. *The Anointed Deliverer*

Isaiah 61:1–3 describes a figure closely similar to the Servant as depicted in Isaiah 42:1–7: both are endued with the Spirit

[197] *Cf.* above, pp. 115–116.
[198] See above, esp. pp. 118–121.
[199] Pp. 122–123.

of Yahweh, open blind eyes,[200] and bring prisoners out of darkness. Both are, in other words, sent and equipped by Yahweh to deliver the oppressed and wretched, and both are characterized by their gentleness. This similarity has led many to regard Isaiah 61:1–3 (and sometimes more of the chapter) as a fifth 'Servant Song'.[201] Modern scholarship has not endorsed this theory.[202] Even if it is right to speak of the 'Servant Songs' as a distinct group of poems within the book of Isaiah (and this is now widely questioned), the conspicuous weakness of this view lies in the complete absence from Isaiah 61:1ff. of that vicarious suffering in which the fourth 'Song' culminated.

The similarity to the 'Servant Songs' is, however, sufficient to render improbable the suggestion that the speaker is the prophet himself;[203] the passage bears a much greater resemblance to passages about the Servant than to any place where the prophet speaks of himself, both in the wording,[204] and in the figure described.[205] If this is not the Servant, it is a Messianic figure of similar character and status. That it was so regarded in the time of Jesus is indicated by Matthew 11:5, where Jesus' use of the passage depends on the recognition by John the Baptist that it describes 'him who is to come'; that Jesus himself so interpreted it we shall see from his use of it.

J. W. Bowman[206] bases his case for Jesus' self-identification with the Servant on the fact that he twice applied Isaiah 61 to himself. This is to go beyond the evidence,[207] for Jesus never

[200] See below, pp. 252–253 for an argument for this meaning in the MT of Is. 61:1 as well as in the LXX.

[201] So esp. W. W. Cannon, *ZATW* n.F. 6 (1929), pp. 284–288; *cf. e.g.* F. Delitzsch, *Biblical Commentary on the Prophecies of Isaiah*[4] (ET Edinburgh, 1890), vol. 2, pp. 395–396.

[202] See esp. J. S. van der Ploeg, *Les Chants du Serviteur de Jahvé* (Paris, 1936), pp. 201–204; C. R. North, *Servant*, pp. 137–138. Note, however, that North (*ibid.*, p. 25) regards these verses as 'belonging to the same complex of passages' as Is. 42 and 53, which amounts to much the same thing.

[203] So J. S. van der Ploeg, *op. cit.*, pp. 204–205, concluding that the passage is not therefore 'a prophecy in the literal sense' but 'a messianic prophecy in the sense of a type'.

[204] Nowhere in Is. 40–66 is the first person used by the prophet in describing his own work and experience. It is, however, used here and in the second and third 'Servant Songs'.

[205] Note esp. that nowhere after 1 Ki. 19:16 is there a reference to a prophet being anointed, even metaphorically. For the resemblance to the Servant see the data adduced by W. W. Cannon, *loc. cit.*, pp. 287–288.

[206] *The Intention of Jesus* (London, 1945), pp. 130–131; *cf.* also *ibid.*, p. 103.

[207] M. D. Hooker (*Servant*, p. 19) criticizes Bowman's position.

suggests that the figure of Isaiah 61 is the Servant, and in his allusions to Isaiah 61 combines that passage with Isaiah 35 and 58, not with the 'Servant Songs'. While he cannot have missed the similarity of these two figures, which he applied to himself, there is no evidence that he identified them. His use of Isaiah 61 can therefore only indirectly confirm that he saw himself as the Servant, in that a very similar figure from the same book of the Old Testament[208] is taken emphatically as a pattern for his mission. The occasions of the two clear allusions are significant.

Luke 4:17–21, quoting Isaiah 61:1–2a, with Isaiah 58:6.[209] The occasion is the beginning of Jesus' public ministry, and the quotation is, as it were, a manifesto setting out his programme. His claim that 'Today this scripture has been fulfilled in your hearing' is a deliberate identification of his work as that described in Isaiah 61:1–3. He is the Lord's anointed; the Messiah has come.

Matthew 11:5 (Lk. 7:22), alluding to Isaiah 61:1 and 35:5–6.[210] The occasion is no less significant. John the Baptist requires proof that Jesus is 'he who is to come', and Jesus furnishes that proof by pointing to his literal fulfilment of these two prophecies, the one a prediction of eschatological blessing, the other (Is. 61) a specifically Messianic prediction. Here then, no less than in Luke 4:17–21, Isaiah 61:1 is employed in a deliberate statement of Jesus' status and mission. God's time of salvation has come, and Jesus is the one anointed to be the bringer of that salvation.

A similar implication may be seen in a further possible allusion: *Matthew 5:3–4*. *πτωχοί* ('poor') may echo the ענוים (LXX *πτωχοῖς*) of Isaiah 61:1, to whom good news is preached, and *οἱ πενθοῦντες . . . παρακληθήσονται* ('those who mourn . . . shall be comforted') is close to לנחם כל-אבלים (LXX *παρακαλέσαι πάντας τοὺς πενθοῦντας*) in Isaiah 61:2, the idea being continued in verse 3. The first is a rather remote allusion, but the close

[208] Jesus was presumably innocent of Deutero- and Trito-Isaiah!

[209] The insertion of a phrase from Is. 58:6 has not been satisfactorily explained, but it does not affect the sense, as it comes from a passage describing the merciful actions God requires, and replaces a phrase ('to bind up the broken-hearted') which is of a similar character.

[210] See above, pp. 95–96 on the combined allusion, and the verbal echoes of Is. 61:1.

proximity of the second lends it credibility. Thus Jesus here describes the blessedness of his disciples in terms of this Old Testament description of the work of the Messiah. The good news for the poor and comfort for the mourners which the Messiah was to bring is now theirs; the Messiah, therefore, has come.[211] Alone, this inference could not be regarded as compelling, but its agreement with the two clear uses of Isaiah 61:1–3 already discussed renders it probable.

We conclude that Jesus saw his mission not only as that of the Servant, but also as that of the similar Anointed Deliverer of Isaiah 61:1–3, and that he proclaimed this self-identification more openly than any we have yet examined.

We may notice, finally, how amply these results confirm our observations on the type of Messiahship envisaged by Jesus.[212] One could scarcely imagine a Messianic ideal more entirely removed from nationalistic and political hopes than the Servant of Yahweh. 'The Servant is a soteriological rather than a political Messianic figure;'[213] and that salvation is achieved not only without force, but by humiliation, suffering and death. The Lord's Anointed in Isaiah 61:1–3 is likewise peaceful and merciful, engaged in a mission of relief, comfort and deliverance; it may be significant that the one note in Isaiah 61:1–3 which might jar against this conception, 'the day of vengeance of our God', finds no echo in Jesus' allusions. The emphasis falls entirely on deliverance, which is fulfilled both in literal healing and preaching (Mt. 11:5), and spiritually in the lives of his disciples (Mt. 5:3–4; probably Lk. 4:17–21 is also so intended).

VII. THE SON OF MAN

The figure of the Son of man in the teaching of Jesus has been the subject of even more debate in recent years than that of the Servant of Yahweh. Fortunately, the main part of that debate is not here our concern, for we are concerned only with Jesus' use of the Old Testament, in this case with his use of Daniel 7,

[211] J. Schniewind (*Matthäus*, p. 43) concludes that in these verses, no less than in Lk. 4 and Mt. 11, 'This allusion is a veiled messianic claim'.

[212] See above, pp. 102, 103, 105–106, 109.

[213] C. R. North, *Servant*, p. 218.

and we shall give reasons shortly for not regarding the title 'Son of man' *as such* as an allusion to Daniel 7. The use of the title in itself can therefore be very briefly dealt with, and our attention will be concentrated on the actual allusions to Daniel 7.

Our inclusion of these allusions at this point depends on the view that Daniel 7:13 may fairly be taken, and was taken by Jesus, as Messianic, as we have defined the term; that is, as looking forward to an individual as 'the figure of salvation'. This view we shall discuss in Excursus 3 below,[214] where we consider the interpretation of Daniel 7. Jewish interpretation of the chapter around and after the time of Jesus is fully discussed in our next chapter,[215] and fully confirms that we are justified in classing the vision as Messianic.

a. *The title 'Son of man'*

That Jesus did in fact use the title 'Son of man' is indicated by its distribution in the New Testament, and is generally agreed.[216] Even the hypothesis of its later introduction into some sayings of Jesus depends on the recognition that he had used it himself. That he used it with reference to himself is more widely questioned, but for our purposes must be assumed, we believe on good grounds.[217]

It is hardly disputed that Jesus derived this title, in part at least, from Daniel 7:13.[218] Some scholars believe not only

[214] Pp. 169–171.

[215] Below, pp. 174–175, 179–183, 185–188, 194–196.

[216] P. Vielhauer (in *Festschrift für Günther Dehn*, ed. W. Schneemelcher (Neukirchen Kreis Moers, 1957), pp. 51–79) rejects any use of the title by Jesus, basing his argument on the denial of any connection in Jesus' teaching between the kingdom of God and the Son of man. His argument is answered, *e.g.*, by E. Schweizer, *JBL* 79 (1960), pp. 119–124, discussed and supplemented by M. Black, *BJRL* 45 (1962/3), pp. 306–311. A full study of the connection between the kingdom of God and the Son of man is given by J. W. Doeve, *op. cit.*, pp. 119ff.

[217] The view associated particularly with the name of Bultmann, that Jesus referred to the Son of man as an eschatological figure distinct from himself, has a wide currency; it is most fully represented by the detailed study of H. E. Tödt, *op. cit.* Among many criticisms of this view, those of E. Schweizer are important (*ZNTW* 50 (1959), pp. 185–209; *JBL* 79 (1960), pp. 119–129; *NTS* 9 (1962/3), pp. 257–261). For recent defences of a more traditional approach see I. H. Marshall, *NTS* 12 (1965/6), pp. 327–351; M. D. Hooker, *Son of Man*, esp. pp. 189–197; R. Maddox, *NTS* 15 (1968/9), pp. 45–74.

[218] J. Y. Campbell (*JTS* 48 (1947), pp. 148–150) stands practically alone in denying this.

that this passage was the major source of the title as used by Jesus, but that it was the only source, beyond Jesus' own creative thinking.[219] The suggestions of the influence of the Similitudes of Enoch,[220] or of the use of the term in Ezekiel (to denote the prophet himself) or even in Psalms 8:5; 80:18 (EVV 8:4; 80:17),[221] are open to the grave objection that whereas, as we shall see, Jesus alluded frequently to Daniel 7, there is no clear allusion to any relevant part of Ezekiel,[222] and we have no indication that Jesus knew the Similitudes of Enoch at all[223] (or even that they were then in circulation[224]); for there is no phrase in the whole of Jesus' teaching which is reminiscent of the Similitudes, which could not as well be derived from Daniel 7, or elsewhere in the Old Testament. On the other hand, there can be no question of his use of Daniel 7 with regard to his own work, and this fact makes it unreasonable to base any argument on any other presumed source of the title. If we assume that it was derived from Daniel 7:13, we shall not be far astray.

But while Daniel 7:13 was the source of Jesus' title 'Son of man', the implications of the title are far wider. We shall show below[225] that 'Son of man' was not current in contemporary Judaism as a recognized name for the figure of Daniel 7:13. The title was not, therefore, in itself an allusion to that figure. John 12:34 shows that the title puzzled the crowds; they recognized from the way Jesus used it that he intended it to be a title with Messianic implications,[226] but, not realizing that it derived from Daniel 7:13,[227] had no background against

[219] *E.g.* T. W. Manson, 'The Son of Man in Daniel, Enoch, and the Gospels' (1949) reprinted in his *Studies in the Gospels and Epistles* (Manchester, 1962), p. 143; W. Manson, *op. cit.*, pp. 117–120.

[220] R. Otto (*op. cit.*, pp. 159–261) argues for Enoch as the major source.

[221] For the Ezekiel derivation see esp. E. A. Abbott, *The Son of Man* (Cambridge, 1910); also A. Richardson, *Introduction*, pp. 128–129, 145–146. It is well criticized by R. H. Fuller, *Mission*, pp. 99–102.

[222] The allusion to Ezk. 34 in Lk. 19:10 (see above, p. 96), even though in a Son of man saying, is not relevant, as the action alluded to is the action of Yahweh, whereas 'son of man' occurs here (v. 2), as always in Ezekiel, as a designation of the prophet.

[223] For the restricted field of influence of the Enochic literature see below, pp. 195–196.

[224] See below, p. 181 n. 38.

[225] See below, pp. 187–188.

[226] See Jn. 12:34a, where 'the Christ' stands parallel to 'the Son of man'.

[227] The phrase was common enough in Aramaic for the derivation not to be obvious.

which to interpret it. This may well have been Jesus' intention in using the title; its source made it a suitable one around which to gather his ideas of Messiahship which, as we have seen, were sharply opposed to current ideas of a political deliverer. Any of the recognized Messianic titles must inevitably carry overtones from this popular expectation, but 'Son of man', not being a recognized title of the Messiah, carried no such implication,[228] and provided a useful vehicle for Jesus' own reinterpretation of Messiahship.[229] It thus became the one title regularly adopted by Jesus, and therefore was made to carry a far wider range of ideas than its original context in Daniel 7 conveyed.[230] It is used to express whatever Jesus knew from the Old Testament must be his work and his fate.

It is for this reason that we stated above that a Son of man saying cannot simply on account of the title be classed as an allusion to Daniel 7. The attempt to trace the contents of all Son of man sayings to a source in Daniel 7 would result in a ludicrous example of 'eisegesis' (the art of reading into a passage what is not there). We have seen an example of this tendency in the attempt to derive the predictions that the Son of man must suffer from Daniel 7;[231] such a saying as Mark 10:45, which, as we have seen, bears no obvious reference to Daniel 7 beyond the title 'Son of man', cannot fairly be considered as deriving its teaching from that chapter, or even as having it consciously in mind. Jesus knew from the Scriptures (pre-eminently from Is. 53) that he must suffer, and therefore taught this as his Messianic destiny. That in so doing he should use the title 'Son of man' is almost inevitable; it was the term he regularly used to describe his role as Messiah. But this does not indicate a reference to the source of that title, Daniel 7. Only where the wording of a saying beyond the actual title is reminiscent of Daniel 7 can we fairly see an allusion to that chapter. To such allusions, therefore, we now turn.

[228] *Cf.* R. H. Fuller, *Mission*, pp. 98, 106.

[229] *Cf.* the occasions when Jesus rejected the title 'Christ' in favour of 'Son of man'; see above, p. 103, and A. Richardson, *Introduction*, pp. 134, 145.

[230] See further, below, pp. 145–146; and *cf.* the similar use of the title in the Similitudes of Enoch: see below, p. 182.

[231] See above, pp. 121, 128–130.

b. The allusions to Daniel 7

We shall consider here seven possible allusions to Daniel 7, not all of which are by any means certain. Six of these contain the title 'Son of man'; one (Mt. 28:18) does not. All are to the two verses 13–14.[232] We shall first discuss the allusions individually, and then in our next section attempt to see Jesus' use of the Danielic vision as a whole.

(i) *Mark 8:38* (Mt. 16:27; Lk. 9:26). In this saying an allusion to Daniel 7:13–14 is suggested not only by the title 'Son of man', but by the verb ἔλθῃ (Mt. ἔρχεσθαι) echoing אתה (Thdt ἐρχόμενος, LXX ἤρχετο), by the idea of glory (δόξα probably alludes to MT יקר, and the whole scene of Dn. 7:13–14 is one of glory, both the glory of the theophany and the 'dominion and glory and kingdom' given to the Son of man), and by the angelic retinue (the *words* are not derived from Dn. 7,[233] but the idea suggests the heavenly host of Dn. 7:10, who were present at the coming of the Son of man). The mention of the kingdom (Mt., the kingdom of the Son of man) in the following verse reinforces this impression. The verse is, therefore, generally seen as based on Daniel 7:13–14. Here, then, Jesus looks forward to a time when he will exercise the power and judgment (so the context of his saying implies) which are to be given to the Son of man.

The following verse states unambiguously that this time will be within the lifetime of some who hear the saying. (The phrase 'the kingdom of God come with power' suggests that the same event is in view, and the Matthean version, 'the Son of man coming in his kingdom', makes it plain that for Matthew at least the same fulfilment of Dn. 7:13–14 was intended.) It is of course possible that the connection of the two verses is not original, but we shall see three further cases where Jesus looks for a fulfilment of Daniel 7:13–14 within the generation;[234]

[232] A further suggested allusion to Dn. 7:22 in Mk. 1:15 (C. H. Dodd, *Scriptures*, p. 69; *cf.* J. W. Doeve, *op. cit.*, p. 159) seems too remote to be considered: the first clause (πεπλήρωται ὁ καιρός) is a not uncommon formula, and does not closely resemble the Aramaic or Thdt, while in the second clause (ἤγγικεν ἡ βασιλεία τοῦ Θεοῦ) neither the verb nor the possessor of the kingdom is the same as in Daniel.

[233] Zc. 14:5 may have influenced the wording; see pp. 157–158.

[234] See below, on Mt. 10:23; Mk. 13:26; 14:62.

it is therefore more natural to take Mark 8:38 of such an imminent event, as its present connection with 9:1 demands.

There is no clear indication in the present context of what sort of fulfilment is envisaged, except that it will be a 'visible' one ('they *see*' – 9:1). We shall see similar language in Mark 13:26 and 14:62. What form this clear manifestation of Jesus' exaltation to power and kingship will take is not here stated, but we shall see that in Mark 13:26 the reference is to the fall of Jerusalem in AD 70. This would meet the temporal limitation to the present generation, and it is tempting to see the same reference here.[235] Further discussion of this point must be postponed until the other allusions have been considered.

(ii) *Matthew 10:23* may be mentioned here because of its close connection with the last passage considered. It too looks for a 'coming of the Son of man' in the near future (before the disciples have completed their mission to Israel). While not in itself so clear an echo of Daniel 7:13, it is plausibly seen as such in the light of its connection with Mark 8:38 – 9:1.

What was said of that passage will apply here too, and again a reference to the coming destruction of Jerusalem as the manifestation of the exaltation and dominion of Jesus seems not unlikely.[236]

(iii) *Mark 13:26* (Mt. 24:30; Lk. 21:27). The fact of an allusion to Daniel 7:13 here is not questioned. We shall discuss the interpretation of this verse in an appendix,[237] concluding that the reference is to the destruction of Jerusalem. That act of judgment will make plain that Jesus has received from God the authority and dominion described in Daniel 7:13–14. The reasons for this interpretation are contained in the appendix, and need not be repeated here.

(iv) *Mark 14:62* (Mt. 26:64; Lk. 22:69 lacks the allusion to Dn. 7:13). Again the allusion to Daniel 7:13 is not in question.

[235] *Cf.* A. Plummer, *Luke*, pp. 249–250; P. Benoit, *L'Évangile selon Saint Matthieu*[2] (La Bible de Jérusalem, Paris, 1953), p. 107.

[236] So, most fully, A. Feuillet, *CBQ* 23 (1961), pp. 182–198. See also M.-J. Lagrange, *Matthieu*, p. 205; P. Benoit, *Matthieu*, p. 75; J. A. T. Robinson, *Jesus and His Coming*, pp. 76, 80, 91–92; C. F. D. Moule, *Birth*, p. 90.

[237] See below, Appendix A, esp. pp. 235–236.

What has been very much in debate in recent years is the sort of fulfilment for which Jesus looks. Until recently it was almost universally assumed that this was a prediction of the Parousia, but this interpretation is now frequently questioned.[238] It is suggested instead that in Mark 14:62 Jesus is taking Daniel 7:13 in just the sense in which it was originally intended,[239] that is, as describing his imminent vindication and exaltation to supreme authority. His judges may accuse and condemn him, but they will soon see that the one they condemn has become their lord and king. The sitting at God's right hand and the coming with clouds are not, then, two events separated by an indefinite period of time, but two figures for the single idea of the vindication and exaltation of the Son of man. His 'coming' is not a coming to earth, but, as in Daniel 7:13, a coming to God to receive power and glory, and is, of course, not to be interpreted literally: a literal 'sitting' and a literal 'coming' could hardly be envisaged together![240]

This exegesis is supported not only by the fact that it is reasonable to assume that Jesus used Daniel 7:13 in its intended sense unless there is evidence to the contrary, but also by the word *ὄψεσθε* ('you will see'), which implies that those sitting in judgment over Jesus will in fact witness the 'coming', *i.e.* that it will occur within their lifetime. This is confirmed by the Matthean *ἀπ' ἄρτι* (Lk. *ἀπὸ τοῦ νῦν*, 'from now on'). If, as Glasson argues, this phrase was originally in Mark,[241] it makes explicit what is already implied in *ὄψεσθε*, that Jesus is not referring to an event in the indefinite future, but to a situation which is to obtain immediately.

The primary note, then, of this allusion to Daniel 7:13 is, as

[238] Some of the more important such treatments are those by W. K. Lowther Clarke, *Theology* 31 (1935), pp. 130–132; T. F. Glasson, *The Second Advent*[3] (London, 1963), pp. 54–62; G. S. Duncan, *Jesus, Son of Man* (London, 1947), pp. 175–177; V. Taylor, *Mark*, pp. 568–569; J. A. T. Robinson, *ExpT* 67 (1955/6), pp. 336–340, and *Jesus and His Coming*, pp. 43–51; M. D. Hooker, *Son of Man*, pp. 167–171. Other exponents of this exegesis are listed in T. F. Glasson, *Advent*, p. 60; G. R. Beasley-Murray, *Mark Thirteen*, pp. 90–91.

[239] See below, p. 169.

[240] For a defence of this exegesis in detail see the works listed in n. 238 above, and also T. F. Glasson, *NTS* 7 (1960/1), pp. 88–93.

[241] T. F. Glasson, *Advent*, pp. 57–59. It is in sy[s], and was probably omitted due to the embarrassment it caused when the verse came to be interpreted of the Parousia.

in the original meaning of that chapter, one of vindication, and the conferment of power and authority on the Son of man. Jesus, the defendant and victim, will be exalted to be lord and king. But while this continuing state is the primary point of the application, ὄψεσθε suggests that some particular manifestation of this lordship within history is in view, and that it will be within the lifetime of his hearers. When we compare this with the similar implication that we have seen in Mark 8:38 and Matthew 10:23, there seems to be good reason for taking all three passages as parallel to Mark 13:26, where the context is explicitly that of the destruction of Jerusalem, and for suggesting that Jesus saw this act of judgment on the nation which judged and rejected him as the visible manifestation of that vindication and lordship which was soon to be conferred on him.[242] In Mark 14:62, where Jesus, the apparently helpless defendant, is addressing the leaders of that nation, this application is singularly appropriate.

(v) *Matthew 28:18* may be considered next, as it reinforces what we have seen to be the primary application of Mark 14:62. ἐδόθη μοι πᾶσα ἐξουσία ἐν οὐρανῷ καὶ ἐπὶ τῆς γῆς ('all authority in heaven and on earth has been given to me') is an echo of Daniel 7:14 ולה יהב שלטן (LXX καὶ ἐδόθη αὐτῷ ἐξουσία; Thdt has ἀρχή at this point, but ἐξουσία for the other two occurrences of שלטן in the verse, as in verses 6 and 27), with its following description of an everlasting dominion over all peoples, nations, and languages.[243] Jesus' application here leaves no room for doubt. After his resurrection he *is* the exalted Son of man, and *has* received the everlasting and universal dominion predicted for that figure. 'Through the Resurrection, Jesus of Nazareth . . . has now been given the authority of the Son of Man triumphant: in short, he has become Lord and Christ.'[244] What he had pointed forward to during his life has now become fact. The kingdom has come, and Jesus reigns as Son of man.

[242] For a similar view, taking the phrase 'the coming of the Son of man' as referring regularly to the destruction of Jerusalem, see G. B. Caird, *op. cit.*, pp. 20–22.

[243] Arguments in favour of this allusion include E. Lohmeyer, *Das Evangelium des Matthäus* (Göttingen, 1956), pp. 416–417; G. Barth, *op. cit.*, pp. 133–134; W. D. Davies, *Sermon*, pp. 197–198.

[244] W. D. Davies, *Sermon*, p. 198.

This goes to confirm our interpretation of Mark 14:62, as referring to a state of exaltation shortly to begin. Daniel 7:13–14 is explicitly so applied here. In his triumph over death Jesus, the victim, is vindicated, and now all power is his. Moreover, it is this fact which makes possible the further application to the destruction of Jerusalem, which we saw implied in Mark 14:62, and explicit in Mark 13:26, as well as possibly intended in Mark 8:38 and Matthew 10:23; for this manifestation of the vindication of Jesus demands the already existing *fact* of that vindication and the consequent authority.

(vi) *Matthew 19:28.* The term 'Son of man', the idea of his reigning, the concepts of glory, thrones and judgment, and the enthronement of the disciples (*cf.* the reign of the 'saints') – all these point to key themes of Daniel 7, and especially to the 'enthronement' of the Son of man in Daniel 7:13–14.

Here we find a new application of Daniel 7, for the word παλιγγενεσία ('regeneration'; RSV 'the new world') stamps the saying as having an eschatological reference in the fullest sense.[245] The picture is of the final judgment, when the reign of the Son of man will be finally consummated.

A further new element in this application is the recognition of the corporate aspect of Daniel 7. Not only will the Son of man reign, but his disciples too, because they belong to him, will reign and judge. The 'saints of the Most High' will indeed receive the kingdom, but they will receive it in association with, indeed through the mediation of, the Son of man. There is no suggestion of a *purely* corporate exegesis of Daniel 7; the Son of man has an independent existence as an individual, and is in fact the prominent figure, but his reign leads to the reign of those who belong to him.

(vii) *Matthew 25:31.* The application of Daniel 7:13–14 here is very similar to that in Matthew 19:28. Again the picture is of the Son of man as king (*cf.* verse 34), sitting on his throne, judging, in glory; all the ideas from Daniel 7 found in Matthew 19:28 are here as well, with the exception of the reign of the saints. In this case we find also the same terminology which led

[245] For the implications of the term see F. Büchsel, *TDNT* I, pp. 686–689.

us to see in Mark 8:38 an allusion to Daniel 7, that of the Son of man coming in glory, with an angelic retinue.[246]

Here again there is nothing in the context to restrict the reference to any event before the final judgment, and it seems clear that this was the intention. Matthew, in placing this passage after the Parousia teaching at the end of chapter 24 and the parables of the virgins and the talents, clearly intended it to be taken thus. Again, therefore, Daniel 7:13–14 is applied to the final consummation of the authority and dominion of Jesus as the exalted Son of man, in the final judgment.

It is to be noted, however, that not even in these two cases is Daniel 7:13 applied to the Parousia as such. Neither passage envisages a coming to earth or an appearance on earth. In each case it is a heavenly judgment scene. There is thus no suggestion even here that Jesus ever understood the 'coming' of Daniel 7:13 as meaning anything other than a coming to God to receive vindication and authority.

The corporate aspect of Daniel 7, which we have seen to have been taken into account in Matthew 19:28, may have influenced this passage too. Jesus states in verses 40 and 45 that what is done to his 'brothers' is done to him. There is thus a sort of identity between the Son of man and his people. However, 'Son of man' is used only of the king himself, and there is no suggestion that his 'brothers' either share his throne or participate in his judgment; they are rather the beneficiaries of that judgment, and are given a kingdom by him (verse 34). Thus, as in Matthew 19:28, the 'saints' are not identified with the Son of man, but the authority given to the latter results in blessing, and a derivative authority, for the former.

c. The use of Daniel 7 – Conclusions

The seven allusions just considered provide a sufficiently wide range of applications to enable us to draw a relatively full picture of the way Jesus understood and used Daniel 7, and especially the key figure in verses 13–14. The following points may be noticed.

[246] As in Mk. 8:38 (see p. 139), the *idea* may be derived from Dn. 7:10. Here, more clearly than in Mk. 8:38, the *wording* echoes Zc. 14:5. See below, pp. 157–158.

1. The keynote of Daniel 7 is that of vindication and exaltation to an everlasting and universal dominion.[247] We have found this same pattern in Jesus' uses of the chapter. Sometimes the note of vindication is prominent (Mk. 14:62), sometimes the reception of power (Mt. 28:18) or the exercise and manifestation of that power, especially in judgment (another theme of Dn. 7). The fidelity to the general tone and pattern of Daniel 7 is clear.

2. The fulfilment is seen as occurring in three stages: (a) Immediately after the resurrection, Jesus, vindicated over those who rejected and judged him, receives the dominion of the Son of man (Mt. 28:18; Mk. 14:62). (b) This dominion is to be manifested in a specific historical act of judgment, which is imminent, and is probably to be identified with the destruction of Jerusalem (Mk. 8:38; Mt. 10:23; Mk. 13:26, and probably as a secondary element in Mk. 14:62). (c) The final manifestation of this dominion will be in the judgment of all nations (Mt. 19:28; 25:31). These three stages form a logical progression, the first being the most direct application of the vision in Daniel 7:13–14 of the reception of power by the Son of man, and the second and third the manifestations of that power, the one imminent and local, the other more remote, universal and final.[248]

3. The application of Daniel 7 is therefore consistently to the period after the resurrection. There is no allusion to Daniel 7 by Jesus with reference to his earthly life and death. This goes to confirm our argument[249] that the use of the title 'Son of man' alone does not necessarily betray a reference to Daniel 7, for the majority of the Son of man sayings do refer to the earthly life or death of Jesus; uses of the term 'Son of man' by Jesus

[247] See below, p. 169.

[248] B. Lindars (*op. cit.*, pp. 48–49, 257) recognizes the first and third of these applications, and sees the latter as an extension by the early church of the former, which was the only use of Dn. 7 made by Jesus. This assumption that a 'shift of application' denotes the work of a later mind underlies much of Lindars' work. It is not shared by G. S. Duncan (*op. cit.*, pp. 176–177), who recognizes the logical connection between stages (a) and (c), and therefore has no difficulty in attributing both to Jesus. Once stage (b) has also been recognized, it falls naturally into the scheme. The different stages in the application, therefore, provide no warrant for denying the authenticity of any of these allusions to Dn. 7 by Jesus.

[249] See above, pp. 137–138.

therefore include a much wider range of application than do his allusions to Daniel 7. In particular, we may note that there is no application of Daniel 7 by Jesus to the necessity of his suffering. For him it described only the exaltation, not the suffering, of the Messiah. The idea that it was from Daniel 7 that Jesus derived his expectation of suffering finds no support in his actual use of the chapter. And in this he is true to its original meaning, for Daniel 7 says nothing of the suffering of the Son of man, and only applies that title to the 'saints' in their vindication and exaltation, not in their subjection.

4. The 'coming' of the Son of man in Daniel 7:13 was a coming to God to receive authority, not a 'descent' to earth.[250] Although, as we shall see,[251] it was interpreted both in Jewish and in Christian circles in the latter sense, Jesus did not so interpret it, but applied it in its original sense, to his own reception of authority. The two fully eschatological applications picture a heavenly judgment scene, not a 'descent' to earth. That Jesus taught a second coming to earth is clear, but it is equally clear that he did not use Daniel 7 as a prediction of it.

5. The point at which there is a real discrepancy between the meaning of Daniel 7 and Jesus' use of it, is in the fact that, whereas in Daniel 7 the Son of man represented the triumph of Israel over other nations, the triumph of Jesus is, in the first instance, over the Jews. This is so both in the reversal of the relation between Jesus and the Sanhedrin envisaged in Mark 14:62, and even more clearly in the application of Daniel 7 to the destruction of Jerusalem. That this discrepancy was not the product of careless exegesis is indicated by two facts. (a) We saw frequently in chapter 3 evidence that Jesus saw his coming as marking the end of the privileged status of the Jewish nation as the people of God, a status which he now assumed in himself, and which would pass to his disciples. (b) At the end of one of the most pronounced statements to this effect (the parable of the tenants) we have found an allusion to Daniel 2:34–35,[252] a passage relating a vision parallel to that of Daniel 7; there again a prediction of the destruction of pagan empires is apparently applied to the rejection of the Jewish

[250] See below, p. 169. [251] Below, pp. 188, 196, 219–220.
[252] Lk. 20:18; see above, pp. 98–99.

leaders. The suggestion is that Jesus' teaching that he himself, and through him his disciples, now constituted the true people of God was deliberately carried to the extent of applying to the unbelieving Jews the Danielic visions of the crushing of pagan opposition. In rejecting Jesus, the Jews, no less than the pagan empires, were the opponents of the kingdom of God.

6. Jesus saw Daniel 7:13–14 as portraying an individual Messiah. T. W. Manson's theory that Jesus used the term 'Son of man' in a purely corporate sense, to include both himself and his disciples,[253] cannot be maintained, at least as far as the explicit allusions to Daniel 7 are concerned. The only cases where the disciples are in any way associated with Jesus are Matthew 19:28 and 25:31, and in these, as we have seen, the distinction is clear; the disciples' authority is only a derivative one, because *Jesus* is the Son of man. Mark 8:38 and Matthew 10:23 clearly differentiate between the Son of man and his disciples. This individual interpretation of Daniel 7:13–14 is, as we shall show below,[254] both true to the accepted understanding of the passage in the time of Jesus, and consonant with the expression of the chapter itself.

7. Jesus' attention is, therefore, largely restricted to verses 13–14. This is the primary reference of each allusion. We have, however, noticed that he was not unaware of the corporate aspect of Daniel 7, and two of his allusions show that it played a part in his application of the chapter to his own work.[255]

8. The frequency of the allusions to Daniel 7:13–14 suggests that the figure of the Son of man was one of the foremost influences on Jesus' conception of his Messianic status and destiny. What did this figure contribute to his teaching about Messiahship? While the title 'Son of man' in itself was used as a vehicle for Jesus' Messianic ideas without giving scope for the perpetuation of current hopes of a political deliverer, the positive content of Daniel 7:13–14 served the same end. It depicts not an earthly conquest, but a heavenly exaltation and authority. Such nationalistic connotations as the original vision had are deliberately put aside by Jesus when he predicts its fulfilment not in the Jewish nation but in himself. And the kingdom of the Son of man is not won by his own power, but

[253] *The Teaching of Jesus*[2] (Cambridge, 1935), pp. 227ff.
[254] See Excursus 3, pp. 169–171. [255] See above, pp. 143–144.

given by God; he is not the conquerer, but the vindicated. The congruity of this conception with the other Messianic figures so far studied is therefore clear. All tend to the same end, a reversal of the popular ideas of Messiahship.

9. But while Daniel 7:13–14 provides a picture of the kingdom Jesus is to receive after his work on earth, and in which his disciples are to share, it does not specify the means of achieving that kingdom. It has no application to his earthly life and death. It thus lends itself admirably to a combination with those other figures from Zechariah and Isaiah which depict the suffering of the Messiah. It has often been asserted that Jesus' conception of Messiahship was based on a combination of the two figures of the Servant of Yahweh and the Son of man;[256] in an oversimplified form it could be stated that he saw his mission as the achievement of the kingdom of the Son of man by means of the suffering of the Servant. This we believe to be a true, if not an exhaustive, account. More accurately it may be stated that Jesus saw in Daniel 7:13–14 a prediction of the ultimate goal and culmination of his Messianic work, the character of which as accomplished on earth he saw depicted in various Old Testament figures, pre-eminently the Servant of Yahweh. The combination of the various figures we have examined, and especially those of the Servant of Yahweh and the Son of man, was Jesus' own work, and it resulted in his own particular teaching, which took even his own disciples by surprise: 'Was it not necessary that the Christ should suffer these things and (thus) enter into his glory?'

VIII. THE MESSIAH ACCORDING TO JESUS – SUMMARY

The various Messianic figures which we have considered may be pieced together to form a rough picture of the nature of Messiahship as Jesus construed it from the Old Testament.

The *status* of the Messiah is not merely that of a descendant of David, *i.e.* an ordinary human king; he is of a greater authority, exercised in a sphere above earthly politics, in a close association with God himself[257] (Ps. 110:1 as interpreted in

[256] For a typical statement of this view see O. Cullmann, *Christology*, pp. 158–161.

[257] *Cf.* our contention in the next section that some of Jesus' OT allusions implied a status no less than divine.

Mk. 12:35–37; *cf.* Dn. 7:13–14). The *work* of the Messiah on earth is one of humiliation, suffering and death (the Servant figure; also Zc. 12:10; 13:7); even his kingship is conceived in terms of lowliness (Zc. 9:9). He heals the sick and preaches good news to the poor (Is. 61:1). The *results* of his work will be the justification of those for whom he has vicariously suffered (Is. 53), comfort and relief for the suffering (Is. 61:1 as interpreted in Mt. 5:3–4 and, probably, Lk. 4:17–21), and peace and prosperity for his people (Zc. 9:9–10). The *outcome* of his humiliation will be his vindication and exaltation by God (Dn. 7:13–14; but the same idea is also present in Is. 53:10–12; Zc. 9:9; and Ps. 110:1), to receive an everlasting and universal dominion (Dn. 7:14; Ps. 110:1; also the echo of Dn. 2 in Lk. 20:18).

The total picture, no less than the individual figures, makes up a view of Messiahship in striking contrast to what was probably the dominant popular hope at the time, of a Son of David who was to reign in Jerusalem, subduing all other nations, and exalting the Jews to an everlasting earthly dominion.[258] Jesus' view has no room for political supremacy, military conquest or earthly power; the only dominion it envisages is a heavenly one, and the position of the Messiah on earth is one of humiliation, not of power. This cannot be less than a deliberate repudiation of the popular conception. Each of the figures considered above is either in itself in direct contrast to such an idea, or, in the case of Psalm 110:1, is so interpreted by Jesus.

The choice of Messianic figures is remarkable. The only two passages in the Old Testament which clearly envisage the suffering of the Messiah are Isaiah 52:13 – 53:12 and Zechariah 9–14. Yet it is these passages, together with Daniel 7, which account for the vast majority of the Messianic allusions by Jesus. And even Daniel 7, while it does not directly teach the suffering of the Messiah, paints a picture of vindication which is well suited to a combination with such teaching. On the other hand, Jesus makes no use of what is generally regarded as

[258] For this sort of Messianic expectation see, *e.g.*, S. Mowinckel, *He That Cometh*, *passim*, esp. chapter 9 and p. 445; more briefly T. W. Manson in *The Background of the New Testament and its Eschatology* (Studies in honour of C. H. Dodd), ed. W. D. Davies and D. Daube (Cambridge, 1956), pp. 218–219; G. E. Ladd, *op. cit.*, p. 146.

the main stream of Old Testament Messianism, the idea of Davidic kingship, found *e.g.* in Isaiah 9; 11; Micah 5; Jeremiah 23:5–6, *etc.*, except, in his use of Psalm 110:1, to lift it to a higher plane. The only other kingly idea used is that of Zechariah 9:9–10, where the king is not only lowly and peaceful, but far from being a conqueror is one saved and vindicated by God. This one-sided emphasis can hardly have been accidental.[259]

We may note finally that through these Messianic passages, and Jesus' application of them, runs the same note of eschatological fulfilment which we noted in the use of non-Messianic predictions. The Messiah is, by definition, an eschatological figure, and Jesus is the Messiah. Thus in his coming the eschaton has arrived. This is the point of Jesus' declaration concerning Isaiah 61:1–2: 'Today this scripture has been fulfilled in your hearing' (Lk. 4:21). 'The idea of fulfilment ... holds in it an eschatological intensity.'[260] The long-awaited time of deliverance is now here. It is true that in his application of Daniel 7:13–14 Jesus still looks to the future, but only to the very near future, the time of his resurrection. The more distant application (to the final judgment) is only the final outworking of that fulfilment. The coming of Jesus, if it was not the end, was the beginning of the end. In that coming all was in principle fulfilled, and it only remained for it to work itself out. To this understanding of his place in the purpose of God, which is contained in Jesus' use of Messianic as well as non-Messianic predictions, we shall apply the term 'inaugurated eschatology'.[261]

IX. THE ASSUMPTION OF THE ROLE OF YAHWEH

Not all the quotations and allusions to be considered in this final category are from specifically predictive passages in the Old Testament, though the majority are. We treat them

[259] C. H. Dodd (*History and the Gospel* (London, 1938), pp. 61–62) notes this selective use of Messianic ideas in the NT as a whole, and attributes it to 'the memory of what Jesus had been, had said, had done, and had suffered'. That the selection was the work of Jesus himself is an even more obvious explanation.

[260] C. F. D. Moule, *Birth*, p. 62, with reference to Lk. 4:21. *Cf.* G. E. Ladd, *op. cit.*, pp. 107–108.

[261] See further, below, p. 162, and n. 303 *ad loc.*

together because they reinforce one another in suggesting that Jesus was not averse to taking upon himself what in the Old Testament was said of Yahweh, and that he saw his Messianic role as involving not only a sharing in the divine activity, but even a divine status. The relevant quotations are not numerous, nor is the implication always clear, but the cumulative effect is to present a striking and daring claim.

We consider first four Old Testament passages which were not specifically predictive; then three indications, either in the Old Testament passage or in Jesus' use of it, that the Messiah was to be at least closely associated with Yahweh; and finally six actual Old Testament predictions of the eschatological activity of Yahweh, which Jesus apparently took upon himself.

a. Non-predictive passages

(i) *Mark 13:31* (Mt. 24:35; Lk. 21:33). There is no verbal allusion here, but the saying recalls Isaiah 40:8. In both cases the permanence of a 'word' is established by contrast with the natural order, and the parallelism is similar. In Jesus' saying, however, the contrast is stronger; grass and flowers are replaced by heaven and earth. Yet the 'word' now in view is not the word of Yahweh, but the word of Jesus. Its permanence is affirmed in terms which even surpass the Old Testament description of the word of Yahweh. (Even if an allusion to Is. 40:8 is doubted, the similar statements of Ps. 119:89, 160, and Jesus' own words in Mt. 5:18 and Lk. 16:17, show that the permanence of the word of God was a common idea.[262]) The claim is a daring one.

(ii) *Matthew 21:16*, quoting Psalm 8:3 (EVV verse 2).[263] The occasion is the Messianic salutation of Jesus by the children at the cleansing of the Temple. In reply to the protest of the authorities, Jesus not only refuses to disown the salutation, but justifies it by quoting an Old Testament verse which states that Yahweh uses the praise of children to silence his adversaries. Jesus' use of the verse depends on its applicability to the

[262] For Jesus' use of the cosmic order as the standard of comparison, *cf.* also Is. 51:6; 54:9–10; Je. 31:35–36; 33:20–21.

[263] See below, pp. 251–252 for the rendering of עֹז by *αἶνον*.

children's praise of *him*, and to *his* adversaries. Unless he is here setting himself in the place of Yahweh, the argument is a *non sequitur.*

(iii) *Luke 10:19.* πατεῖν ἐπάνω ὄφεων καὶ σκορπίων ('to tread upon serpents and scorpions') is a possible allusion to Psalm 91:13 על־שחל ופתן תדרך תרמס כפיר ותנין (LXX ἐπ᾽ ἀσπίδα καὶ βασιλίσκον ἐπιβήσῃ καὶ καταπατήσεις λέοντα καὶ δράκοντα). Not only the details, but the idea of protection given to the faithful, suggest the allusion.[264] The expression is of a proverbial type, but it is perhaps not insignificant that Jesus explicitly affirms that he has given to his disciples an immunity which in the Old Testament was the gift of Yahweh to his devoted followers.

(iv) *Luke 20:18* (?Mt. 21:44). The allusion to Daniel 2:34–35, 44–45 in the second half of the verse has been considered above,[265] but the clause πᾶς ὁ πεσὼν ἐπ᾽ ἐκεῖνον τὸν λίθον συνθλασθήσεται ('everyone who falls on that stone will be broken to pieces') alludes to Isaiah 8:14–15, where Yahweh is described as a stone of offence and a rock of stumbling to Israel, on which many will stumble and fall and be broken. There may be a verbal allusion to verse 15 ונפלו ונשברו (LXX πεσοῦνται καὶ συντριβήσονται), but in any case the metaphor is clearly parallel. The context in Isaiah is the threat of invasion, in face of which Isaiah calls for fear not of conspiracy and invasion, but of Yahweh. The verses in question state that Yahweh will be a sanctuary for those who fear him, but for those who do not he will be a rock indeed, but a rock on which they will stumble and be broken.[266] The application of the passage by Jesus may well intentionally echo this contrast: he is the head corner-stone, the one to be trusted and relied on, but for those who reject him (as the tenants in the parable), this same stone will be a stumbling-block, and they will be broken. The results of men's response to him will be the same

[264] So, *e.g.*, M.-J. Lagrange, *Luc*, p. 303. An allusion to Dt. 8:15 is also possible, but the similarity in both wording and context is less obvious.

[265] See above, pp. 98–99.

[266] Interpretations of this passage vary in detail, but the main theme as outlined above is generally agreed. See, *e.g.*, B. Lindars, *op. cit.*, p. 175, and the fuller exposition by E. J. Young, *The Book of Isaiah* (Grand Rapids, 1965–), vol. 1, pp. 311–313.

as the results of their response to Yahweh. At least it is clear that here Jesus applies to himself an Old Testament description of Yahweh.

b. Messianic passages

The three passages to be mentioned here have all been discussed above, and we shall not repeat what was stated there. Here our concern is with the implication of a close association, amounting virtually to identification, between the Messiah and Yahweh.

(i) *Zechariah 12:10.* The figure of the martyr, which we have argued was seen by Jesus as a prediction of his own fate, has one remarkable characteristic: the text reads literally: 'They shall look on *me* whom they have pierced.' The reading אלי has been emended (*e.g.* to אליו[267]), but the MT is supported by the older versions,[268] and by the difficulty of the reading, an obvious target for emendation; the variety of expedients adopted is sufficient evidence that the exegetical difficulty is the only reason for questioning the text.[269] The martyr is described elsewhere in the third person, and this strange first person must be accounted for by the recognition that 'this character is the representative of Yahweh to such an extent that the latter considers that he himself has been pierced through his representative'.[270] The significance of this fact will become more apparent when we add the evidence of Zechariah 13:7, for,

[267] So RSV and JB, both claiming the support of Thdt (though RSV has dropped the note from editions after 1962). The chief witnesses to the text of Thdt, however, include the first person pronoun of the MT (πρός με), possibly combined with a further phrase representing a third person: so Field restores from the Syro-Hexaplar πρός με εἰς ὅν. (*Cf.* the remarkable compromise of NEB: 'They shall look on me, on him whom they have pierced.')

[268] The awkward and unnecessary מן קדמי in the Tg paraphrase must be due to a first person in the original. The LXX is unequivocal. P. Lamarche (*op. cit.*, p. 82) lists also the Syriac, Talmud, Aquila, Symmachus, Thdt, and Vg as supporting the MT (on Thdt see the last note).

[269] For some of the suggestions see H. G. Mitchell, *op. cit.*, pp. 334–335; B. Otzen, *Studien über Deuterosacharja* (Copenhagen, 1964), p. 264. P. Lamarche (*op. cit.*, pp. 80–84) gives a full defence of the MT.

[270] P. Lamarche, *op. cit.*, p. 107; *cf. ibid.*, pp. 83–84, and F. F. Bruce, *This is That*, p. 112.

as we have seen,[271] these are aspects of the same Messianic conception.

(ii) *Zechariah 13:7*. Here again we are concerned with a single phrase of the Old Testament description of the suffering Messiah. Yahweh describes him as רעי . . . גבר עמיתי (RSV 'My shepherd . . . the man who stands next to me'). עמית implies kinship; its only other use in the Old Testament is to describe a 'fellow-Israelite',[272] and it is probably derived from a root denoting 'family connection'.[273] This figure is thus more than Yahweh's 'associate' or even 'companion';[274] he is his 'kinsman'.[275] Thus the two passages Zechariah 12:10 and 13:7 together suggest a relationship between Yahweh and his representative, the smitten Shepherd-King, which amounts at least to a close 'kinship', even to identification. And these two passages are both applied by Jesus to himself. In neither case is the phrase in question actually cited, but the identification of himself with this Messianic figure, which Jesus' allusions take for granted, could not have been made without an awareness of the implication that he was closely related to Yahweh, and that his suffering was the suffering of Yahweh himself.

(iii) *Daniel 7:13–14*. The Old Testament passage in itself seems to be speaking here too of something more than a human ruler, if, as we shall argue,[276] it is right to see an individual figure here at all. The clouds of heaven with which he comes are in Old Testament thought the vehicle or accompaniment of the coming of Yahweh,[277] and the kingship he receives is

[271] Above, pp. 104–105.

[272] So eleven times in Leviticus.

[273] Assyrian *emû*: so BDB, p. 765. They translate 'associate, fellow, relation'. Note that in Lv. 19:17 עמית stands in parallelism with אח (brother).

[274] So H. G. Mitchell, *op. cit.*, p. 317.

[275] G. A. Smith (*The Book of the Twelve Prophets* (London, 1898), vol. 2, p. 478) suggests 'compatriot'. *Cf.* E. Sellin, *Das Zwölfprophetenbuch* (Leipzig-Erlangen, 1922), p. 517: 'עמית, strictly, *fellow-countryman* (Volksgenosse).' P. Lamarche (*op. cit.*, p. 91) comments, 'As an Israelite is "close" to another Israelite, so this shepherd struck by the sword is "close" to Yahweh.' See further M. F. Unger, *Zechariah* (Grand Rapids, 1963), pp. 231–232.

[276] See Excursus 3, pp. 169–171.

[277] See below, p. 236, and further, W. K. Lowther Clarke, *Theology* 31 (1935), pp. 63–65.

everlasting and universal: more could not be said of the kingship of Yahweh himself. We shall see shortly that Jesus in fact goes still further, and envisages himself as assuming the status and function of the Ancient of Days himself.

c. Predictions of the coming and judgment of Yahweh

The passages in this group relate predominantly to the future work of judgment. This might be seen as implying that Jesus expected to be entrusted with divine functions in his future exaltation, but made no such claim for his earthly work. This is disproved, however, by the previously considered passages, all of which except the last imply a divine function and status for Jesus on earth, and also by two of this present group, which apply Old Testament predictions of the coming of Yahweh to judge and to save to Jesus' earthly work. These two cases may be considered first.

(i) *Mark 9:12–13* (Mt. 17:11–12); *Matthew 11:10* (Lk. 7:27); *Matthew 11:14*. These references to Malachi 3:1 and 3:23–24 (EVV 4:5–6) have been considered above.[278] We argued there that the 'messenger' of 3:1 and the figure of Elijah *redivivus* in 3:23–24 both refer to the same prophetic forerunner, whose coming would prepare the way for the imminent 'great and terrible day of Yahweh', when Yahweh himself would come to judge his people (3:5). There is no third person, no Messiah, involved; first 'my messenger'/Elijah, then Yahweh.[279] And, as Jesus affirmed on more than one occasion, the former had appeared in the person of John the Baptist. But while Elijah was to prepare the way for Yahweh, John prepared the way for *Jesus*. The implication is as clear as it is startling: the reference to 3:23–24 implies that the 'day of Yahweh' is at least imminent, if not already present in the work of Jesus; that to 3:1 can hardly imply less than that the coming of Jesus is the coming of Yahweh for judgment.[280]

[278] See above, pp. 91–92.

[279] *Cf.* J. A. T. Robinson, *Twelve New Testament Studies*, pp. 35–37.

[280] 'The coming of Jesus is as important as that of God himself, hence the appearance of the Forerunner' (P. Bonnard, *Matthieu*, p. 163). *Cf.* J. Schniewind, *Matthäus*, p. 143. Note also the parallel implication of the use of Is. 40:3 of John the Baptist (Mk. 1:3; Mt. 3:3; Lk. 3:4–6): there too the forerunner is to prepare the way for Yahweh himself.

(ii) *Luke 19:10*, alluding to Ezekiel 34:16, 22.[281] While the later part of Ezekiel 34 introduces a Messianic shepherd figure, David, in the earlier verses Yahweh states what he himself will do for his sheep, and it is to these earlier verses that Jesus here alludes. Thus Jesus' statement of the purpose of his coming is in words which in the Old Testament contained the promise of what Yahweh would do for his people.

In these two cases, therefore, Jesus applies predictions of Yahweh's coming, both to judge and to save, to his own ministry on earth. In that ministry the 'day of Yahweh' has begun. In the remaining cases, however, its consummation is still seen as future, when Jesus will perform the final judgment which the Old Testament foretold as the work of Yahweh.

(iii) *Matthew 13:41*, alluding to Zephaniah 1:3. The MT includes המכשלות את־הרשעים,[282] 'the stumbling-blocks with the wicked',[283] as part of a list of things which Yahweh is going to 'sweep away'; it is preceded by man and beast, birds and fish, and is followed by the cutting off of all mankind. The phrase fits strangely in its context, but the fact that the next three verses go on to castigate Baalism and idolatry suggests that it is not out of place, as it refers probably to idols and their worshippers.[284] Matthew 13:41 *τὰ σκάνδαλα καὶ τοὺς ποιοῦντας τὴν ἀνομίαν* (lit. 'the stumbling-blocks and those who practise

[281] See above, p. 96 for the fact and significance of the allusion.

[282] The authenticity of the phrase is suspected. It is absent from the LXX (except W* and some MSS of the Lucianic revision, where it is fairly clearly a late correction to the MT), but the LXX text here is in a poor state. In place of this phrase the main MSS read *καὶ ἀσθενήσουσιν οἱ ἀσεβεῖς*, which probably points to the presence of הרשעים at least in the Hebrew text used. The MT is supported also by the Tg תקלת רשיעיא, and the present allusion lends it further weight. The apparent lack of logical connection with the preceding phrases (see, however, our treatment in the text) is hardly sufficient ground for an alteration of the text in an apocalyptic section of the prophets.

[283] The only other OT occurrence of מכשלה is in Is. 3:6, where it means a 'heap of ruins' (RSV). The meaning 'stumbling-block', however, is indicated by the cognate מכשול, and by the root meaning of כשל.

[284] So BDB, p. 506. *Cf.* the use of מכשול־עון for idols in Ezk. 7:19; 14:3, 4, 7; 18:30; 44:12.

lawlessness') is a close verbal parallel to this phrase,[285] and is a very likely allusion to it. Jesus thus transfers to himself in his final judgment what the Old Testament predicts as the eschatological work of Yahweh. According to Zephaniah, Yahweh will sweep away 'the stumbling-blocks with the wicked'; Jesus says that he will send out his angels to gather 'the stumbling-blocks and those who practise lawlessness' to burn them. The similarity between this passage and Matthew 25:31 ff. is marked, especially at this point in the idea of an eschatological division of men into the good and the bad, and of the fire as the lot of the latter. As we shall go on to show, that passage shows still more clearly an assumption by Jesus of what the Old Testament describes as the work of Yahweh.

(iv) *Matthew 19:28; 25:31ff.*, alluding to Daniel 7. Not only does Jesus cast himself in the Messianic role of the Son of man, but he also adds to that role the royal status of the Ancient of Days (*i.e.* Yahweh): whereas in Daniel 7 it was the Ancient of Days alone who sat on the throne (verse 9), in these two allusions the Son of man sits 'on his glorious throne'. He is even unambiguously referred to as the king (25:34). Moreover, Daniel 7 takes the form of a court scene, with the Ancient of Days as judge;[286] in Jesus' use of the chapter in these two places the scene is again one of judgment, but the judge is now the Son of man (and in 19:28 derivatively his disciples). Thus the essential function and status of Yahweh in the vision becomes for Jesus his own central role at the final consummation.

(v) *Matthew 25:31.* We have noted[287] that while the idea of an angelic retinue may be derived from Daniel 7:10, the wording, both here and possibly in Mark 8:38, seems to echo Zechariah 14:5. *καὶ πάντες οἱ ἄγγελοι μετ' αὐτοῦ* ('and all the

[285] R. H. Gundry (*op. cit.*, p. 138) describes *τοὺς ποιοῦντας τὴν ἀνομίαν* as 'a targumic expansion for הרשעים'. T. W. Manson (*BJRL* 34 (1951/2), p. 322) describes it as 'an independent rendering of the Hebrew'.

[286] See esp. verses 10, 22, 26. C. F. D. Moule (*Phenomenon*, p. 90) suggests that the saints later become the judges. This depends on translating in verse 22 'Judgment was given *to* the saints' (so RV), rather than 'for the saints', *i.e.* in their favour (so RV mg, RSV, NEB, JB). Most commentators prefer the latter version; see, *e.g.*, J. A. Montgomery, *The Book of Daniel* (Edinburgh, 1927), pp. 309–310.

[287] See above, p. 139 n. 233 and p. 144 n. 246.

angels with him') here is close to the phrase כל־קדשים עמך (LXX *καὶ πάντες οἱ ἅγιοι μετ' αὐτοῦ*). Mark 8:38 *μετὰ τῶν ἀγγέλων τῶν ἁγίων* ('with the holy angels') is not so close, and the parallels in Matthew and Luke are still less close. Matthew 25:31 is, therefore, the only really clear allusion to Zechariah 14:5. The MT second person, עמך ('with *you*'), may well be corrupt;[288] if so the allusion is still more obvious. But even if the second person were read, the New Testament context would necessitate its alteration to a third person, so that even if the MT were the true text, the allusion would still be a likely one. Here then Jesus pictures himself as Yahweh is pictured in the Old Testament, coming with an angelic retinue.[289] Zechariah 14:5 is a scene of the day of Yahweh, his eschatological coming to judge and to save; Jesus transfers the picture to his own role in the final judgment. Even if the allusion to Zechariah 14:5 be doubted, it cannot be denied that this is the language of theophany; in Daniel 7:10 the angelic retinue is again that of Yahweh, and the Old Testament knows no other figure who is so honoured (*cf.* Dt. 33:2).

(vi) *Matthew 25:32.* The gathering of all nations for judgment is reminiscent of Joel 4:1–12 (EVV 3:1–12). *συναχθήσονται . . . πάντα τὰ ἔθνη* ('all the nations will be gathered') may be an echo of verse 2 וקבצתי את־כל־הגוים (LXX *καὶ συνάξω πάντα τὰ ἔθνη*), and verses 11–12 repeat the idea, with the specific statement of Yahweh's intention of judging them. Daniel 7, which also lies behind this passage, contributes the idea of the Son of man's dominion over all nations, but not, at least explicitly, his judgment, so that probably Joel 4:1–12 also lies behind Matthew 25:31ff. The picture in Joel is probably eschatologically conceived; certainly Jesus must have interpreted it so. But in any case it describes the judgment of

[288] The description of the coming of Yahweh is in the third person, leaving עמך unattached. Clearly the angels must be accompanying Yahweh, and the correction to עמו is commonly made, being attested by Tg, LXX, and the other versions. B. Otzen (*op. cit.*, p. 268) writes, 'As far as we can see, all commentators correct v 5b to עמו, "with him".' The MT is, however, clearly the harder reading, and is defended by Otzen (*ibid.*) as 'a quotation – perhaps of cultic origin'. P. Lamarche (*op. cit.*, p. 95) points out the frequency of such alternation of persons in Hebrew poetry.

[289] *Cf.* J. W. Doeve, *op. cit.*, pp. 150–151.

Yahweh, and that judgment Jesus takes as a model for his description of his own eschatological judgment.

Thus in Matthew 25:31ff. we have seen echoes of Daniel 7, Zechariah 14 and Joel 4, all of which describe the judgment of Yahweh. We might add also that the division of sheep from goats in verse 32 echoes a similar metaphor for the judgment of Yahweh in Ezekiel 34:17. The whole passage is reminiscent of such Old Testament scenes, and expressions appropriate only to a theophany mingle with specific allusions to predictions of Yahweh's judgment. Yet here, as in the similar passage Matthew 13:37–43, the central figure in the whole picture, the judge on his throne, is not Yahweh, but Jesus, the Son of man.

The passages considered in this section add up to the conclusion that, pre-eminently in his expectation of the central role in the final judgment, but also with reference to his work on earth, Jesus did not scruple to apply to himself and his work words and ideas which the Old Testament used to describe the attributes and work of Yahweh. The number of such cases is not large, and the implication seldom made obvious in Jesus' words, but the remarkable fact is that this transfer could be made without comment and without argument; its validity is assumed.

If even a few of these sayings are genuine (and we see no reason to question most of them), this aspect of Jesus' use of the Old Testament goes to confirm what other parts of his teaching suggest, that he thought of his work as the work of God, his coming as the coming of God, and himself as closely related to God in a relationship which was more than merely functional. That the Messiah would be God's agent and representative would be no very new idea. But Jesus seems to have gone further, and suggested not only that he had come to do the work of God, but that he and his Father were one.

X. CONCLUSIONS

In our study of the Old Testament predictions applied by Jesus to himself and his work we have distinguished three categories: the non-Messianic eschatological predictions, the Messianic predictions, and predictions of the activity of

Yahweh. The significance of each group individually has been examined above.[290] Though they are only a small selection from among the numerous expressions of eschatological hopes in the Old Testament, together they cover a wide range, representing most aspects of the hopes both of judgment and of salvation, including both the material and (far more prominently) the spiritual aspects of the latter. The one striking omission is that of the Davidic hope as popularly conceived in political and nationalistic terms, which is superseded by what is in the Old Testament the less prominent figure of a lowly, suffering and dying Messiah.

It remains only to comment on the implications of our study for Jesus' view of his place in the over-all pattern of the purpose of God, the *Heilsgeschichte*. Does his use of the eschatological hopes of the Old Testament throw any light on his own eschatological conception and teaching?

We may note first that the predictions used by Jesus were almost without exception in their original intention eschatological, in the fullest sense which that word can convey when applied to the Old Testament; *i.e.* they looked forward to the day of Yahweh, that decisive act of God which should bring to an end the present order of things, and, through a work of judgment and purification, bring in a new order of peace and blessedness.[291] Only in three cases is it probable that there was a primary reference to some work of deliverance in the near future, viz. Isaiah 35:5–6 (Mt. 11:5); 56:7 (Mk. 11:17); Ezekiel 34:16, 22 (Lk. 19:10).[292] Even in these cases, two of the passages are shown by their context to have a secondary eschatological reference,[293] and the context of the third, while it does not demand such a reference, does not exclude it, and was so interpreted at the time of Jesus;[294] we have seen in the introductory section how closely a historical and an eschatological reference were connected.[295] Thus Jesus drew consistently on the eschatological strata of Old Testament prediction

[290] See the summaries on pp. 97, 148–150, 159.

[291] See above, pp. 83–86.

[292] The passages cited on pp. 151–153 were not predictive at all, and were not so regarded by Jesus.

[293] See above, pp. 95–96 on Is. 35:5–6; Ezk. 34:16, 22.

[294] See above, pp. 93–94 on Is. 56:7.

[295] See above, pp. 84–86.

when sketching the Old Testament background to his own mission.

This means that the earthly life and future glory of Jesus of Nazareth is presented as the fulfilment of the Old Testament hopes of the day of Yahweh. Features from many different expressions of such hopes are drawn together into a single comprehensive fulfilment. The coming of Jesus is that decisive act of God to which the Old Testament looked forward, and in his coming all the hopes of the Old Testament are fulfilled; the last days have come.

This is the meaning of the declaration with which his ministry began: 'The time is fulfilled, and the kingdom of God is at hand' (Mk. 1:15). What was said of Isaiah 61:1–2, 'Today this scripture has been fulfilled' (Lk. 4:21), could have been said of any of the Old Testament passages considered above. In Jesus' coming they found their fulfilment.

This conclusion agrees with the implication that we saw in Jesus' typological use of the Old Testament, that in his coming the last days had arrived.[296] There the emphasis was on the rejection of the Jewish nation, and the status of Jesus and his followers as now constituting the true Israel, in whom the hopes and destiny of Old Testament Israel were now being fulfilled. What was there largely a matter of implication and suggestion, though in fact firmly rooted in the basic principles which make typology possible, is here explicit and indeed emphasized. The time is fulfilled; the last days have come.[297]

Our study does not, however, sanction a complete repudiation of 'Consistent Eschatology' and an unconditional acceptance of 'Realized Eschatology' in the teaching of Jesus,[298] if this be taken as meaning that there was no more to look forward to. As G. E. Ladd points out,[299] there is now a consensus of opinion that in Jesus' teaching about the kingdom of God one must recognize both a present and a future aspect.

[296] See above, pp. 79–80.

[297] For this note of eschatological fulfilment in the preaching of Jesus *cf.* G. E. Ladd, *op. cit.*, esp. pp. 106–110; for the NT as a whole, with reference both to typology and the appeal to prediction, *cf.* R. Bultmann, *ST* 2 (1948), pp. 21–22 and the ensuing article.

[298] For the terms, and their various exponents, see the excellent survey by G. E. Ladd, *op. cit.*, pp. 4–23.

[299] *Ibid.*, pp. 23–38; see esp. n. 154 (pp. 35–36) for an extensive bibliography.

The kingdom both has come and will come. This is what our study also suggests. While the emphasis falls strongly on the fact that in Jesus' coming the eschaton has arrived, the fulfilment is not viewed as restricted to the period of his earthly mission. He looks forward to a final judgment at some time in the future. The use of Daniel 7:13–14 is particularly instructive, for here we have distinguished at least three phases in the fulfilment, the first at the resurrection, the second some time within the living generation, and the third, the final consummation, at some unspecified time in the future. Jesus looked for a Parousia and final judgment at some time subsequent to the fall of Jerusalem;[300] he consistently refused to give a date for it. He envisaged, therefore, an indefinite period during which the salvation and blessing he had come to bring would be worked out in the world. He had come to institute a new order, the golden age to which the Old Testament prophets had looked forward; with his coming that new order had begun, but 'the Gospels constantly represent Jesus as teaching that the consummation of the Old Testament promise of God's Kingdom, which is in process of fulfilment, will occur only in the age to come'.[301]

For this view of Jesus' coming as 'fulfilment without consummation'[302] we may adopt the term 'Inaugurated Eschatology'.[303] In his coming the 'last days' to which the Old Testament looked forward arrived, but they have not yet run their course; the Christian church is still living in this eschaton. Jesus' first coming inaugurated it; his second will consummate it. The coming of Jesus was, therefore, the beginning of the end.

Jesus places himself in the centre of the history of the world's salvation. It is *in him* that the prophecies are fulfilled, and *in his coming* that the new order is inaugurated. His life and ministry is the pivotal point of the *Heilsgeschichte*. His coming

[300] See esp. Mk. 13:32ff., and below, pp. 232–233, 239.

[301] G. E. Ladd, *op. cit.*, p. 110.

[302] This is the heading of the relevant section of Ladd's book, pp. 110–117.

[303] *Cf.* above, p. 150. J. A. T. Robinson's use of the term in *Jesus and His Coming*, p. 101 (*cf. ibid.*, p. 161) is in a similar sense: 'thenceforward (i.e. from the first coming of Jesus) men are in the presence of the eschatological event and the eschatological community;' but in his treatment a second coming of Jesus is dispensed with. *Cf.* E. Haenchen's term *sich realisierende Eschatologie*, adopted by J. Jeremias, *Parables*, p. 230.

is that decisive event to which the Old Testament looked forward, the 'day of Yahweh'. The Jews hoped for the time when God himself would come to visit and save his people, and now their hopes are fulfilled, for Jesus presents himself, not only in his work, but in his very nature, as one with God. In a fuller sense than perhaps they intended, the crowd at Nain expressed the truth: 'God has visited his people!' (Lk. 7:16).

EXCURSUS 2
THE PREMISES OF MARK 12:35–37

We concluded our exegesis of the pericope about the Son of David as follows: 'The argument may thus be seen to rest upon three premises, that the speaker in Psalm 110 is David, that the person addressed by Yahweh in verse 1 is the Messiah, and that the use of the term אדני ('my lord') implies the superiority of the one so described. Without any one of these premises the argument would be invalid.'

The aim of this excursus is to discuss the validity of these three premises. They may conveniently be considered in reverse order.

I. THE IMPLICATION OF SUPERIORITY IN THE TERM אדני

This is almost universally admitted and assumed. B. Lindars, indeed, calls it a 'gratuitous assumption',[1] but the Old Testament does not endorse this view. The majority of uses of אדון are with reference to Yahweh, where the implication of superiority is obvious. Where אדני is used to address a man, the context involves the same implication in nearly every case. It is applied to the following: master, husband, prophet, prince, king, father, Moses, priest, theophanic angel, captain, and as a 'general recognition of superiority'.[2] If then David the king

[1] *Op. cit.*, p. 47.

[2] BDB, p. 11.

uses the term אדוני, it must be of someone superior to a mere king;[3] that is all that Jesus' argument requires.

II. THE MESSIANIC REFERENCE OF THE PSALM

a. The interpretation in the first century AD

P. Billerbeck[4] argues strongly that the evidence of the New Testament alone demands an accepted Messianic reference in the first century. It is clear that Jesus' argument in Mark 12:35–37 would be useless if not based on this common assumption ('*e concessis*'). Moreover, Psalm 110 is quoted more than any other Old Testament passage in the New Testament;[5] in all such quotations a Messianic reference is assumed, not argued, which implies that this was the accepted interpretation. Further indications of such an interpretation are the strong reaction of the Sanhedrin to Jesus' application of Psalm 110:1 (with Dn. 7:13) to himself in answer to the question whether he was the Messiah (Mk. 14:61–64), and the application of verse 4 to David as 'prince in the world to come' in the Tg.[6]

On the other hand, Billerbeck has shown convincingly[7] that in rabbinic literature there is no trace of such an interpretation before 250. With remarkable consistency the Rabbis from 130 (the earliest dated reference) until about 260 applied the psalm to Abraham. This interpretation is as confidently assumed as is the Messianic interpretation of the New Testament. From R. Ḥama ben Ḥanina (*c.* 260) the Messianic interpretation reappears, and quickly becomes commonplace, alongside the Abrahamic, and an occasional reference to David. Beside Billerbeck's list of authorities we may place the testimony of Justin[8] that in his day the Jews referred the psalm to Hezekiah; Tertullian[9] testifies to the same interpretation. Thus we have a consistent picture of non-Messianic inter-

[3] *Cf.* O. Cullmann, *Christology*, p. 131. [4] SB IV, p. 452.

[5] V. Taylor (*Mark*, p. 492) lists eighteen NT quotations from or allusions to this psalm, to which Billerbeck adds a further five, more or less convincing.

[6] The date at which this Tg originated is, of course, unknown, but it may well reflect an early interpretation; it can hardly be due to Christian influence, as is probably the heading in the Peshitta, which interprets the psalm as a 'prophecy concerning the Messiah and his victory over his accuser'.

[7] SB IV, pp. 453–458. [8] *Dial.* 33.1; 83.1. [9] *Adv. Marc.* v. 9.7.

pretation in the second and early third centuries, contrasted with an accepted Messianic interpretation in the first century.

Billerbeck's explanation of this phenomenon[10] revolves around the figure of R. Ishmael, whose interpretation of the psalm is the first recorded non-Messianic interpretation. His period (*c.* 100–135) was that at which the conflict between church and synagogue came to a head, and the anti-Christian imprecation was inserted into the Shemoneh Esreh. In this development Ishmael was a prominent and fanatical leader. Billerbeck therefore concludes that it was this anti-Christian zealot who introduced the non-Messianic interpretation of Psalm 110, to counter Christian claims which were based on it, and that it was only more than a century later, when the church was sufficiently separate from the Jewish community to be safely ignored, that the Messianic interpretation gradually regained its place. Whether or not Ishmael was responsible may be left in doubt, but that there was a deliberate *volte-face* away from a previously agreed Messianic interpretation, in order to escape an embarrassing Christian claim, accords well with the evidence.

We therefore conclude, despite the lack of rabbinic evidence before 250, that in the time of Jesus Psalm 110 was agreed to refer to the Messiah.

b. The original intention of the psalm

Psalm 110 is generally regarded today as a typical Royal Psalm. As such it is an address, full of hope and confidence, to the king by a loyal subject. Such psalms, as we have seen above,[11] are expressed in extravagant terms, because they express the ideal of kingship, and look beyond the present king to that future king who will perfectly embody the ideal. As such they have a proper, though secondary, Messianic reference. This is probably the dominant view of Psalm 110 today.

If this were all that could be said of Psalm 110, then Jesus' argument is based on a false premise; if the psalm was written about a historical king, and not by David about the Messiah, however justifiable a Messianic application may be, its terminology cannot be used to determine the Messiah's status.

[10] SB IV, pp. 458–460.

[11] Above, pp. 85–86.

A study of the wording of the psalm, however, suggests that it is not a typical Royal Psalm. It has even been questioned whether it is royal at all, as it contains no specifically royal terminology.[12] But even if a royal element is recognized, there are good reasons for maintaining with E. J. Kissane[13] that it 'deals not with an historical king, but with the Messiah'.

The main reason is the attribution to the person addressed of a priesthood (verse 4), and one not in the hereditary Aaronic line, but, like that of Melchizedek, independent of his ancestry, and for ever. This is inappropriate to any of the historical kings. It has been applied to the Hasmonean priest-kings; but the psalm is almost certainly pre-exilic, as we shall see below, and in any case the Hasmoneans were born priests, of the Aaronic line. However, the union of the two offices is no more appropriate to the pre-exilic monarchy; 1 Samuel 13 and 2 Chronicles 26:16–21 show that they were entirely separate, and there is no instance before the Exile of an Israelite king who was also a priest.[14] Nor is there any parallel in the Royal Psalms to this attribution of priesthood, still less an eternal priesthood.[15] If then Psalm 110:4 were applied to any historical king, it would be more than the extravagant language of a Royal Psalm; it would be either nonsense, or verging on blasphemy. It is best seen as referring to the Messiah.

When we add to this the sitting at God's right hand, which goes beyond the language of any of the Royal Psalms (and is unique in the Old Testament unless it is implied in Dn. 7:9–14, a Messianic passage), and the lack of specifically royal

[12] So R. Tournay, *RB* 67 (1960), pp. 5–41, esp. pp. 38–40. He points out that such terms as 'king', 'kingdom', 'throne', *etc.* are absent (the 'sceptre' of v. 2 is no more royal than Aaron's rod), and concludes that the psalm emanates from post-exilic priestly circles, and refers solely to the (priestly) Messiah.

[13] *Psalms*, vol. 2, p. 189; *cf.* C. A. Briggs, *Psalms*, vol. 2, pp. 373–376.

[14] *Cf.* H. H. Rowley in *Festschrift für Alfred Bertholet* (Tübingen, 1950), pp. 470–472. A. Weiser (*Psalms*, p. 695) speaks of a 'union of throne and altar' continuing through the historical Davidic dynasty, and of 'royal priesthood' as an element in the conception of kingship (*ibid.*, p. 63), but offers no evidence for either statement beyond Ps. 110. David was never called a priest, and a regular priesthood is amply attested in his reign (2 Sa. 8:17; 20:25, *etc.*); for a hereditary royal priesthood in the dynasty there is not a scrap of evidence (David's sons were priests, but not kings, 2 Sa. 8:18).

[15] *Cf.* H. H. Rowley, *loc. cit.*, p. 471, esp. n. 1.

language, there is good reason for distinguishing this from the Royal Psalms, despite certain similarities of terminology, in that the Messianic reference which in them is secondary is here primary.

It is also clear that if the speaker in verse 1, with its confession of superiority, is in fact David, then the reference could hardly be to anyone other than the Messiah. This question must now be examined, but we may note that the two questions are closely connected. To recognize David as the speaker is to demand a Messianic reference; to recognize a Messianic reference is, as we shall see, to remove the main objection to Davidic authorship. Neither position alone can act as evidence for the other, but independent evidence for the one will automatically strengthen the other.

Thus to the argument of A. Plummer[16] that the authority of Jesus' own interpretation demands that we accept a Messianic reference in Psalm 110, we may add that the evidence of the psalm itself also suggests it.

III. THE DAVIDIC AUTHORSHIP OF THE PSALM

The suggestion of G. Bickell and G. Margoliouth that the first four verses form an acrostic on the name שמען (*i.e.* Simon Maccabaeus) is now almost universally abandoned.[17] Since the work of H. Gunkel a post-exilic date has ceased to be favoured, since the psalm is now generally regarded as one of the Royal Psalms of the pre-exilic monarchy. Thus to the earlier commentators who argued for an early, perhaps Davidic, date,[18] we may now add H. H. Rowley,[19] who gives an unequivocally Davidic dating and mentions the support of such scholars as A. Bentzen and A. R. Johnson, and S. Mowinckel,[20] who describes the psalm as 'very old', 'very "old-fashioned" '. Detailed evidence for this view is provided by E. R. Hardy Jr.,[21] who mentions the frequent occurrence of

[16] *Luke*, p. 472.

[17] W. O. E. Oesterley (*The Psalms* (London, 1939), vol. 2, p. 461) describes it as 'fantastic'. It is strange to find it still advanced by V. Taylor, *Mark*, p. 491. The evidence of Qumran now rules out a Maccabaean date.

[18] A. F. Kirkpatrick, *Psalms*, pp. 663–664; C. A. Briggs, *Psalms*, vol. 2, pp. 374–375; W. E. Barnes, *The Psalms* (London, 1931), vol. 2, pp. 534–535.

[19] *Loc. cit.*, pp. 466–472.

[20] *Psalms*, vol. 1, p. 125; vol. 2, p. 153.

[21] *JBL* 64 (1945), pp. 385–390.

the name Yahweh, the formula נאם יהוה, the poor state of the text, the character of the king in contrast with Psalm 72, and the use of the figure of Melchizedek 'to impress and at the same time conciliate the Jebusite population', and H. G. Jefferson,[22] who suggests, on the grounds that 71% of its words are paralleled in Ugaritic (the highest proportion in the psalms), that it is an early adaptation from a Canaanite poem, perhaps connected with David's conquest of Jerusalem.[23]

Given an early date (and in the opinion of many scholars a Davidic date is more likely than any other in the period of the monarchy), the only considerable objection to actual Davidic authorship is the belief that this is a Royal Psalm, and is therefore *about* David, not *by* him. We have, however, given a number of reasons above for believing that this psalm is not like the Royal Psalms, and that its primary reference is not to David or any other Old Testament king, but to the Messiah. If these arguments are valid, the one objection to Davidic authorship of the psalm is removed, and we are able to give full weight to its ascription to David.[24] The prophecy of Nathan to David (2 Sa. 7:5–16), with its promise of a descendant who shall be called God's son, and of an everlasting kingdom, and David's own reflections on that prophecy (2 Sa. 23:2–5), may encourage us to see in Psalm 110 David's own description of the glory and triumph of the Messiah.

If it cannot be claimed that the Davidic authorship, and with it the Messianic reference, of Psalm 110 has been proved, it may at least be affirmed that the question is more open than many scholars would admit.

Of the premises on which Jesus' argument is based, we have seen that the first is unassailable; of the second and third we may now conclude not only that they were unanimously

[22] *JBL* 73 (1954), pp. 152–156.

[23] For a survey of other work to this effect see A. Caquot, *Semitica* 6 (1956), pp. 49–52).

[24] R. D. Wilson (*Princeton Theological Review* 24 (1926), pp. 393–394) came to this conclusion on the basis of an exhaustive study of the headings of the psalms. F. Godet (*A Commentary on the Gospel of St. Luke* (ET[5] Edinburgh, n.d.), vol. 2, pp. 250–251) argued for Davidic authorship on stylistic grounds. The same conclusion is accepted by E. J. Kissane, *Psalms*, vol. 2, p. 190, and is most recently argued by R. H. Gundry, *op. cit.*, pp. 228–229.

accepted by the Jews of Jesus' day, but that there is a strong possibility that they accord with the facts.

EXCURSUS 3
THE SON OF MAN IN DANIEL 7

We have taken the 'Son of man' in Daniel 7:13 as a Messianic figure,[1] and have argued that Jesus saw it in this light, and applied it to himself accordingly. Our aim in this excursus is to justify that interpretation by a brief study of the figure in its Old Testament context.

Daniel 7 describes a vision and its interpretation. The vision is of four beasts appearing in succession, and exercising an increasingly oppressive power, until at last 'one that was ancient of days' sits in judgment over them. Then 'one like a son of man' comes with the clouds of heaven to the 'ancient of days', and is given an everlasting and indestructible dominion over all peoples. In the interpretation the four beasts are found to represent four successive empires, while the human figure represents 'the saints of the Most High' who, previously oppressed by the fourth kingdom, are now, in this act of judgment by God, vindicated and exalted to their due place of dominion over all other powers. The keynote is thus one of vindication and exaltation, of the inauguration of the kingdom of the 'Son of man', which supersedes the human kingdom which had previously opposed God and oppressed his saints. The 'coming' of the Son of man in verse 13 is a coming to God to receive authority, not a coming to earth.[2]

Is this figure to be seen as an individual ruler, or merely as a personification of the 'saints of the Most High'?[3] Since T. W.

[1] An *individual* interpretation of the figure must surely, in the context, be a *Messianic* one in terms of our definition (above, p. 87).

[2] *Cf.* T. W. Manson, *Studies in the Gospels and Epistles*, p. 126.

[3] We assume here that this phrase denotes either Israel or a spiritual remnant within Israel. This almost universal assumption is challenged by J. Coppens and L. Dequeker, *Le Fils de l'Homme et les Saints du Très-Haut en Daniel, VII* (Louvain, 1961). They see it as a description of the heavenly

Manson's *The Teaching of Jesus* (1931) the emphasis has fallen largely on the corporate aspect of the figure, sometimes to the total denial of the individual. J. Y. Campbell,[4] while recognizing that the four beasts stand for the individual kings of 'four autocratic heathen empires', writes anachronistically, 'But the Jewish "kingdom" was to be a democracy.' Such an extreme position is perhaps uncommon. More typically, C. H. Dodd[5] regards the Son of man, like the Servant of Yahweh, as 'a pure personification of Israel (or of the faithful remnant of Israel)', but regards the Christian 'individuation of this corporate conception', resulting in the idea of the Messiah as the '"inclusive representative" of the people of God', as a legitimate development. But was the Son of man so purely corporate, even in its original intention?

The key to the understanding of this figure, as of the Servant of Yahweh, must surely lie in the Hebrew ability to combine the ideas of a community and the individual who is its representative into a single concept, where the individual and corporate aspects are both really present. It has been pertinently observed that whereas the 'man' is here a figure for the nation, the beasts are figures for kings, the representatives of their empires, which may indicate that the 'man' was also so conceived.[6] This is confirmed by the fact that the fourth beast is interpreted in verse 17 as a king, and in verse 23 as a kingdom. This indicates that to the Hebrew mind the distinction between a community and its individual head is an unreal one. 'Democracy' as we know it had no meaning for them. The figures of Daniel 7 do indeed stand for communities, but they also envisage the individual heads who represent those communities. The Son of man stands for the community of the saints, but also for its representative head.[7] While the author may not have thought out clearly the relationship between

---

host of the angelic attendants of Yahweh, pictured in v. 10. The basis of this position is an unsatisfactory dissection of Dn. 7 into two independent sources.

[4] *JTS* 48 (1947), p. 149.

[5] *Scriptures*, pp. 117–119.

[6] *Cf.* O. Cullmann, *Christology*, p. 140, following H. Gressman, *Der Messias* (Göttingen, 1929), pp. 345ff.; also R. H. Fuller, *Foundations*, p. 36.

[7] *Cf.* A. Jeffery, in *The Interpreter's Bible*, vol. 6, pp. 460–461. See T. W. Manson, *loc. cit.*, p. 142 for a considerable modification of his earlier views in the same direction.

individual and community (this is, after all, a 'vision by night'!), it is not doing violence to his thought to see in an individual, the head of a community, the fulfilment of the vision.[8]

It must be noted, of course, that the essential feature of the vision is neither the saints nor their leader, but the kingdom. It is a parable of vindication, exaltation and dominion given by God to his people. But an essential ingredient in the picture of the kingdom is the figure of the king.

Our conclusions on the meaning of Daniel 7 are amply confirmed by the later Jewish use of the chapter. Indeed the individual interpretation of verses 13–14 so predominates that the corporate language of the later part of the chapter finds no place in Jewish thought, except possibly at Qumran. In the Pseudepigrapha and the Rabbis verses 13–14 are consistently interpreted as a description of the Messiah,[9] even though, outside a restricted apocalyptic circle, the term 'Son of man' was not current as a title for this figure.

We find, therefore, that, as in the case of the Servant of Yahweh, Jesus' application of the figure to himself in Messianic terms was not only consistent with current exegesis, but a valid use of the Old Testament passage. Again we may call to mind his view of himself as summing up in himself the status and destiny of Israel, as its representative head, and even as its individual embodiment. Here, however, as in the case of the Servant, the individuation of Israel was already present in the Old Testament passage used, which looked, at least in part, for an eschatological figure who, himself the representative of Israel, should receive the dominion which was their due as the people of God.

[8] R. H. Gundry (*op. cit.*, p. 233) actually sees in Dn. 7 a description of 'an eschatological Messianic figure'. On pp. 231–232 he presents a detailed argument for this view. *Cf.* more fully E. J. Young, *Daniel's Vision of the Son of Man* (London, 1958). R. H. Fuller (*Foundations*, p. 36) postulates an original 'individual eschatological figure' to which the author of Daniel has added the corporate interpretation.

[9] See below, pp. 174–175, 179–183, 185–188. *Cf.* SB I, p. 956, and the detailed argument of J. Bowman, *ExpT* 59 (1947/8), pp. 283–288.

CHAPTER FIVE

THE ORIGINALITY AND INFLUENCE OF JESUS' USE OF THE OLD TESTAMENT

I. INTRODUCTION

Our study of Jesus' application of the Old Testament to his own mission has revealed certain clearly characteristic lines of approach, as well as numerous points of detail. Our aim in this section is to try to assess how these characteristics fit into the environment of the first century AD. How far was Jesus in agreement with, and how far independent of, his Jewish contemporaries, in the use of the Old Testament? And was his a decisive influence on the use of the Old Testament in the Christian church? We aim, then, to assess both the originality and the influence of Jesus' use of the Old Testament.

We shall, therefore, first attempt to discover how the relevant parts of the Old Testament were used in the Jewish environment in which Jesus lived and taught. Contemporary information is scarce. We have material from the isolated sect of Qumran, and the Pseudepigrapha provide evidence of more widespread, though not necessarily orthodox, currents of thought; but for the more orthodox Jewish use of the Old Testament we have to rely on rabbinic sources which are almost without exception subsequent to the time of Jesus, though they may well embody earlier traditions. These three groups will be considered in turn, and Jesus' relation to them then assessed.

Secondly we shall attempt to estimate the influence of Jesus' own use of the Old Testament on that of the Christian church, as seen both in the rest of the New Testament, including the contributions of the Evangelists themselves which are not recorded as *verba Christi*, and in the patristic writings of roughly the first two and a half centuries of the Christian era.

This programme is clearly too ambitious to be carried through over the whole range of Old Testament passages we have studied. We are accordingly restricting our study to two passages of the Old Testament which were of particular importance in Jesus' own thought, viz. Daniel 7 and Zechariah 9–14. It will be recalled that these two passages together accounted for a large part of Jesus' applications of Messianic predictions to himself, as well as providing a number of contributions to our other sections. While not covering every nuance of agreement and disagreement in the use of the Old Testament, it is hoped that a study of the use of these two passages will disclose the essential relationships in this field between Jesus and both his fellow-Jews and his followers.[1]

II. JESUS AND CONTEMPORARY JUDAISM

a. Qumran

The Qumran sect was not a major influence in first century AD Palestine. It kept itself to itself. We have no evidence of any direct connection of Jesus with the sect, though an indirect connection through John the Baptist has been postulated.[2] Attempts to identify Jesus with the 'Teacher of Righteousness' have now been abandoned, and assessments of Jesus and the early church as dependent to any considerable degree on the teaching and practice of the sect are now out of fashion.[3] Indeed, this sect inevitably receives attention out of all proportion to its contemporary significance, because of the accident of the preservation of many of its writings. But as it is our one first-hand source of knowledge of a non-orthodox Jewish community of the period, we may use it as evidence of the

[1] It is suggested that readers who do not wish to examine the full documentation from the original sources, but only to follow the main lines of the argument, should pass over the detailed discussion on pp. 173–193, 202–214. The summaries given after each of these sections should be enough to make our conclusions intelligible.

[2] See esp. W. H. Brownlee in *The Scrolls and the New Testament*, ed. K. Stendahl (London, 1958), pp. 33–53.

[3] In favour of such dependence see A. Dupont-Sommer, *The Essene Writings from Qumran*[2] (ET Oxford, 1961), esp. pp. 368–378, 395–397; *cf.*, less judiciously, J. M. Allegro, *The Dead Sea Scrolls* (Harmondsworth, 1956), pp. 155–162. See *contra* the essays of O. Cullmann and K. Schubert in *The Scrolls and the New Testament*, pp. 18–32, 118–128; F. F. Bruce, *NTS* 2 (1955/6), pp. 176–190. Two good discussions of the importance of Qumran for the NT are P. Benoit, *NTS* 7 (1960/1), pp. 276–296; H. H. Rowley, *BJRL* 44 (1961/2), pp. 119–156.

use of the Old Testament in at least one stream of Jewish thought outside the dominant Pharisaism.

(i) *Daniel 7*. The Qumran texts so far published contain no explicit quotation from this chapter. With the exception of the Damascus Document, however, they are not much given to explicit quotations, except in the course of a systematic commentary on a passage. It is in their use of Old Testament language that their interpretation of Old Testament passages appears, even where there is no formal quotation.[4]

The 'human figure' of Daniel 7:13 is later identified as 'the saints of the Most High' (קדישי עליונין), verses 18, 22, 25; 'the people of the saints of the Most High' (עם קדישי עליונין), verse 27. These phrases may have been the root of one of the sect's descriptions of itself. The term קדושים ('holy ones'), though often denoting the angels, is frequently used in this way,[5] and clearer echoes occur, such as קדושי עליון (CD B 20:8), עם קודש (1QM 12:1), and עם קדושים (1QM 10:10; 12:8).[6]

Further, in Daniel 7:22 judgment is given לקדישי עליונין ('to/for the saints of the Most High'). It is probable, as we have mentioned above,[7] that the ל denotes 'for', not 'to'; it means not that they are themselves constituted judges, but that judgment is pronounced in their favour. The former meaning could, however, have been read from the words of Daniel 7:22, and in any case seems to be implicit in the dominion received by the saints, on any reading of the chapter. Perhaps it was this concept which led the sect to see itself as destined to judge the nations (1QpHab 5:3–6).[8]

It seems likely, then, that in the 'saints of the Most High' the community saw itself depicted.[9] F. F. Bruce[10] infers from

[4] *Cf.* C. Rabin, *JTS* 6 (1955), p. 174.

[5] The following seem to be clear cases: 1QM 3:5; 6:6; 16:1; 1QSb 3:26; 4:23; 4QFlor 1:4. It is very often impossible to decide whether the reference is to the community or the angels: see below, p. 178 for some clear uses with reference to the latter.

[6] Reading עַם, not עִם, in the last case, with Y. Yadin and J. Carmignac (commentaries *ad loc.*) and A. S. van der Woude, *Die messianischen Vorstellungen der Gemeinde von Qumrân* (Assen, 1957), pp. 136–137, against J. van der Ploeg, A. Dupont-Sommer and G. Vermes in their respective editions.

[7] See above, p. 157, n. 286.

[8] See F. F. Bruce, *Biblical Exegesis in the Qumran Texts* (London, 1960), pp. 63–64; H. H. Rowley, *BJRL* 44 (1961/2), p. 152.

[9] See further, B. Gärtner, *op. cit.*, pp. 127–129.

[10] *Exegesis*, p. 64.

the use of the later part of the chapter that they must also have identified themselves collectively with the 'Son of man' of verse 13. This may be so, but the inference demands a 'scientific' method of interpretation which, while it seems necessary to the modern exegete, was foreign to Qumran. It would be not at all impossible for a Qumran exegete to take Daniel 7:13–14 of any figure, past, present or future, to whom the form of words could be adapted, and to go on to apply the interpretation of the vision to the community itself. So while we may say that the only interpretation of Daniel 7 discernible at Qumran is in a corporate sense, applied to the community, we have no example of the use of verses 13–14, nor any means of telling whether they were interpreted in this or some other way.

We may note finally a probable allusion to Daniel 7 found in a liturgical fragment (4QSl 40),[11] where the stream of fire of Daniel 7:10 recurs in a description of the angels surrounding the throne of God. This is, therefore, a straightforward application of the theophanic imagery.

(ii) *Zechariah 9.* There is one possible echo of Zechariah 9:9 in 1QM 12:13, repeated in a slightly abbreviated form in 19:5. The words are, in Yadin's translation, 'Zion, rejoice exceedingly, and shine forth in songs of joy, O Jerusalem, and be joyful, all ye cities of Judah.' Such exhortations are not infrequent in the Old Testament,[12] the closest parallels being Zephaniah 3:14, which has the threefold form, and Zechariah 9:9, which alone has 'exceedingly' (מאד, *cf.* 1QM מאדה). Some commentators therefore regard Zechariah 9:9 as the source of the expression.[13] But the verse is best seen as an echo of a general Old Testament idiom, and specific reference to Zechariah 9:9, appropriate though this would be in a battle-hymn looking forward to eschatological victory, is not likely.

We may note, however, that the sect did see in Genesis 49:10 a prediction of the Messiah. In a fragment known as 4Q Patriarchal Blessings[14] the mysterious שילה is glossed as 'the Messiah of Righteousness, the Shoot of David'. J. M.

[11] Cited by A. Dupont-Sommer, *op. cit.*, pp. 333–334.

[12] *E.g.* Is. 12:6; 52:9; Zp. 3:14; Zc. 2:14 (EVV v. 10); 9:9. Also, though not in the imperative, Ps. 48:12 (EVV v. 11); 97:8.

[13] So J. Carmignac, Y. Yadin, *ad locc.*; *cf.* J. de Waard, *op. cit.*, p. 72.

[14] Published by J. M. Allegro, *JBL* 75 (1956), pp. 174–175.

Allegro[15] points out the close relationship between Genesis 49:10–11 and Zechariah 9:9,[16] and suggests a parallel between the עד בוא משיח הצדק of 4Q Patr. Bl. and Zechariah 9:9 מלכך יבוא לך צדיק. It is certainly probable that a group which interpreted Genesis 49:10–11 of the Messiah would regard the similar prophecy of Zechariah 9:9 in the same light, but the fact is that we have no clear allusion to Zechariah 9:9 in this or any other sense.[17] It is possible that it was used as a Messianic prediction at Qumran, but we cannot yet be sure.[18]

(iii) *Zechariah 13:7*. The one formula quotation at Qumran of any of the passages with which we are concerned is that of Zechariah 13:7 in MS B of the Damascus Document (CD B 19:7–9). The relationship of the two MSS here is not clear,[19] but the general opinion is that both are versions of a single archetype.[20] If this is so, there is a considerable section omitted from MS B immediately before the quotation of Zechariah 13:7.[21] This means that we do not know what immediately preceded the quotation, and this makes the interpretation placed on Zechariah 13:7 very uncertain, but the following tentative conclusions may be drawn.

The flock will be the community, as the sequel shows, and the shepherd therefore presumably a leading member of the community. The only such character known to us is the Teacher of Righteousness, and the identification is made, *e.g.*, by C. Rabin[22] and A. S. van der Woude.[23]

[15] *Ibid. Cf.* his *Scrolls*, pp. 152–153.

[16] See below, pp. 188–189 for rabbinic and Christian combination of the two passages.

[17] Note also that in such hints as we have there is no mention of the ass, though it is probable that 4Q Patr. Bl. went on to expound Gn. 49:11.

[18] An allusion to Zc. 9:13 in 1 QH 6:30, suggested by M. Mansoor and S. Holm-Nielsen, *ad loc.*, is too remote to add any weight to the case.

[19] The two versions are clearly set out in parallel columns in A. S. van der Woude, *op. cit.*, pp. 39–42. *Cf.* also C. Rabin, *The Zadokite Documents* (Oxford, 1954), pp. 28–33. The quotation of Zc. 13:7 introduces a short passage peculiar to B, while A has a longer catena of quotations which is absent from B. Neither MS shows evidence of a lacuna, and the wording of each can be construed satisfactorily without assuming a break.

[20] See *contra*, however, E. Wiesenberg, *VT* 5 (1955), p. 307.

[21] So, *e.g.*, C. Rabin, *Documents*, pp. viii, 30–31, and esp., with full argument, A. S. van der Woude, *op. cit.*, pp. 38–39, 61–64.

[22] *Documents*, p. 31.

[23] *Op. cit.*, pp. 64–65, with detailed argument. *Cf.* A. Michel, *Le Maître*

Against this interpretation, F. F. Bruce[24] sees the quotation as a threat to a wicked ruler.[25] This interpretation depends on a continuous reading of MS B, without postulating an omission in line 7. Given this reading, it is indeed hard to avoid such an interpretation, but the very fact that, as Bruce recognizes, it involves the improbable description of a wicked ruler by God as 'the man who is my kinsman' may be seen as an additional argument against the integrity of the B text as it stands.

It is probable, then, that Zechariah 13:7 was applied to the persecution of the Teacher of Righteousness and his community. The persecutions in which he (probably) died and to which they were continually subjected, were a testing which would result in their purification and escape in the coming time of judgment 'when the Messiah of Aaron and Israel shall come'. The application of Zechariah 13:7 is, therefore, not Messianic (the Teacher of Righteousness is not the Messiah at Qumran); it looks to a figure of the past and the experiences of the community in the present.

We may mention here also the use of the phrase 'the poor of the flock' (עניי הצאן) in the same context (CD B 19:9). The wording makes it a clear reference to Zechariah 11:11, and the use of עני and ענו by the community to describe itself[26] makes the application clear. It is to the sect, in the time of persecution before the coming of the Messiah of Aaron and Israel. It seems, then, that the sect took Zechariah 11:4–14 and 13:7–9 together as passages relating to its experiences in the days of persecution between the suffering of the Teacher of Righteousness and the coming of the Messiah.

(iv) *Further Uses of Zechariah 9–14.* The War Scroll contains a few other allusions to these chapters, which, while they have no close parallels in the teaching of Jesus, serve to illustrate the sect's approach to this portion of the Old Testament.

de Justice (Avignon, 1954), p. 270; and, with reservation, A. Dupont-Sommer, *op. cit.*, p. 137 n. 4.

[24] *BJRL* 43 (1960/1), p. 343. *Cf.* J. A. Fitzmyer, *NTS* 7 (1960/1), p. 326. In *This is That* (1968) Bruce has apparently abandoned this identification.

[25] Or ruler*s*; so B. Lindars, *op. cit.*, p. 280, presumably adopting Rabin's tentative reading 'shepherds' for 'little ones', which has the support of LXX A in Zc. 13:7, but no support at all in CD.

[26] 1QH 2:34; 5:13, 14, 21; 18:14. *Cf.* the similar use of אביונים.

In 1QM 1:5–6 and 4:7 we find the phrases מהומה גדולה, מהומת אל ('a great panic', 'a panic of God').[27] These may well be derived from Zechariah 14:13 מהומת־יהוה רבה ('a great panic of Yahweh').[28] This panic is to be sent by God on the enemies of the community in the great battle, as in Zechariah it is sent on 'all the people that wage war against Jerusalem' (14:12) in the eschatological victory.

1QM 11:10 provides an allusion to Zechariah 12:6, in the simile of a flaming torch among sheaves;[29] as in Zechariah Yahweh will make the clans of Judah like a flaming torch devouring its way among the sheaves, *i.e.* destroying their enemies in the great battle against all the nations, so at Qumran he will cause the 'downcast of spirit'[30] to destroy the Kittim.

In 1QM the term קדושים ('holy ones') is applied several times to the angelic retinue of God (see esp. 12:1, 4, 7). The most probable Old Testament sources for this usage (which is not common in the Old Testament) are Deuteronomy 33:2; Psalm 89:6, 8 (EVV verses 5, 7); Zechariah 14:5. The context in 1QM 12 especially favours a reference to Zechariah 14:5, where the description is of Yahweh's triumphant visitation with his angels in the eschatological conflict. However, as with the possible derivation of such phrases as עם קדושים from Daniel 7, this is more likely a case of the unconscious influence of the Old Testament language than of intentional allusion.[31]

1QM includes therefore at least possible references to Zechariah 9:9; 12:6; 14:5; 14:13. The inference is suggested that these chapters were well known to the author, who, even if not deliberately alluding to them, applied their predominantly eschatological tone and terminology to the subject in hand, viz. the great battle in which the Kittim (*i.e.* probably the

[27] *Cf.* also 1QH 3:25 מהומות רבה, which S. Holm-Nielsen (*ad loc.*) sees as also derived from Zc. 14:13, and used of 'eschatological terrors'.

[28] So J. Carmignac *ad locc.*, Y. Yadin on 4:7. While there are other possible OT sources for the phrase (*e.g.* Dt. 7:23; 1 Sa. 5:9,11; 14:20), Zc. 14:13 has the use of ־יהוה in an almost adjectival sense, probably echoed in the מהומת אל of 1QM 4:7.

[29] So J. Carmignac, J. van der Ploeg, Y. Yadin *ad loc.*

[30] *I.e.* the sect; *cf.* אביונים in line 13.

[31] The same may be said of 1QSb 4:24–28; so R. B. Laurin, *Journal of Semitic Studies* 3 (1958), pp. 352–353. The suggestion of a verbal reference is here still less obvious.

Romans, seen as symbolizing all worldly opposition to true religion) were to be decisively defeated, and the theocracy established, in a setting which seems to combine heaven and earth in very much the same way as Zechariah 14. The ideas of the two books are similar in many ways, and the application is an entirely natural one, if it be granted that the Qumran community was, as it believed, exclusively the chosen people of God.

b. The Pseudepigrapha

This convenient term is used to cover a varied collection of works coming from roughly the period 150 BC – AD 100, ranging from extravagant apocalypticism to ethical platitude. The diversity within the corpus is considerable, and there is no guarantee that a view expressed in any one of these books commanded any wide following. Numerous later redactions make the date of a given section hard to determine, and there are not a few Christian interpolations. In the following study we shall attempt to eliminate all Christian elements, and try where possible to build up a picture of a consensus of opinion on the interpretation of a given Old Testament passage among the various Jewish 'schools' and individuals represented. Unfortunately, the material hardly renders this possible except in the case of Daniel 7.

(i) *Daniel 7 in the Pseudepigrapha excluding the Book of Enoch.* The use of Daniel 7 in the Enochic literature is sufficiently copious and also sufficiently individual to warrant a separate treatment. In the remaining books it is not so much in evidence.

Two apocalyptic works dated around the end of the first century AD, but, at least in the relevant parts, lacking any sign of Christian influence, make use of the general plan of the vision in Daniel 7. Both the Ezra Apocalypse (*i.e.* 2 Esdras 3–14) and the Apocalypse of Baruch (*i.e.* 2 Baruch, or Syriac Baruch) have visions in which hostile empires are destroyed, and the Messiah is revealed as the final and eternal ruler. 2 Esdras 11–12 concentrates on the final hostile empire, portrayed as an eagle (clearly Rome), and identified as 'the fourth kingdom which appeared in vision to thy brother Daniel' (12:11), but the other three beasts of Daniel 7 are also mentioned (11:39–40). 2 Baruch 36–40 does not use the imagery of beasts, but speaks explicitly of the four empires, of which the first is clearly Babylon, and the last Rome (39:3–5). Both works stress how much worse the fourth empire is than its predecessors. Clearly then, at least within the circles in which these works circulated, Daniel 7 was known (it could be assumed, and used as an agreed basis) and used as a prophecy of the Messiah's conquest, the fourth empire being seen as Rome, and the end therefore imminent.

Numerous parallels of terminology and imagery between Daniel 7 and the Pseudepigrapha could be listed, but they are not sufficiently close to be classed as allusions. Rather they are apocalyptic stock-in-trade, in some cases perhaps originated by Daniel 7, but not used with specific reference to it. Thus a great sea (Dn. 7:2) reappears in 2 Baruch 53:1;[32] the horn 'speaking great things' (Dn. 7:8, 11, 20) may be echoed in Ass. Mos. 7:9, and the three horns plucked up by the roots (Dn. 7:8) in Sib. Or. 5:222; the whole idea of imagery based on animals recurs in 2 Esdras 11 and 1 Enoch 85–90; the vision of God on the throne (Dn. 7:9) *may* lie behind 2 Esdras 7:33, and the books of judgment (Dn. 7:10) are found in 2 Esdras 6:20 and 2 Baruch 24:1.

The only other part of the chapter specifically referred to is verses 13–14. Daniel 7:13 is clearly the source of the vision of 2 Esdras 13, of the 'form of a man'[33] who emerged from the sea and flew with the clouds of heaven.[34] The figure of Daniel 7:13 is here interpreted as an individual Messiah ('the Man'). (The 'other multitude' of verse 12, the subjects of the Messiah, may be derived from the 'saints of the Most High' in Daniel 7; they are distinct from the Messiah.) This interpretation of the figure as an individual Messiah appears also in the visions of 2 Esdras 11–12 and 2 Baruch 36–40, constructed on the model of Daniel 7, both of which contain a figure corresponding to

[32] *Cf.* also the clouds of 53:1–2, *etc.*?

[33] So the Syriac version; the clause is omitted from the Latin by *homoioteleuton*. (See G. H. Box in *The Apocrypha and Pseudepigrapha of the Old Testament*, ed. R. H. Charles (Oxford, 1913), vol. 2, p. 616; W. O. E. Oesterley, *II Esdras* (London, 1933), p. 149.)

[34] The vision is interpreted in vv. 25–26. Further allusions to Dn. 7 may be seen in v. 2 (the wind on the sea; Dn. 7:2), and in the fact that the nations fight against the Man (Dn. 7:21, 25).

the 'Son of man' (a lion and a vine), who is explicitly interpreted as the Messiah (2 Esdr. 12:31–34; 2 Bar. 39:7 – 40:3). A further probable allusion to Daniel 7:13–14 is in Sib. Or. 5:414–416,[35] again in the same sense of an individual Messiah. Finally, an earlier allusion to verse 14 possibly occurs in Ps. Sol. 17:31–32 (29–30), where the Messiah judges nations, the nations serve under his yoke, and his glory is world-wide.[36] This exhausts the pseudepigraphic allusions to Daniel 7 excluding the Enochic literature.

We note, then, that there is no use made of the corporate aspects of Daniel 7, and no allusion to the later part of the chapter.[37] Verse 13 is invariably taken to portray an individual Messiah, whose coming will bring to an end the oppressive power of the fourth empire, viz. Rome.

(ii) *Daniel 7 in the Book of Enoch.* The 'Book of Enoch' consists of several different pieces of Enochic literature of different dates and origins. Of particular interest to us is the 'Similitudes of Enoch' (1 Enoch 37–71), an independent work generally agreed to be Jewish, and probably pre-Christian.[38]

The use of Daniel 7 outside the Similitudes is slight. The only considerable passage clearly based on Daniel 7 is 14:18–22, where various details of the vision of God and his angels are

[35] Even if *νώτων* be translated not as 'billowy clouds' (Bate) but, more accurately, as 'vaults' (*cf.* Charles 'plains'), the allusion remains a likely one, esp. in view of the apocalyptic uses of Dn. 7:13–14 already noted.

[36] A reference to the same verse in Test. Joseph 19:12 is probably a Christian interpolation.

[37] A possible allusion to v. 22 in Wisdom 3:8 stands entirely alone in this period, except for the possible use in 1QpHab (see above, p. 174).

[38] The non-appearance of this section of the book among the fragments of Enochic literature at Qumran has led to a questioning of its pre-Christian date, and even of its Jewish origin. So esp. J. T. Milik, *Ten Years of Discovery in the Wilderness of Judaea* (ET London, 1959), pp. 33–34. Such a drastic conclusion from the silence to date of a separatist group in an isolated part of the desert, with many fragments still to be examined, is too sweeping. For a more cautious statement see M. Black, *BJRL* 45 (1962/3), p. 312, and for arguments against Milik, A. Dupont-Sommer, *op. cit.*, pp. 299–300; G. H. P. Thompson, *ExpT* 72 (1960/1), p. 125. The question is still open. That the Similitudes were of an independent origin was already recognized, but the Qumran finds do not help us to decide when and what that origin was. The consensus of opinion seems still to be that it was Jewish, and around, if not before, the time of Jesus. The Similitudes may fairly be taken, therefore, as an indication of the use made of Dn. 7 in at least a restricted part of Jesus' Jewish environment.

drawn from Daniel 7:9–10. Other possible allusions are in 5:4, to the horn 'speaking great things' (Dn. 7:8, 11, 20), in 90:9, a very likely use of the horn imagery of Daniel 7:8, and in 90:20, where the books of judgment (Dn. 7:10) again occur.

In the Similitudes, on the other hand, Daniel 7 is constantly in use. We may list the parallels as follows. The theophany of Daniel 7:9–10 is echoed in 46:1; 47:3; 71:10 (the description of God himself); 40:1; 47:3; 71:8, 13 (the angelic attendants); 71:2, 5–6 (the stream of fire); 47:3 (the books). In 46:1–2 the Messianic figure normally called 'the Elect One' is presented as 'the Son of man', and described as having 'the appearance of a man' and as being with God. 'Son of man' is thereafter adopted as one of the titles of the Elect One. Among his functions and attributes the following recall Daniel 7, in some cases verbally, in others by the idea alone; he has a universal and eternal dominion (48:5; 49:2; 62:6, 9); he acts as judge (45:3; 46:4–6; 49:4; 55:4; 61:8–9; 69:27); he sits on a glorious throne (45:3; 51:3; 55:4; 61:8; 62:2–5; 69:27, 29).

It is interesting that the Similitudes never allude to verse 13 of Daniel 7 except in the title 'Son of man' and the initial description in 46:1–2. The angelic figure to whom this title is given is far more than a mere transcript of the image of Daniel 7. He is basically a new creation, Daniel 7 being simply used to supply some of the details.[39] While we may say, therefore, that the author knew and used Daniel 7, seeing verse 13 as a description of a Messianic figure,[40] it would not be true to describe the Elect One as *derived from* Daniel 7. Moreover, the *context* of Daniel 7:13 is ignored in the Similitudes, in that no reference is made to the beast-empires, though this need not be taken as meaning that the author was unaware of them. It simply means that he used the figure and the term 'Son of man'[41] as a convenient description of his 'hero', and utilized some of his attributes, but without tying his work closely to Daniel 7 as a whole.

In the Book of Enoch, then, we find a broad picture similar

[39] *Cf.* Jesus' use of the title 'Son of man' in a way which goes far beyond the limits of Dn. 7; see above, pp. 137–138, 145–146.

[40] See SB I, pp. 485–486, 956–958.

[41] This phrase, as a technical term for the Messiah, is found only in 1 Enoch among the Pseudepigrapha. For the significance of this fact see below, pp. 187–188.

to that in the other Pseudepigrapha, despite differences of detail. The essential agreement is on the fact that verse 13 presents an individual Messianic figure, and this is reinforced by the striking agreement of all the Pseudepigrapha in ignoring completely the corporate interpretation of the later part of the chapter. The beast-empires (where they are referred to at all) are consistently interpreted as leading up to that of Rome, which the Messiah will destroy; Enoch, however, makes no reference to them. The other apocalyptic language of Daniel 7 is used sporadically in a way which is not of particular interest to us, but is in the same sense as that intended by the author of Daniel.

(iii) *Zechariah 9–14.* The use of this portion of the Old Testament in the Pseudepigrapha is meagre in the extreme. The only passage for which one can reasonably claim a recognized use is 9:9–10. Three passages are, with varying degrees of probability, seen as based on these verses. Test. Jud. 24:1[42] is perhaps, at least in the longer Greek version, based more obviously on Numbers 24:17, and perhaps also Psalm 45:5 (EVV verse 4), but the Messianic figure ('the Star') there depicted has the attributes of peace, meekness and righteousness,[43] all of which occur in Zechariah 9:9–10, and only there all together.[44] 1 Enoch 71:14–15 combines peace and righteousness as attributes of the Son of man, and the 'proclaiming peace' of verse 15 is a near echo of Zechariah 9:10. Ps. Sol. 17:35–39 (32–35) includes for the Messiah the attributes of kingship, righteousness and peace, and the repudiation (verse 37) of horse, rider and bow recalls the cutting off of chariot, horse and bow in Zechariah 9:10. While we may not see explicit allusions to Zechariah in all these passages, it seems likely that Zechariah 9:9–10 has exercised a fairly widespread influence on the Messianic ideas of these circles in the first two centuries BC. However, the motif of the ass does not occur, and the idea of meekness only in Test. Jud. 24:1.

There is no obvious use of Zechariah 10–13 at all anywhere

[42] A Jewish origin for this work cannot be regarded as certain. The debate is usefully summarized by M. Smith in *The Interpreter's Dictionary of the Bible* (New York, 1962), vol. 4, pp. 575–579.

[43] So in both the Greek and the Armenian versions.

[44] Nu. 24:17 and Ps. 45:5 are both in warlike contexts.

in this literature. The shepherd figure, the thirty pieces of silver, and the mourning over the one pierced are all absent.

Zechariah 14 fares little better. The cutting of the Mount of Olives in verse 4 may have suggested the cutting out of the mountain by the Messiah in 2 Esdras 13:6, but this is a very remote possibility. The same is true of the suggested echo of the internecine fighting of verse 13 in 1 Enoch 56:7 (*cf.* 100:2). Neither of these is capable of bearing any weight. The 'holy ones' of verse 5 *may* lie behind the use of this term for angels in 1 Enoch *passim*,[45] and the description in 1 Enoch 1:9 of God's coming with his holy ones to execute judgment could well have been suggested by verse 5, though a more obvious source would be Deuteronomy 33:2. Certainly there is never in the Pseudepigrapha any suggestion of an angelic retinue coming with *the Messiah.*[46]

c. *The Rabbis*

Surviving sayings of orthodox teachers of the first century AD are very few and far between, at least as far as explicit interpretations of the Old Testament are concerned. Even in the later Tannaites the number of quotations is not great in proportion to the volume of the literature. It is only from the third century that Old Testament quotations become common, in both talmudic and midrashic sources. However, many interpretations handed down anonymously may in fact be very old, and those attributed to Amoraic teachers may have a much longer pedigree. We must, therefore, trace the references back as far as dated quotations will allow us, and then trust to the consensus of interpreters to tell us how the passage is likely to have been interpreted in the earlier period.[47] In fact we shall find that in most cases this method will produce fairly clear results.

Our study will be restricted almost entirely to the Rabbis

[45] For references see R. H. Charles, *Apocrypha*, vol. 2, p. 189n.

[46] *Cf.* J. W. Doeve, *op. cit.*, pp. 136–137.

[47] Clearly the disruption of AD 70, involving the end of the old order centred on the Temple, must have had a profound effect on rabbinic thought, but it is not likely to have led to a large-scale recasting of the basic principles of scriptural interpretation, or of the essential understanding of individual OT passages, except those directly concerned with Jerusalem and the Temple cult.

of the first three centuries AD. In order to avoid excessive length, we shall generally simply mention the teacher concerned, and the source of the reference, except where a presentation of the argument and its context seems essential.

(i) *Daniel 7*. The four beast-empires are universally interpreted respectively as Babylon, Persia,[48] Greece,[49] and Rome.[50]

Verses 9–10 are in very common use as a source of details in describing the glory of God and his appearing for judgment.[51] Two strange uses of these verses are those by R. Meir (*c.* 150), apparently applying them to the punishment of rebellious *Israelites*,[52] and R. Joshua ben Levi (*c.* 250), who translated 'thrones were cast down', *i.e.* overturned in mourning for the exile of Israel.[53] A standard use of verses 9–10 from early times seems to have been as a description of God's coming in peace, in contrast with his coming for war.[54] None of these seem of great significance for our purpose.

The figure of verse 13 was apparently always in the early period applied to the Messiah. Before coming to the rabbinic literature proper, we may note three pieces of earlier evidence. First, Tg Ps 80 indicates that בן אדם in Psalm 80:18 (EVV verse 17) was read as a Messianic title,[55] though of course this could have been due to the influence of the Similitudes of Enoch; the influence of Daniel 7, Messianically interpreted, is, however, probable. Secondly, Tg 1 Chron 3:24 glosses the name ענני with the phrase 'He is the King Messiah'; that ענני as a name of the Messiah was derived from the description of the Son of man in Daniel 7:13 as coming עם־ענני שמיא

[48] R. Joḥanan (d. 279): Kid. 72a, *cf.* Yom. 77a; R. Ammi (*c.* 300): Kid. 72a; R. Joseph (d. 333): Kid. 72a, *cf.* Meg. 11a, A.Z. 2b.

[49] Mekiltha *Wayehi Beshallaḥ* §1 (on Ex. 14:5).

[50] Mekiltha *Yithro Baḥodesh* §9 (on Ex. 20:18); *cf. Wayehi Beshallaḥ* §1 (on Ex. 14:5); R. Joḥanan (d. 279): A.Z. 2b, *cf.* Shebu. 6b (reading רומי for פרס, as Goldschmidt, and Silverstone in the Soncino edn.). Rome is commonly referred to as 'Edom'. For the four kingdoms together see Gen R. 99:2.

[51] Among many examples, see Aboth 2:1 (*c.* 200); Ḥag. 13b–14a (*c.* 200); Lev R. 31:6 (*c.* 200); Est R. 1:6 (*c.* 260); Sifre Dt §49 (on 11:22).

[52] Ex R. 30:18.

[53] Lam R. 1:1 §1.

[54] Mekiltha *Hashira Beshallaḥ* §4 (on Ex. 15:3), *Yithro Baḥodesh* §5 (on 20:2); *cf.* Sifre Num §42 (on 6:26); R. Simeon (*c.* 280): Num R. 11:7.

[55] The Tg balances בר נש in v. 18b with the phrase מלכא משיחא in the parallel v. 16b.

('with the clouds of heaven') is stated in so many words in Tanḥuma.[56] Though no targumic interpretation can be dated with certainty, we have here evidence of a very early, perhaps pre-Christian, Messianic interpretation of Daniel 7:13 in Palestinian Judaism. Thirdly, for the early Christian period we may cite Justin,[57] who attributes a Messianic interpretation to Trypho; while we may credit Justin with embellishments, a complete falsification of his opponent's position would hardly further an apologist's purposes.

The rabbinic sources proper begin from this period. A Messianic interpretation of the chapter is implied by R. Akiba (d. 135) in his interpretation of the 'thrones' of verse 9 as one for God and one for David;[58] it is likewise implied in R. Nathan's (*c.* 160) conscious opposition to 'our Masters', who used Daniel 7:25 to date the coming of the Messiah, which means that up to the first half of the second century verse 27 at least must have been generally applied to the Messiah's reign with the saints;[59] it becomes explicit in R. Joshua ben Levi (*c.* 250)[60] and R. Samuel ben Naḥman (*c.* 260),[61] both of whom assume the interpretation as common and accepted; and it probably lies behind the title בר־נפלי used by R. Naḥman (d. 320) for the Messiah.[62] R. Joḥanan's (d. 279) use of verse 13 to prove that clouds come from above earthwards[63] *may* imply that he took it of the Messiah's coming to earth, but this cannot be pressed. An undated quotation[64] which has been placed 'probably no later than c. A. D. 200'[65] proves the wide extent of the Messiah's dominion from Daniel 7:13–14, and further, presumably later, Messianic applications are listed by SB.[66]

[56] See SB I, pp. 67, 486.
[57] *Dial.* 31–32:1.
[58] Ḥag. 14a; San. 38b. In the latter case the verse is quoted as one used by the 'Minim' (*i.e.* Christians), and Akiba's explanation is rejected as too dangerous; alternative interpretations are suggested, which are not liable to a heretical understanding. Here we may perhaps see anti-Christian polemic beginning to undermine the previously agreed Messianic interpretation of the chapter.
[59] San. 97b. Justin may be referring to this use of v. 25 when he mentions (*Dial.* 32:3–4) Jewish attempts to make it demand at least 350 years' dominion for the 'little horn'. So W. A. Shotwell, *The Biblical Exegesis of Justin Martyr* (London, 1965), p. 73.
[60] San. 98a.
[61] Midr. Ps 21 §5 (on v. 7).
[62] San. 96b. *Cf.* W. D. Davies, *Paul*, p. 280 n. 1.
[63] Gen R. 13:11.
[64] Num R. 13:14.
[65] J. Bowman, *ExpT* 59 (1947/8), p. 285.
[66] SB I, pp. 483, 957; III, p. 639.

In contrast to this considerable number of individual Messianic interpretations of Daniel 7:13–14, the only collective uses of the chapter we have been able to find in Talmud and Midrashim are two anonymous, and therefore undated, midrashic quotations, one of which[67] applies verse 27 to the future sovereignty of Israel, and the other[68] takes Daniel 7:13–14, along with Isaiah 42:1; 52:13; Psalm 110:1; and Psalm 2:7, as applying to 'the children of Israel'. It is surely remarkable that even verses 18–27, which are expressed in clearly collective terms, are apparently never so applied in the early period. For the period up to AD 300, SB[69] rightly conclude: 'Dan. 7.13f. was nowhere interpreted by the old synagogue collectively of the "people of the saints" (= Israel, Dan. 7.27), but regularly individually of the Messiah.'

An important distinction must be drawn with regard to the term 'Son of man'. The use of this term as a title for the Messiah is not the same thing as a Messianic interpretation of Daniel 7:13.[70] In all the pseudepigraphic and rabbinic literature up to AD 300 the only occurrences of the title as such are in the Similitudes of Enoch,[71] possibly the Tg Ps 80, and a use by R. Abbahu (*c.* 300),[72] which is clearly an anti-Christian polemic, and therefore derives the term from Christian use (though he does not dispute its Messianic significance).[73] Yet Daniel 7:13 is consistently interpreted, in both apocalyptic and rabbinic circles, of an individual Messiah; no other interpretation is known. This distinction has not always been observed,[74] but it is important. It leads us to the conclusion that the figure in Daniel 7:13 was interpreted consistently from at least as early as the time of Jesus as an individual Messiah, but that he was not generally dubbed 'Son of man', this title being restric-

[67] Num R. 11:1.

[68] Midr. Ps 2 §9 (on v. 7).

[69] SB I, p. 956. They deal with Dn. 7 in I, pp. 67, 483, 485–486, 956–959; III, p. 639.

[70] *Cf.* J. W. Doeve, *op. cit.*, p. 138; L. Gaston, *No Stone on Another* (Leiden, 1970), pp. 374–375.

[71] See above, p. 182 n. 41.

[72] pTaan. 2:1 (65b).

[73] *Cf.* SB I, pp. 958–959.

[74] *E.g.* T. W. Manson (*Studies in the Gospels and Epistles*, pp. 127–128) treats the two together, unjustifiably restricting the evidence to Enoch, Justin, and two rabbinic passages, one of which deals, like Enoch, with the Son of man, the other, like Justin, with the Messianic use of Dn. 7:13.

ted to the Similitudes of Enoch, and perhaps a few similar circles. He was known more clumsily by such phrases as 'the one who came with the clouds of heaven', or ענני.

Two further points may be noted in view of Jesus' application of Daniel 7:13. Firstly, the 'coming' of this verse is apparently generally regarded as a coming *to earth*, where the exegesis of this point can be discerned.[75] But in one case[76] the reference is to the presentation of the Messiah before God in heaven, by the angels.

Secondly, the Rabbis seem to have been innocent of the idea sometimes canvassed today that Daniel 7:13 portrays a suffering Messiah. In all the above passages he is a victorious and majestic figure,[77] and in all the passages cited by SB[78] for the idea of a suffering and a dying Messiah there is no use of Daniel 7.

(ii) *Zechariah 9:9*. Here again there is an apparently unanimous application to the Messiah in the earliest sources. This is found in the following authorities: 'the Rabbis' (cited together with R. Judah and R. Neḥemiah, and therefore *c.* 150),[79] R. Samuel (d. 254),[80] R. Joshua ben Levi (*c.* 250),[81] R. Levi (*c.* 300),[82] R. Isaac (*c.* 300),[83] and R. Joseph (d. 333).[84] In the first, the reference is to 'the royal Messiah' in explicit contrast to 'the anointed for war' (*i.e.* the Messiah ben Joseph, the precursor of the Messiah ben David),[85] and the reference is clearly the same in all these cases.[86] Only three anonymous (and therefore probably later?) references apply the verse to the coming of *God* to bring salvation.[87]

Two points are worth noting on the rabbinic use of this

[75] This is clearly so in San. 98a; Gen R. 13:11. [76] Midr. Ps 21 §5.

[77] NB San. 98a, where he is set in contrast with the lowly Messiah of Zc. 9:9.

[78] SB II, pp. 273–299.

[79] Gen R. 75:6; 98:9. For the dating see SB I, p. 842. [80] San. 98a.

[81] *Ibid.* [82] Midr. Sam 14:9 (45b).

[83] Ecc R. 1:9 §1; Gen R. 56:2.

[84] San. 99a. [85] See below, p. 191.

[86] In a much later reference (Pesiqta Rabbathi 34 (§159b)) Zc. 9:9 is expounded of the redemptive suffering of the Messiah. W. A. Shotwell (*op. cit.*, p. 76) dates this about the ninth century, and regards it as the earliest evidence for such a belief in Judaism.

[87] Cant R. 1:4 §2; Dt R. 4:11; Ex R. 30:24.

verse. (1) In two passages[88] it is brought into connection with a Messianic use of Genesis 49:10–11. The connection is a fairly obvious one, and is paralleled in Christian circles.[89] (2) The stress is overwhelmingly on the second half of the verse, *i.e.* on 'lowly and riding on an ass', not on the triumphant words 'righteous and saved' which precede them. The actual words cited in each of the above cases[90] show that all the early and Messianic applications stress the lowliness of the Messiah's coming,[91] whereas the later applications to the coming of God stress the rejoicing and triumph.

The early rabbinic application of Zechariah 9:9, then, is to the expected coming of the Messiah ben David, the royal Messiah, and its particular use is to stress the lowliness of his coming.

(iii) *Zechariah 11:13.*[92] The main point of interest for the Rabbis in Zechariah 11 was the mention of the thirty pieces of silver in verses 12–13. There were two conflicting interpretations of these. (1) The Tg *ad loc* glosses them as the few faithful men who respected the worship of Yahweh, and a record of whose faithfulness he caused to be deposited in the Temple. This 'exegesis' is then combined with a tradition going back at least to R. Simeon ben Joḥai (*c.* 150)[93] that there must always be thirty good men in the world. Zechariah 11:13 is interpreted of these thirty champions by R. Simeon ben Jehozadak (*c.* 225),[94] Rab (d. 247),[95] and Rab Judah (d. 299).[96] (2) The other interpretation is that these are thirty commandments

[88] Gen R. 98:9; 99:8.

[89] Justin, *Apol. I* 32; Clem. Alex. *Paed.* i. 5:15. *Cf.* also above, p. 176 for a possible parallel at Qumran.

[90] The latter part of the verse alone is cited (or referred to) in Gen R. 75:6; 98:9; San. 98a (bis); Ecc. R. 1:9 §1; Gen R. 56:2; 99:8. The first half alone is cited in Cant R. 1:4 §2; Ex R. 30:24. The whole verse, with no obvious emphasis on either half, is cited in San. 99a; Dt R. 4:11.

[91] This is particularly clear in San. 98a.

[92] This chapter is not clearly referred to by Jesus, but it will be necessary to consider the rabbinic use of it in view of its use by Matthew, to be considered below.

[93] Gen R. 35:2.

[94] Ḥul. 92a; the thirty have now become 45, divided between Palestine and Babylonia, and Zc. 11:13 proves that thirty of them are in Palestine.

[95] Gen R. 98:9; pA.Z. 2:1 (40c), however, makes 'the Rabbis' take this line *against* Rab, to whom the other interpretation is attributed.

[96] Ḥul. 92a.

which the Gentiles will agree to accept from the Messiah when he comes. So R. Joḥanan (d. 279),[97] R. Ulla (*c.* 280),[98] and R. Ḥanin (*c.* 300).[99]

One point of interest is the lack of agreement among the Rabbis as to the time to which the chapter applies. Sometimes it is thought that Zechariah is recounting past history; according to R. Ulla the thirty commandments were taken upon themselves in the past by the 'sons of Noah',[100] and the three shepherds of verse 8 were interpreted as figures of the past.[101] The worthless shepherd of 11:17, however, is applied to recent history by R. Joḥanan (d. 279), viz. to Bar Kochba,[102] and the same authority, as we have seen, applies verse 13 to the Messianic age.[103] The interpretation concerning the thirty champions refers to past, present and future, since they must always exist as long as the world continues.

Thus there is no agreement among the Rabbis as to the application of chapter 11 as a whole, or of verse 13 in particular.

(iv) *Zechariah 12:10–14.* Among the various applications of these verses there is apparently a tendency to regard them as describing an eschatological work of God, drawing men closer to himself. The eschatological element is implied in R. Judah's (d. 217) use of this verse among four 'outpourings' for good, the other three being eschatological,[104] and may lie behind the use of the verse during the days of the Temple, with reference to the time when 'the Evil Inclination will have no power over them', as reported by Rab (d. 247).[105] The idea of drawing men close to God appears in the interpretations of 'the spirit of grace' in verse 10; R. Eliezer ben Jacob (*c.* 150) expounded this as the Holy Spirit,[106] and 'the Rabbis' (contemporary with R. Joḥanan and Resh Lakish,

[97] Gen R. 98:9 against Rab. See n. 95 above for the contradiction in pA.Z. 2:1 (40c).

[98] Ḥul. 92a. [99] Gen R. 98:9. [100] Ḥul. 92a.

[101] R. Jose ben Judah (*c.* 180) and R. Levi (*c.* 300) applied the verse to Moses, Aaron, and Miriam: Tos. Sot. 11:10; Cant R. 4:5 §2. Taan. 9a rejects this identification in favour of the manna, the pillar of cloud, and the rock of the wilderness wanderings.

[102] pTaan. 4:5 (68d); *cf.* Lam R. 2:2 §4.

[103] *Cf.* R. Aḥa (*c.* 320), who sees the covenant-breaking of v. 11 as still future: Gen R. 34:11. [104] Lam R. 2:4 §8 = 4:11 §14.

[105] Suk. 51b–52a. [106] Mekiltha *Bo* §13 (on Ex. 12:36).

therefore *c.* 250) used it to illustrate the highest degree of intimacy between God and man.[107]

The cause of the mourning is discussed in Suk. 52a. R. Dosa (either *c.* 90 or *c.* 180)[108] explains the 'piercing' as the death of the Messiah ben Joseph, 'the Rabbis' as the killing of the Evil Inclination (יצר הרע); the latter is given a rather forced explanation by R. Judah (d. 217). The Messiah ben Joseph, otherwise known as 'the anointed for war', to whom this may be the earliest explicit reference,[109] is a figure who is to appear before the coming of the 'true' Messiah, the Messiah ben David (the 'royal Messiah'); his function is to recapture Jerusalem from the Romans, and lead Israel against the onset of the forces of Gog and Magog. In this latter battle he will be killed, and Israel will escape to the wilderness, until God defeats Gog and Magog, and brings the Messiah ben David.[110] It is this interpretation which probably lies behind Tg Zech 12:10, which, according to SB,[111] reads literally, 'They will plead from before me for him on whose account they went into exile' (ויבעון מן קדמי על דאטלטלו). SB, in a full discussion of the doctrine of the Messiah ben Joseph,[112] conclude that it arose in the mid second century,[113] suggested by Deuteronomy 33:17, and crystallized by Zechariah 12:10,[114] a verse believed to be Messianic, but not applicable to the Messiah ben David, who was not to die. They attribute the development to reflection on the claims and fate of Bar Kochba, not to the pressure of the Christian use of Zechariah 12:10 and the preaching of the cross. At any rate, it is unlikely that such a developed doctrine

[107] Gen R. 29:4.

[108] There seems to be no means of deciding whether this is R. Dosa ben Harkinas, an older contemporary of Rabbis Joshua ben Ḥananiah, Eleazar ben Azariah, and Akiba (Yeb. 16a), or R. Dosa the Elder (*c.* 180). For the former view see E. G. King, *The Yalkut on Zechariah* (Cambridge, 1882), p. 107; also J. Klausner, *op. cit.*, pp. 491–492. For the latter see W. D. Davies, *Paul*, pp. 276–277.

[109] Gen R. 75:6 (*c.* 150?) may be earlier, if the later R. Dosa is here meant. *Cf.* also Tg Ps-Jon Ex 40:11.

[110] For the full story see R. Levi (*c.* 300) in Leqach Tob Num 24:17 (SB II, p. 298).

[111] SB II, pp. 583–584.

[112] SB II, pp. 292–299. *Cf.* J. Klausner, *op. cit.*, pp. 400–401, and full discussion, *ibid.*, pp. 483–501.

[113] Identification of R. Dosa in Suk. 52a as Dosa ben Harkinas would necessitate a first-century date.

[114] *Cf.* J. Klausner, *op. cit.*, pp. 204, 485–487.

existed in the time of Jesus. It may perhaps indicate, however, that Zechariah 12:10 was felt to have a Messianic relevance, and caused some difficulty to orthodox minds at that time.

(v) *Zechariah 13:7*. This verse was almost completely ignored by the Rabbis.[115] The only reference which has any claim to be early is a legendary account[116] of the martyrdoms of R. Ishmael and R. Simeon ben Gamaliel. R. Ishmael cites the verse, in a commendatory sense ('Awake, O sword, against my *friend* . . .'), as R. Simeon dies. The use is clearly an isolated one.

(vi) *Zechariah 14*. This chapter was in fairly common use as a source of details and terminology for the description of God's eschatological work of conquest of the enemies of Israel, and the establishment of Israel as his people in undisputed sovereignty, prosperity and blessing.[117] A slightly different application of the chapter is to the future life (*i.e.* after death), by R. Joshua ben Levi (*c.* 250) and other Rabbis of the third and early fourth centuries,[118] but this is not widespread. We may notice especially the application of verse 2 to the temporary suffering of the Messiah ben David and his generation,[119] and of verse 3 to God's attack on Gog and Magog after the defeat of the Messiah ben Joseph.[120] However, verse 5, with its mention of the 'holy ones' who come with God, does not seem to have been used, except by R. Joḥanan (d. 279) to describe the

[115] SB have no entry under Mt. 26:31, and the verse is not quoted in the Talmud or in any of the earlier Midrashim.

[116] Aboth R. N. (A) 38. The dates of the two Rabbis alone (d. 135 and *c.* 140 respectively) show it to have no historical value. The work may date from the third or fourth century (so J. Goldin's edition, p. xxi), but it was subject to later recension and addition.

[117] For some examples see R. Eliezer (*c.* 90) using v. 9: Lam R. 3:66 §9; R. Eleazar of Modiim (d. *c.* 135) using vv. 3 and 9: Mekiltha *Amalek Beshallaḥ* §2 (on Ex. 17:14); R. Joḥanan (d. 279) using v. 10: B.B. 75b, Cant R. 7:5 §3; R. Ḥiyya (*c.* 280) using v. 8: Gen R. 48:10.

[118] Pes. 50a.

[119] So R. Eleazar of Modiim (d. *c.* 135): Cant R. 6:10 §1; R. Jonathan (*c.* 220) or (according to SB II, p. 285) R. Joḥanan (d. 279): Ruth R. 5:6; R. Judan (*c.* 350); Midr. Ps 18 §5. See SB II, p. 285 for the importance of Zc. 14:2 for the doctrine that the Messiah ben David must first suffer.

[120] R. Levi (*c.* 300) (see above, p. 191 n. 110; also in Lev R. 27:11 and Est R. 7:23); *cf.* also, without specific mention of the Messiah ben Joseph, Sifre Num §76 (on 10:9).

multitudes of forgotten prophets, whose message God will bring to light 'in the time to come'.[121] The picture is of a generally agreed eschatological reference, but without any very clearly fixed details in the application.

d. Summary of Jewish interpretation

Our results are inevitably far from conclusive. The paucity of clear allusions at Qumran and in the Pseudepigrapha, the diversity of ideas expressed in the latter, and the relatively late date of the rabbinic sources, all conspire to frustrate a neat summary of Jewish interpretation in the first century AD. The following points, however, emerge comparatively clearly.

(i) *Daniel* 7. The chapter as a whole was in use as a model for apocalyptic visions, and the four empires were almost always identified as Babylon, Persia, Greece and Rome, the last of which was to be overthrown by the Messiah. The details of verses 9–10 provided materials for theophanic descriptions by all the groups examined, including Qumran. The figure of Daniel 7:13 was invariably understood as an individual Messiah, generally seen as coming from heaven to earth, and always as a victorious figure. He was not normally given the title 'Son of man', this being virtually restricted to the Similitudes of Enoch. The use of verses 13–14 at Qumran is unknown, the principal use of the chapter there being of the corporate interpretation in verses 18ff., which is ignored with striking unanimity by the pseudepigraphic and rabbinic literature. The Qumran sect apparently saw itself as 'the people of the saints of the Most High', both in its present status as the chosen people of God, and in its future function as judge of the nations.

(ii) *Zechariah* 9:9. The king riding on an ass was seen in rabbinic literature as the Messiah ben David, and the verse was used especially to stress the lowliness of his coming. Only in later centuries was it applied to God, with a shift of emphasis from the lowliness to the victory. A Messianic use of Genesis 49:10–11 suggests that Zechariah 9:9 was similarly interpreted at Qumran, and there are hints of its influence on the conception of the Messiah's reign in the Pseudepigrapha; lowliness, however, is not emphasized in these sources.

[121] Cant R. 4:11 §1 = Ruth R. Proem 2; *cf.* Ecc R. 1:11 §1.

(iii) *Zechariah 11:12–13.* Here there is no agreed application. Rabbinic sources apply the verses to past, present and future events, and interpret the thirty pieces of silver either as the thirty righteous men who must always be in the world, or as the thirty commandments given by the Messiah to the Gentiles. The Qumran sect saw the suffering of 'the poor of the flock' as predicting its own past and present persecution. Chapters 10–13 find no echo in the Pseudepigrapha.

(iv) *Zechariah 12:10–14.* The passage is applied by Rabbis to the eschatological blessing of Israel, but the cause of the mourning, *i.e.* the 'piercing', is not explained until the post-Christian doctrine of the Messiah ben Joseph emerges. Neither the Pseudepigrapha nor the Qumran literature show any use of this passage.

(v) *Zechariah 13:7.* The Qumran sect saw this probably as a prediction of the death (?) of the Teacher of Righteousness (a *past* event). The resultant persecution of the sect would end in the coming of the Messiah and the deliverance of the now purified community. The Pseudepigrapha and rabbinic sources ignore the verse.

(vi) *Zechariah 14.* The chapter as a whole was used as a quarry for details in the picture of God's eschatological visitation and conquest of the enemies of Israel. The hope of the Qumran sect of an imminent vindication by God over their enemies (especially the Romans?) seems to have been influenced by this chapter (and by much of Zc. 9–14). The angelic retinue of God in his eschatological coming (verse 5) possibly finds an echo in 1QM and 1 Enoch.

e. Jesus and his contemporaries

(i) *Daniel 7.*

1. For Jesus, as for the Jews as a whole, the figure of Daniel 7:13 is an individual, the Messiah, who receives universal power and glory for ever. With the exception of the Qumran literature, where the use of this verse is not known, this agreement is complete. In using the term 'Son of man' for this figure, however, Jesus follows a usage of the Simili-

tudes of Enoch, which was not apparently characteristic of Judaism as a whole. As we have seen reason to question whether Jesus was in fact influenced by this work,[122] this is best seen as an independent and original development by Jesus.

2. The corporate interpretation of the vision in verses 18ff., which was completely ignored by Judaism as a whole, but was the part on which, apparently, the Qumran sect concentrated, while not prominent in Jesus' use of Daniel 7, is not ignored by him.[123] He envisages his disciples as sharing in his authority as Son of man. Thus, in contrast with the purely individual application of the Rabbis and Pseudepigrapha, and the (apparently) purely corporate interpretation at Qumran, we find an unprecedented integration of the individual and corporate aspects of the chapter, which comes nearer to the intended sense of Daniel 7 than any other known interpretation of the time.

3. The widespread use of the general apocalyptic language and ideas of Daniel 7 by Jewish writers finds no echo in Jesus' teaching. His attention is restricted to verses 13–14, except for the recognition of the corporate interpretation mentioned above. The Jews seem to have been keen to establish the identity of the four kingdoms, and were virtually unanimous in looking for the overthrow of the last (Rome) at the coming of the Messiah. In Jesus' teaching we hear nothing of the four kingdoms, nor of an overthrow of the Roman power. Even while the Roman rule is unbroken, Jesus can declare that Daniel 7:14 has been fulfilled; his kingdom is 'not of this world'. In this he may perhaps find a parallel in 1 Enoch, which likewise has no speculation on the four kingdoms, nor prophecies of the downfall of Rome; the Son of man of the Similitudes is an angelic judge of sinners, not a political conqueror. 1 Enoch, however, if not an entirely isolated work,[124] is evidence only for a restricted apocalyptic current within Judaism, whose widespread influence is more a matter of conjecture than of evidence; its influence on Jesus is highly

[122] See above, p. 137, and below, para. 3.

[123] See above, pp. 143–144.

[124] *Cf.* C. H. Dodd, *Scriptures*, pp. 116–117: 'an isolated and probably eccentric authority'. *Cf.* also SB I, pp. 486, 957, suggesting that the Enochic use of Dn. 7:13 was the author's own idea, not a traditional interpretation.

questionable.[125] And not even 1 Enoch can parallel Jesus' conception that the judgment will in fact fall on the Jewish nation itself.[126]

4. For the most striking and characteristic aspect of Jesus' application of Daniel 7 there is, and can be, no non-Christian parallel. In all the Jewish literature, the fulfilment is to come. It may be imminent, but the Messiah has not yet appeared. Even at Qumran, where the chapter was applied to the already existing community, its fulfilment in their role as judge of the nations was still future. The Jews as a whole were characterized by waiting. But for Jesus the time is fulfilled. He is the Son of man, and within a generation his vindication will be seen. Already after his resurrection Daniel 7:14 has been fulfilled. Here is the characteristic note of Jesus' use of the Old Testament, his 'inaugurated eschatology'. There is no need to speculate on the four kingdoms, or to build up an elaborate apocalyptic scheme. The Son of man has already come. Attention is focused simply on the triumphant figure of verses 13–14, and the fulfilment of the vision is announced – in himself. No Jew had ever applied Daniel 7 like that.

5. The 'coming' of verse 13 was generally understood as a coming from heaven to earth, though at least one rabbinic passage is an exception. Such a view is implied by the Pseudepigrapha, which see the Messiah as acting on earth.[127] This exegesis is consonant with the predominantly earthly application of Daniel 7, in terms of political conquest.[128] For Jesus, however, as for the original author of Daniel 7, verse 13 depicts a coming before God to receive authority. Here again Jesus is more faithful to the intended sense than the Jews as a whole.

(ii) *Zechariah 9:9–10.*

1. As far as our sources allow us to see, the contemporary exegesis of this passage as a Messianic prophecy was unani-

[125] On the date of the Similitudes see above, p. 181 n. 38.

[126] See above, pp. 146–147.

[127] J. A. T. Robinson (*Jesus and His Coming*, pp. 50–51n.) points out that in 2 Esdras 13 'the Man' *ascends* (*cf.* v. 32) from the sea into the clouds. His work, however, is still earthly. There is no coming to God.

[128] 1 Enoch, which does not share this application, has no explicit allusion to the 'coming' of v. 13, though an allusion has been seen, rather improbably, in 14:8 (so T. F. Glasson, *Advent*, pp. 3–4), where an 'ascent' is in view.

mous. As in the case of Daniel 7:13–14, Jesus was in complete agreement on this point.

2. The Jewish sources seem to have differed on the aspect of Messiahship which they stressed. The few possible allusions in the Pseudepigrapha stress the triumphant reign of righteousness and peace; meekness is only once mentioned.[129] The one possible allusion at Qumran is in a battle-hymn, and victory was more to their taste than lowliness. The Rabbis, on the other hand, stress almost exclusively the aspect 'lowly and riding on an ass', and attention is drawn to the paradoxical nature of their great deliverer's appearance. On this point Jesus sided with the Rabbis. The one unmistakable feature of his acted quotation was the ass, which does not appear in the Pseudepigrapha or (so far) at Qumran. This was, of course, the only obvious 'pictorial' way to refer to the passage, and no doubt Jesus had the whole figure of Zechariah 9:9–10 in mind, but his entry to Jerusalem was noticeably lacking in regal splendour. He was a king, but a lowly one. Thus he drew attention to the very aspect of this portrait of the Messiah which the Pseudepigrapha ignored, and the Rabbis found interesting, but rather embarrassing. His conquest and reign were not to be of the type looked for by Pseudepigrapha and Rabbis alike; there was to be no earthly pomp and power.

3. As in the use of Daniel 7:13–14, we find here the same essential and inevitable difference between Jesus and his contemporaries. They looked forward to the fulfilment of Zechariah 9:9–10 in the future; for him it was already present – in himself.

(iii) *Zechariah 12:10–14.*[130]

1. Apparently the Rabbis looked for this outpouring of God's grace as an eschatological event. In applying it to the time of the destruction of Jerusalem, Jesus gave to it a place peculiar to his own eschatological system. It belongs to a phase *within* the last days which he has inaugurated, but not to their consummation (though for the Jewish nation it will mark

[129] Test. Jud. 24:1 – possibly a Christian work.

[130] We omit Zc. 11:12–13, as this was nowhere alluded to by Jesus. Its inclusion above was necessary in view of its use by Matthew, to be considered below.

what is in a sense the end). Jesus' whole scheme of inaugurated eschatology is foreign to Jewish expectation, and inevitably leads to a different application.

2. The Rabbis, in accordance with the original meaning, saw the mourning as leading to the salvation of the mourners, Israel, by giving them the opportunity of restoration to fellowship with God. Jesus, however, sees the salvation as coming to God's elect in all parts of the world, not to the mourning Jews.[131] Thus his idea of the Christian community as the true Israel leads to an unprecedented application of Zechariah 12:10ff. In this case, the rabbinic application, as far as it can be ascertained, is closer to the original sense.

3. The Rabbis seem to have found the 'piercing' of verse 10 embarrassing. They felt that the person concerned was a Messianic figure, yet could not accept the apparent teaching of the death of the Messiah. Their dilemma later resulted in the creation of a lower Messianic figure, the precursor Messiah ben Joseph, to whom the 'piercing' could be attributed. Jesus, on the other hand, boldly grasped the nettle which stung the Rabbis. He was the Messiah, but his idea of Messiahship included suffering and death. (Perhaps this passage was among those which led him to this conviction.) He had no need to foist the 'piercing' upon another Messiah. He was the true Messiah, and as such he must be 'pierced'.

(iv) *Zechariah 13:7.*

This verse was apparently of little interest to the Jews. It simply does not appear, except at Qumran, until at least the third century, and then not in a Messianic application. In all the literature we have studied there is no Messianic use of Zechariah 13:7.

The application of verse 7 at Qumran to the death (?) of the Teacher of Righteousness and the persecution of the sect is at first sight similar to Jesus' use of the verse: the fate of the leader is followed by the suffering of the group. But while at Qumran the smiting of the shepherd was a past event of no soteriological significance (the Teacher of Righteousness was not the Messiah), Jesus saw his death as his Messianic destiny,

[131] See above, p. 90.

which was the means of salvation for his followers. He therefore stood alone among his contemporaries in regarding the smiting of the shepherd in Zechariah 13:7 as both Messianic and of soteriological significance. Yet this, as we have argued above,[132] seems to have been the intention of the author, who drew in 9:9–10; 11:4–14; 12:10 – 13:1; 13:7–9 four different sketches of the career of the same suffering yet triumphant Messiah. Jesus alone seems to have been aware of this intention, and to have used the passages concerned in accordance with it. His application reveals a consistent exegesis unmatched in Jewish circles.

(v) *Zechariah 14.*

1. The chapter was quite freely used in Jewish writings as a quarry for details in constructing an eschatological scheme. The general sense of the verses used is quite faithfully adhered to, and the scheme constructed is in the main quite similar to that of Zechariah 14, though with the addition of Gog and Magog, the Messiah ben Joseph, *etc.* As with the apocalyptic details of Daniel 7, Jesus does not share this interest. He makes no use of the battle scene, and his possible acted allusion to Zechariah 14:21[133] is to claim a present fulfilment of that to which the Jews looked forward as the glorious future.[134] The parallel to the use of Daniel 7 is close; Jesus does not look for a future fulfilment in apocalyptic terms, but sees a fulfilment in the present.

2. Jesus' one possible verbal allusion is to verse 5, the 'coming with the holy ones'. This phrase, ignored by the Rabbis except for R. Joḥanan's strange application to the unsung prophets, probably lay behind the description of God's coming with his angels to bring victory in battle (1QM) or to judge (1 Enoch). Jesus' application of the verse is novel and daring; he attributes the angelic retinue not to God's coming to judge, but to his own. Nowhere in Jewish literature is there a suggestion of an angelic retinue for the Messiah; it is the prerogative of God alone. Yet this Jesus claims for himself in his coming authority as king and judge.

[132] See above, pp. 104–109.
[133] See above, p. 92–93.
[134] See Pes. 50a for the use of Zc. 14:21 in this way.

) *Summary and conclusion.*

Exegesis. On most basic points Jesus is in agreement with emporary exegesis. Of particular importance is the agreement on the Messianic significance of Daniel 7:13–14 and Zechariah 9:9–10, and on the eschatological reference of most of the passages considered. The one exception to this last point is Zechariah 13:7, where the only surviving contemporary use is not in an eschatological sense.

The points at which Jesus' exegesis is most conspicuously different from that of his contemporaries are the following. (1) In Daniel 7 Jesus recognizes not only the individual but also the corporate aspects of the chapter. He is thus closer to the original sense than any of the Jewish sources. (2) In Daniel 7:13 Jesus differs from most Jewish exegetes in seeing the 'coming' as to God in heaven, the sense in which it was originally intended. (3) In Zechariah 12:10ff. Jesus' application of the hopes of Israel to his disciples as the true Israel leads him to the exegetical liberty of differentiating between the mourners and the recipients of the resultant blessing. (4) In Zechariah 13:7 Jesus is apparently alone in giving a Messianic and soteriological significance to the smiting of the shepherd; this is due to his recognizing the connection of the various Messianic figures of Zechariah 9–14 as parts of a single over-all conception, which we believe to have been the original intention.

Thus in every case but one where Jesus' exegesis differed from that of his contemporaries it was in the direction of a greater fidelity to the intended sense of the Old Testament passage.

2. *Application.* Here the agreement ends. The reason for this is simple and obvious: Jesus applied these passages to himself and his own work.[135] This results in two basic divergences from current interpretation. (1) Different aspects of Messiahship are emphasized. Jesus is not interested in the Jewish

[135] On this fact and its implications in contrast with the use of the OT at Qumran see F. F. Bruce, *Exegesis*, pp. 75ff.: 'The New Testament interpretation of the Old Testament is not only eschatological but Christological' (*ibid.*, p. 77). For the same point in contrast with rabbinic interpretation see J. W. Doeve, *op. cit.*, pp. 28–29n.; W. D. Davies, *Sermon*, pp. 420–421.

preoccupation with earthly empires and their overthrow. The construction (using, *e.g.*, Dn. 7 and Zc. 14) of detailed pictures of the eschatological battle, with the vindication of Israel and the discomfiture of her enemies, finds hardly an echo in his teaching. Thus he applies Daniel 7 not to earthly conquest, but to a dominion which can coexist with the earthly empire of Rome, because it refers to a different sphere, and which can even involve the judgment rather than the vindication of the Jewish nation. The Messianic king of Zechariah 9:9–10 is presented in his aspect of lowliness; the 'pierced one' of Zechariah 12:10 is unashamedly identified as the Messiah; and the smiting of the shepherd in Zechariah 13:7 is seen as an integral part of the Messianic function. Yet together with this portrait of lowliness and suffering goes a claim to glory far beyond anything the Jews ever attributed to the Messiah, God's own angelic retinue, when he comes to exercise God's own function as judge. Jesus thus applies these passages to a Messiah whose divine glory and power yet embrace an earthly life of lowliness and suffering, because his kingdom is 'not of this world'. (2) While the Jews all looked forward to a Messiah for whose coming they hoped and prayed, Jesus proclaims that this Messiah has already come; he is the Messiah. In himself and his work the eschatological, Messianic age has arrived, and thus these passages are applied generally not to the future but to the present. His application of Daniel 7:13–14 and Zechariah 12:10–14 to future events is not to a new era to come, but to the inevitable outworking of the eschatological work he has already begun. Already the era of salvation is present, and his disciples are the purified, blessed Israel of the Messianic age. Jesus' inaugurated eschatology can have no parallel in non-Christian Judaism. However close his *exegetical* agreement with his contemporaries, he was bound to differ on the *application*, and to apply to the present what they looked for in the future.

We conclude that in his use of the Old Testament Jesus stood alone among his Jewish contemporaries, and that not because he took unusual liberties with the text (he was in general unusually faithful to its intended meaning), but because he believed that in him it found its fulfilment. It is from this basic fact that all the differences noted above spring.

III. JESUS AND EARLY CHRISTIANITY

We shall first survey the use of Daniel 7 and Zechariah 9–14 in the New Testament outside the words attributed to Jesus, including the uses in the Synoptic Gospels which are not attributed directly to him. This will uncover practically all that can be known of the use of these chapters in first-century Christianity. Our next section will carry the story briefly into the next century and a half, aiming to present not an exhaustive study, but rather the main lines of early patristic intepretation of the relevant parts of these chapters. Our question is how far the church's use of the Old Testament echoes the distinctive usage of Jesus, how far it is derived from the Jewish environment as we have outlined it, and how far it is original.

a. The New Testament

(i) *Daniel 7.* The general apocalyptic structure and imagery of Daniel 7 finds no place in the New Testament except in the book of Revelation. There, however, it is in frequent use. Thus Revelation 7:1 echoes the picture of the four winds of heaven stirring up the sea (Dn. 7:2), and 13:1 shows a beast emerging from the sea (Dn. 7:3). The beast imagery is in constant demand, and may be seen reproduced, often in considerable detail, in Revelation 11:7; 12:3; 12:14; 13:1–3, 5, 7; 17:3, 8, 12; 19:20. There is, however, no division into four beasts, but the characteristics of all four are combined into a single centre of opposition. In 11:7 and 13:1–10 the symbolism seems to indicate the concentration of pagan world power in opposition to God and his church, without specific identification, but in 12:9 the dragon, who bears the same characteristics, is identified as Satan, and in 17:9 the beast is clearly Rome. There can be little doubt that it is pagan Rome which is principally in mind throughout, though the identification of the activity of Rome with that of Satan presents little difficulty to the author.[136] Thus the fourth empire of Daniel is stressed to the exclusion (or rather absorption) of the other three, and is identified with Rome. Its overthrow will mark the eschaton, the final judgment and the end of the world. But this final

[136] Rev. 13:2 states that the power and authority of the beast are given to it by the dragon (*i.e.* Satan).

overthrow is nowhere described in terms of Daniel 7:13–14. In fact verses 13–14 are never used in connection with the beast imagery.

Revelation also makes use of the theophany of Daniel 7:9–10. In 5:11 the application is simply to the angels surrounding the throne of God, though their praise is addressed to the Lamb, Jesus. In 20:11–12 the one who is seated on the throne is presumably God himself, but since in 22:1, 3 it is 'the throne of God and of the Lamb', it may well be that here Jesus is regarded as sharing in the judgment depicted in Daniel 7:9–10. All doubt is dispelled by 1:14, where the actual personal characteristics of the Ancient of Days are used in describing the exalted Jesus. For this author, then, Jesus has become identified with God in his function as ruler and judge, and therefore Daniel 7:9–10 is applicable to him.

The crucial verses 13–14 are surprisingly little in evidence. Outside the book of Revelation there is again no clear use, though possible allusions occur in Acts 1:9–11; 7:55–56; 1 Thessalonians 4:17. The first and third of these[137] are hardly likely, the only sign of an allusion being the mention of clouds, in the first case as part of the narrative, and in the second as a piece of conventional eschatological scenery, derived more likely from Jesus' own words than direct from Daniel 7:13. The case for Acts 7:55–56 is not much stronger: beyond the actual term 'Son of man', which is also more likely to be derived from Jesus' usage than from Daniel 7:13, there is no clear allusion to Daniel 7. The wording is perhaps based on Mark 14:62, implying that Jesus' prediction of his imminent exaltation and glory has been fulfilled. The allusion to Daniel 7:13 and Psalm 110:1 is then a second-hand one. If Daniel 7:13 is in mind at all, the application is identical with that by Jesus in Mark 14:62, *i.e.* to his exaltation after his passion, not to the Parousia.[138] The New Testament outside Revelation therefore shows no use of Daniel 7:13–14 independently of Jesus.[139]

The application of these verses in Revelation varies. Revelation 1:13 provides a clear application of verse 13 to Jesus in

[137] The allusion is suggested by C. H. Dodd, *Scriptures*, p. 67.

[138] *Cf.* B. Lindars, *op. cit.*, p. 48.

[139] C. H. Dodd (*Scriptures*, p. 81) sees in Lk. 1:32–33 a 'glance' at Dn. 7:14 together with Is. 9:7 and 2 Sa. 7:13, 16. There is no evidence of a specific allusion.

his exaltation and glory, proceeding in the next verse to ascribe to him certain attributes of the Ancient of Days. This application is in line with that by Jesus in Mark 14:62, *etc.* But in Revelation 1:7 the reference seems to be to the Parousia. The combination of texts is the same as that by Jesus in Matthew 24:30, but the reference cannot now be to the fall of Jerusalem. The author has either misunderstood Jesus' words, or deliberately transferred the texts quoted from the judgment on Jerusalem to the Parousia. The latter is not improbable; Jesus too applied Daniel 7:13–14 elsewhere to the final judgment, though not specifically to his coming to earth. A further allusion to Daniel 7:13–14 may be seen in Revelation 14:14, where the scene depicted is apparently the final judgment. No actual 'coming' is mentioned, though it is the earth which the 'one like a son of man' reaps from his cloud. This use is reminiscent of Jesus' applications of these verses to the final judgment.[140]

The New Testament has some possible allusions to the corporate interpretation of the vision in Daniel 7:18ff. The concept of the reign of the saints recurs a number of times (1 Cor. 4:8; 2 Tim. 2:12; Rev. 1:6; 3:21; 5:9–10; 20:4, 6; 22:5), and though no certain verbal allusion to Daniel 7 appears[141] this might well be the ultimate source of the concept. It may perhaps have been received by way of Jesus' words in Matthew 19:28, since both 2 Timothy 2:12 and Revelation 20:4, 6 envisage the saints reigning *with Jesus*, thus preserving Jesus' unique combination of the individual and corporate application of Daniel 7. The idea of judgment by the saints, found in 1 Corinthians 6:2, may be derived from Daniel 7:22, reading ל as meaning 'to';[142] Paul's 'Do you not know . . . ?' implies some well-known and authoritative teaching, and no other Old Testament background to the idea seems likely. The same verse is probably echoed in Revelation 20:4, 'Judgment was given to them'.

Thus clear uses of Daniel 7 in the New Testament outside the words of Jesus are virtually restricted to Revelation, and there the emphasis is far more on the general apocalyptic structure than on the Messianic aspect of the chapter.

[140] A further possible allusion to Dn. 7:14 is in Rev. 11:15, the everlasting reign of the Messiah (or of God?), but this is not probable.

[141] Compare, however, Rev. 22:5 with Dn. 7:18.

[142] See above, p. 157 n. 286, and p. 174.

(ii) *Zechariah 9:9–10.* The only use of this passage in the New Testament is its quotation by Matthew and John as a comment on the entry to Jerusalem (Mt. 21:5; Jn. 12:15), making explicit the allusion which was already clearly implied in Jesus' action. There is thus no use of this prophecy independently of the 'acted quotation' by Jesus. It did not enter into the preaching or teaching of the early church except in connection with the Gospel narrative itself.[143]

Both Matthew and John omit the words צדיק ונושע (RSV, 'triumphant and victorious'; better, 'vindicated and saved'), and John also omits עני ('humble'). The stress thus falls on the two points which we have seen to be those to which Jesus intended to draw attention, the fact of his kingship, and the lowly nature of that kingship ('riding on an ass').[144] There is then no new application here; the Evangelists simply make explicit what we have already seen to have been Jesus' intention.

(iii) *Zechariah 11:12–13.* The only use of this chapter in the New Testament is by Matthew. The clause 'they paid him thirty pieces of silver' in Matthew 26:15 is a probable allusion to Zechariah 11:12, and verses 12–13 are quoted explicitly in Matthew 27:9–10, as well as alluded to in the story of the death of Judas leading up to this quotation (verses 3–8).

A detailed study of the problems raised by this quotation is outside our scope.[145] It has been cited as a clear New Testament example of the procedure seen in the Qumran 'pesharim',

[143] There is therefore very scanty evidence for Lindars' statement that Zc. 9:9 was 'in use in the church's teaching and apologetic about Jesus' to prove that it was as Messiah that he suffered (*op. cit.*, pp. 111–115). The inference is never drawn, nor is the passage even alluded to except in making explicit Jesus' own allusion.

[144] *Cf.* G. Barth, *op. cit.*, pp. 129–131. Barth sees Matthew's emphasis as falling predominantly on the idea of meekness.

[145] See, *e.g.*, K. Stendahl, *op. cit.*, pp. 120–126; B. Lindars, *op. cit.*, pp. 116–122. The latter postulates an elaborate midrashic development involving not only various Jeremiah texts, but also Ex. 9:12. J. W. Doeve (*op. cit.*, pp. 185–186) makes a similar attempt, but adduces different texts, and postulates a quite different development. Both treatments seem more abstruse than the text warrants. On the attribution to Jeremiah, see K. Stendahl, *op. cit.*, pp. 122–123; B. Lindars, *op. cit.*, p. 119; F. F. Bruce, *BJRL* 43 (1960/1), p. 341. None of the various explanations advanced seems fully satisfactory.

especially that on Habakkuk;[146] an Old Testament text is seen as applying to, and fulfilled in, some specific event of recent history, and the details are interpreted accordingly, using all devices such as textual variants, homonyms, *etc.*, and where necessary adapting the text to fit the facts to which it is applied. This is true in that the fulfilment motif is present here, and the wording has indeed been adapted to fit the facts;[147] it is also possible that both the MT יוצר ('potter') and a variant אוצר ('treasury') were used, in the manner of 1QpHab.[148]

Two differences must, however, be noted. Firstly, Matthew alters the Old Testament wording far more than was ever done at Qumran. His version is hardly even a paraphrase of Zechariah 11:12–13, and is expanded with phrases either drawn from elsewhere in the Old Testament or added to bring out the desired interpretation; at Qumran the textual adaptation seldom went further than a suffix or at most two letters in a word.[149]

Secondly, despite this drastic reworking of the text, Matthew shows far more respect for the original intention of the Old Testament author than the Qumran exegetes. Whereas they would apply Old Testament words to situations of quite a different order from the original, the situation to which Matthew applies Zechariah 11:12–13 bears considerable literal similarity to that envisaged by Zechariah. Besides the literal payment of thirty silver pieces as a price for the Messiah (which was no doubt the feature which drew attention to this passage), we may notice that the scene is in fact in the house of the Lord, where the money is really cast down. Matthew even applies the enigmatic יוצר in its literal sense. There is nothing here to compare with the allegorical interpretations of the thirty

[146] See esp. K. Stendahl, *op. cit.*, pp. 196–198.

[147] That the words are adapted to fit the facts, and not *vice versa*, is argued by K. Stendahl, *ibid.*, pp. 196–197.

[148] It is possible, however, that an interpretation of יוצר as meaning a Temple official connected with the treasury was known; the Tg uses אמרכלא, an official described by Jastrow (*s.v.* אמרכול) as a 'trustee superintending the cashiers' in the Temple. According to F. F. Bruce (*This is That*, p. 109), the יוצר was 'the man who melted down precious metal in the temple mould or foundry'. In that case Matthew would be using two meanings of the same word in his references to the treasury (v. 6) and the potter (vv. 7, 10).

[149] See K. Stendahl, *op. cit.*, pp. 185–190 for details.

silver pieces by the Rabbis,[150] nor with such allegory as the explanation of the net and the seine of Habakkuk 1:16 as the Roman standards and weapons.[151] Only where complications arise, *e.g.* in the presence of the traitor and of the chief priests, does Matthew have to abandon a literal application of the Old Testament text, and he does it not by allegory, nor by any of the hermeneutical devices of Qumran, but simply by altering and supplementing the text to fit the facts. That is why his textual surgery is far more drastic than that of Qumran. His use of Zechariah 11:12–13 is, therefore, quite original. In fact it is unique.

(iv) *Zechariah 12:10–14*. The two New Testament quotations of these verses outside the words of Jesus are in John 19:37 and Revelation 1:7. The former is as a comment on the piercing of Jesus' side with a spear at the crucifixion; there is no reference to the mourning, only to the piercing. It is a simple and obvious use of Zechariah 12:10 for one who believed that passage to be Messianic, and Jesus to be the Messiah. In Revelation 1:7 the verse is conflated with Daniel 7:13, as in Matthew 24:30, and the whole is given as, apparently, a description of the Parousia and its effect. The emphasis is, therefore, as in Matthew 24:30, on the mourning, but the fact that the mourners are those who pierced him is mentioned. What form that piercing took is not specified, but it is impossible to believe that these words could have been applied to Jesus after the crucifixion without interpreting the 'piercing' of that event. The mourning is then, we may fairly assume, occasioned by the sight of the returning Messiah whom the mourners had previously crucified. Thus John 19:37 concentrates on the past fact of the piercing, and Revelation 1:7 on its future effect.

We may note a discrepancy between Matthew 24:30 and Revelation 1:7, in that the first applies the mourning to the time of the fall of Jerusalem, the second to the Parousia, and therefore probably to 'all the nations of the earth' rather than to 'all the tribes of the land' (as in Mt. 24:30).[152] On the

150 See above, pp. 189–190.

151 1QpHab 6:2–5.

152 For the latter point see below, pp. 236–237; for the discrepancy between Mt. 24:30 and Rev. 1:7 see above, pp. 203–204.

Messianic reference of the passage, and its application to the crucifixion of Jesus and its effect on those who killed him, there is agreement in all three uses.

(v) *Zechariah 13:7.* The influence of this chapter on the New Testament outside the words of Jesus is, if anything, even less than that of the other chapters of Zechariah so far studied. Of two suggested verbal allusions, one (1 Pet. 1:7)[153] is merely a matter of the use of a common proverbial simile, while the other (Jn. 16:32),[154] if it is to be classed as an allusion at all, is more likely derived from Jesus' actual quotation of Zechariah 13:7 at this time, as recorded in Mark 14:27, than from an independent use of the text; neither is, therefore, relevant to our purpose.

Zechariah 13:7 is, however, an example of a recurrent theme of these chapters of Zechariah, that of the shepherd and the flock.[155] Israel is the flock of God, which he visits and saves (Zc. 9:16; 10:3, 8–10), which is sometimes afflicted by bad shepherds (10:2–3; 11:5–6, 8, 15–17), but over which he will set a good shepherd, the Messiah (11:4–14; 13:7–9). The metaphor is taken up and used both by Jesus and by the rest of the New Testament. Its normal application by Jesus is to his disciples as the flock and himself as the shepherd: this we have seen in Mark 14:27, where he quotes Zechariah 13:7; it appears also in Mark 14:28;[156] Luke 12:32 (with a possible allusion to the 'little ones' of Zc. 13:7 and/or the 'poor of the flock' of Zc. 11:7, 11);[157] John 10:1–16, 26–28, and is probably implied in the parables of Matthew 18:12–14 and Luke 15:3–7.[158] Correlative to this use is the description of Israel as lost sheep in Matthew 10:6 and 15:24, since this implies their need to be included in the flock over which Jesus is shepherd. One other and derivative use is that in John 21:15–17, where the pastoral office is delegated to Peter.

[153] C. H. Dodd, *Scriptures*, p. 66 suggests an allusion to the idea of gold being refined in the fire (Zc. 13:9).

[154] *Cf.* K. Stendahl, *op. cit.*, p. 80 for σκορπισθῆτε as an allusion to Zc. 13:7.

[155] On this subject see F. F. Bruce, *BJRL* 43 (1960/1), pp. 343–347.

[156] *Cf.* C. F. Evans, *JTS* 5 (1954), pp. 3–18, esp. p. 11.

[157] So Bruce, *loc. cit.*, p. 346.

[158] Mt. 25:32–33, being simply an illustrative simile, is not relevant.

These uses of the shepherd theme by Jesus find a very close parallel in its use in the rest of the New Testament. The picture of Jesus as the shepherd and his church as the flock is again predominant (Acts 20:28; Heb. 13:20; 1 Pet. 2:25; Rev. 7:17), and that of the rest of Israel as lost sheep needing a shepherd is found in Mark 6:34; Matthew 9:36 (very likely based on what Jesus himself had said, and quite possibly derived from the similar description in Zc. 10:2). The derivative use where the pastoral office is delegated to the leaders of the church is now rather more prominent, as would be expected in the situation of the early church (Acts 20:28–29; 1 Pet. 5:2–3).

Zechariah 9–13 is not the only part of the Old Testament where the theme of shepherd and flock is found.[159] In these chapters, however, it is particularly prominent, and we have noted above possible allusions to Zechariah 10:2 and 11:7, 11 or 13:7, in addition to Jesus' explicit quotation of 13:7. The frequent use of these chapters by Jesus, and in the rest of the New Testament, strengthens the suggestion that Zechariah 9–13 was an important source for this theme.

(vi) *Zechariah 14*. Again the book of Revelation shows some interest in the imagery of this apocalypse, and weaves some features of it into the description of the New Jerusalem: there will be no night (Zc. 14:7; Rev. 21:25; 22:5), no curse (Zc. 14:11; Rev. 22:3), and the fountain of living waters will flow out from Jerusalem (Zc. 14:8; Rev. 22:1–2; *cf.* 21:6; 22:17).[160] Here, as with the use of Daniel 7, Revelation stands alone among the books of the New Testament.

A possible use of the 'holy ones' of Zechariah 14:5 is suggested in 1 Thessalonians 3:13.[161] The wording is not far from that of Zechariah 14:5. It is not possible to be sure whether by ἅγιοι here Paul means the angels, or, in accordance with his usual

[159] In Lk. 19:10 Jesus probably alluded to Ezk. 34, where this theme governs the whole chapter. Other passages which could have led to the use of the same metaphor include Is. 40:11; Je. 23:1–6; 31:10; Ezk. 37:24; Mi. 5:3 (EVV v. 4).

[160] The major source for the idea is clearly Ezk. 47:1–12, but the phrase ὕδωρ (τῆς) ζωῆς in these last references suggests that Zc. 14:8 מים־חיים (LXX ὕδωρ ζῶν) was also in the writer's mind.

[161] C. H. Dodd, *Scriptures*, p. 66.

use of the term, Christian believers. However, ἅγιοι is not unknown in the New Testament as a description of angels, and the context here favours an angelic retinue, parallel to that in Matthew 25:31. The application here, as in Matthew 25:31, is to the angels appearing *with Jesus*[162] at the time of the Parousia and final judgment.

b. Early patristic writers

(i) *Daniel* 7. In accordance with Jesus' usage, patristic attention is mainly focused on verses 13–14 of this chapter. There is, however, some interest in the four kingdoms, or rather in the fourth. The 'little horn' is the Antichrist, or the 'man of sin',[163] who is expected very soon,[164] to be shortly followed by the Parousia. Hippolytus' Commentary on Daniel is alone in the early period in giving the standard rabbinic interpretation of the four kingdoms as Babylon, Persia, Greece and Rome;[165] the Antichrist is not elsewhere explicitly regarded as arising from Rome.[166] The fourth kingdom is in all cases either present or future; it is never regarded as already past.

It is therefore not surprising to find verses 13–14 generally interpreted as applicable to a future triumph, the Parousia. In most cases this application occurs in what becomes an almost stereotyped comparison of the weakness and humility of Jesus' first coming with the glory and power of the second, with a fairly standard grouping of texts on either side of the comparison.[167] Other passages apply Daniel 7:13–14 to the Parousia or final judgment without specific comparison with the first coming.[168] Hippolytus does not specifically apply verses 13–14 to the Parousia, but follows his exposition of the fourth kingdom by predicting the coming of Jesus from heaven

162 Here the LXX κύριος is unambiguously identified as Jesus.

163 Barnabas 4:4–5; Justin, *Dial.* 32:3–4; 110:2; Irenaeus, *Adv. Haer.* v. 25:3; Hippolytus, *Comm. Dan.* iv. 12; *cf. ibid.*, iv. 5:3.

164 See esp. Justin, *Dial.* 32:3–4.

165 *Comm. Dan.* iv. 1–8.

166 This is explicit in *Comm. Dan.* iv. 12:4. *Cf.* later Cyril of Jerusalem, *Cat.* xv. 13.

167 So, for Dn. 7:13–14, in Justin, *Apol. I* 51:9; *Dial.* 14:8; 31:1; 110:2 (the allusion to Dn. 7 here is not quite certain); Irenaeus, *Adv. Haer.* iii. 19:2; iv. 33:1, 11; Tertullian, *Adv. Marc.* iii. 7:4; *Adv. Jud.* 14:4; Hippolytus, *De Antichristo* 44.

168 Justin, *Dial.* 120:4; Tertullian, *Adv. Marc.* iii. 24:11; iv. 10:12; iv. 39:11.

as judge to crush the rule of Rome and Antichrist and establish his own eternal kingdom.[169]

There are, however, a few cases where verses 13–14 are applied not to a coming to earth, but to Jesus' coming to the Father to receive kingship, without any specification of the time.[170] Hippolytus' exposition of these verses is a sober presentation of the original sense, picturing Jesus as brought *to the Father* on a cloud by the archangels, to receive all power from him;[171] the surrounding commentary, however, forbids us to say that he saw this as an event which had already occurred[172] – perhaps he saw it as a prelude to the coming to earth.

It is thus all the more remarkable to observe as late as Cyprian a reversion to Jesus' primary application of Daniel 7:13–14. He applies the verses to the eternal power and kingship received by Jesus *cum resurrexisset*, the Parousia being treated later, and quite separately, and Zechariah 9:9 used for the kingship *after* the Parousia.[173] An explicit application to the ascension appears in another North African writer at the beginning of the fourth century.[174]

The corporate interpretation at the end of the chapter is not much in use, but is applied to a reign of the saints on earth after the Parousia;[175] thus the corporate interpretation, where it is noticed, in no way embarrasses the individual application of verses 13–14, which was never questioned.

(ii) *Zechariah 9:9*. This prophecy is applied in two complementary ways. In some cases it occurs in the comparison of the two comings of Christ, on the opposite side to Daniel 7:13–14, *i.e.* it is used to stress the weakness and humility, and even suffering, of the first coming.[176] On the other hand it is applied to the power and kingship received by Jesus after the Parousia.[177] Three further quotations are simple references to

[169] *Comm. Dan.* iv. 10.

[170] Justin, *Dial.* 76:1; 79:2; Irenaeus, *Adv. Haer.* iv. 20:11.

[171] *Comm. Dan.* iv. 11.

[172] See esp. iv. 15ff., where he proceeds to discuss the date of the Parousia, clearly because he saw in vv. 13–14 a prediction of this.

[173] Cyprian, *Test.* ii. 26.

[174] Lactantius, *Div. Inst.* iv. 21.

[175] Irenaeus, *Adv. Haer.* v. 34:2; Hippolytus, *Comm. Dan.* iv. 13–14.

[176] Irenaeus, *Adv. Haer.* iii. 19:2; iv. 33:1, 12. This aspect may be implied also in Justin's addition of πτωχός to the text, *Dial.* 53:3.

[177] Cyprian, *Test.* ii. 29.

the fulfilment of the prophecy at the time of the entry to Jerusalem,[178] though Justin goes on to allegorize the two animals as the Jews and the Gentiles.[179] This latter tendency is fully developed by Origen, who stresses the Messianic relevance of the prophecy, and decries literal applications: it is too unworthy a thing to imagine that Jesus needed an ass.[180]

(iii) *Zechariah 11:12–13.* This passage is apparently ignored except for a paraphrase of Matthew 27:3ff. by Irenaeus,[181] using Matthew's 'pesher' text virtually unaltered,[182] and complete with the attribution to Jeremiah.

(iv) *Zechariah 12:10–14.* As in the New Testament, there is complete agreement that whereas the piercing of verse 10 took place in the earthly life of Jesus, the mourning will be in the future. The piercing is apparently normally applied to the crucifixion.[183] Tertullian, however, has his own peculiar interpretation of the piercing, as meaning the Jewish failure to recognize Jesus as the Messiah at his first coming, because of the humility of that coming; this will cause their mourning at his second coming.[184] The mourning is by all writers expected at the Parousia,[185] and the verse is used, like both Daniel

[178] Justin, *Apol. I* 35:11; *Dial.* 53:3; Irenaeus, *Epideixis* 65.

[179] *Dial.* 53:4.

[180] *Comm. Mat.* xvi. 14–18; *Comm. Joh.* x. 26–32 (17–18). *Cf. De Princ.* iv. 2:1, where he castigates those who look for a literal fulfilment of Zc. 9:10.

[181] *Epideixis* 81.

[182] The variation from Matthew is certainly not sufficient to suggest (as J. R. Harris, *Testimonies I* (Cambridge, 1916), p. 68) that Irenaeus used a source other than Matthew, especially when we consider that what we have is only an Armenian version of Irenaeus' original Greek.

[183] This is virtually certain from the context in Justin, *Dial.* 32:2, and explicit in Cyprian, *Test* ii. 20; Lactantius, *Div. Inst.* iv. 18. The same application is probably also intended in the versions *confixerunt* (*v.l. compunxerunt*) and *convulneraverunt* given by Tertullian, *De Carne Christi* 24:4; *De Res. Carnis* 51:1. In the following cases an application to the crucifixion, though not explicit, seems probable: Justin, *Apol. I* 52:11–12; *Dial.* 14:8; 64:7; 118:1; Irenaeus, *Adv. Haer.* iv. 33:11.

[184] Tertullian, *Adv. Marc.* iii. 7:6; *Adv. Jud.* 14:6. The allusion in *De Res. Carnis* 22:10 does not specify the cause of the mourning. Justin (*Dial.* 126:1) may possibly reflect a similar interpretation in the use of ἐβλασφημεῖτε before the prophecy of mourning at the Parousia.

[185] So in all the passages quoted in the last two notes (except those from Cyprian and Lactantius, where only the piercing is considered). In *Dial.* 121:2–3 Justin seems to see the mourning as taking place as a result of the

7:13–14 and Zechariah 9:9, in the traditional comparisons of the two comings, the piercing belonging to the first,[186] and the mourning to the second.[187]

(v) *Zechariah 13:7.* With one exception, this verse is always applied to the suffering of Jesus. In Barnabas 5:12 the text is altered to *ὅταν πατάξωσιν τὸν ποιμένα ἑαυτῶν* ('when they shall smite their own shepherd'), an alteration for which there is no precedent,[188] but which is used to prove the responsibility of the Jews for Jesus' death. In Justin and Irenaeus the application is exactly as in Mark 14:27, though the imperative of Zechariah (*πάταξον*, for NT *πατάξω*) is used, and the verse is quoted from the beginning.[189] Origen[190] has the Marcan text as a testimony for the necessity of the crucifixion.

The one other application is by Tertullian,[191] who, using apparently the text of LXX W, makes the verse into a threat against false shepherds, *i.e.* for him, Christian leaders who fled in persecution. This is an entirely individual use, and for our purposes may be disregarded.[192]

(vi) *Zechariah 14:5.* The application of the angelic retinue of God to Jesus in his Parousia is carried a stage further. On the one hand the idea of an angelic retinue seems to be established, though the source of the idea is more probably Jesus' words in Matthew 25:31 than direct recourse to Zechariah 14:5. It sometimes appears in connection with the application of Daniel 7:13–14 (or Mt. 24:30) to the Parousia.[193] On

---

first coming, in the repentance and faith of the Gentiles, but in view of so many clear applications to the Parousia elsewhere by Justin this can carry no weight.

[186] Justin, *Dial.* 32:2.

[187] Justin, *Dial.* 14:8; 32:2; Irenaeus, *Adv. Haer.* iv. 33:11; Tertullian, *Adv. Marc.* iii. 7:6; *Adv. Jud.* 14:6.

[188] J. de Waard (*op. cit.*, p. 38 n. 4) prefers the Old Latin version, which retains the first person singular verb, and so is closer to the text in Mark, but Barnabas' application is the same in either version.

[189] Justin, *Dial.* 53:5–6; Irenaeus, *Epideixis* 76.

[190] *Hom. in Exod.* 11:2.

[191] *De Fuga in Pers.* 11:2.

[192] The only parallel to such an application would be at Qumran, if a lacuna were not postulated in the B text of CD; see above, p. 177.

[193] So Justin, *Apol. I* 51:9; in *Dial.* 79:2 there is certainly no allusion to Zc. 14:5, and the angelic attendants on the Son of man are more probably derived from Dn. 7:10 (so P. Prigent, *Justin et l'Ancien Testament* (Paris,

the other hand, in Didache 16:6 the description of God's coming in Zechariah 14:5, not just the angelic retinue, is applied directly to the Parousia of Jesus, again in connection with Matthew 24:30, the *ἅγιοι* being incorrectly interpreted as Christian believers. Clearly then Jesus' appropriation of the divine attributes has taken root in the Christian church.

c. Summary of early Christian interpretation

(i) *Daniel 7.* In the New Testament outside the book of Revelation there is no clear use of this chapter, though it may underlie the notion of the future reign and judgment to be given to believers; even here the clearest echoes are in Revelation. A probable reminiscence of Mark 14:62 preserves Jesus' use of verse 13. Revelation, however, makes considerable use of the apocalyptic ideas of Daniel 7, identifying the beasts as Rome, whose overthrow is predicted, but not in terms of verses 13–14. Patristic writers go on to identify the 'little horn' as Antichrist. In Revelation the divine attributes of verses 9–10 are in part ascribed to Jesus, and verses 13–14 are applied partly to Jesus in his present exaltation and glory, partly to his future coming and judgment. The latter application is regular in the Fathers, often in contrast with the humility and suffering of the first coming. Traces of the former application survive, however, and in North Africa Daniel 7:13–14 is seen as fulfilled in the ascension. In all these writings the corporate interpretation in verses 18ff. is noticed but not stressed. The individual exegesis of verses 13–14 is unanimous.

(ii) *Zechariah 9:9–10.* The only New Testament use is in the Gospel narrative, to make explicit Jesus' 'acted quotation'. The stress falls on the complementary factors of kingship and lowliness. In the Fathers the latter is most prominent, as a contrast with the glory of the Parousia. Its fulfilment is generally noted without comment, though a tendency to allegorize the two asses begins to appear.

(iii) *Zechariah 11:12–13.* An entirely original use by Matthew, applying these verses to the treachery and fate of Judas, and

1964), p. 22); the transfer of the divine retinue to the service of the Messiah is in that case even more remarkable.

altering the wording drastically to fit the facts, is echoed once in the patristic literature. Otherwise the verses are ignored.

(iv) *Zechariah 12:10–14.* All sources agree that the piercing took place at the crucifixion (or, according to Tertullian, the Jewish rejection of Jesus), and the resultant mourning of the Jews will be at the Parousia.

(v) *Zechariah 13:7.* The Fathers, with one exception, apply this verse to the suffering of Jesus. The New Testament does not allude to it, but in its use of the shepherd motif, probably derived, at least in part, from these chapters, it closely follows Jesus' application to himself as shepherd and the church as the flock, with an occasional transfer of the pastoral office to Christian leaders.

(vi) *Zechariah 14.* The apocalyptic imagery again finds several echoes in Revelation. The 'holy ones' of verse 5 are once applied in the New Testament to the angelic retinue of Jesus at the Parousia, and the same idea seems to be established in patristic thought, though probably more on the basis of Matthew 25:31 than from a direct use of Zechariah 14:5.

d. Jesus and his followers

(i) *Daniel 7.*

1. The unanimous agreement of Jewish exegetes, shared by Jesus, that verses 13–14 depict an individual Messiah, is followed in all early Christian writings. The picture is never, in Jewish or Christian sources, of a suffering figure, but of majesty and victory (in patristic writings in explicit contrast with the suffering of Jesus on earth).

2. Jesus' teaching that, because he was to become king and judge, his disciples too would share in this reign and judgment, is echoed in Christian allusions to the later part of Daniel 7, in the idea of reigning *with Christ*[194] and judging the world. This combination of an individual application of verses 13–14 with a corporate application of verse 22, *etc.* has no Jewish precedent;[195] it was Jesus' original creation.

[194] For Hippolytus the reign of the saints is given by, rather than shared with, Jesus (*Comm. Dan.* iv. 14:3), but this is not the NT emphasis.

[195] The probable use of v. 22 at Qumran, while not dissimilar to that in 1 Cor. 6:2, lacks an individual use of vv. 13–14 to balance it.

3. In striking contrast to Jesus' frequent use of Daniel 7:13–14, the rest of the New Testament apart from Revelation virtually ignores the whole chapter. This strange silence is paralleled neither by the Jewish sources (except, so far, Qumran) nor by Revelation and later Christian writing, where Daniel 7 comes into its own again. In the Fathers the emphasis falls, as in Jesus' teaching, on verses 13–14.

4. The apocalyptic imagery of the chapter, especially of the four beast-kingdoms, which was so much used by Jewish writers, was of no interest to Jesus. In this he is followed by the New Testament except for the book of Revelation, where this aspect of Daniel 7 is far more prominent than the Messianic figure of verses 13–14. The author lays special stress on the fourth kingdom, which he identifies as Rome;[196] it is, therefore, still extant, and its imminent overthrow is looked for in an eschatological encounter. The Fathers unanimously follow this lead, though the hostile power is further specified as that of Antichrist (the 'little horn'), sometimes but not always regarded as soon to arise out of Rome.[197] The contrast with Jesus' application of Daniel 7 is complete. He saw in verses 13–14 the overthrow of spiritual opposition, which took place at and as a result of his resurrection and ascension. At the time of his ascension Daniel 7:14 was already fulfilled, though its final manifestation must still be realized. The 'political' application by the author of Revelation is thus inevitably different from that of Jesus; the former looked to the future for what the latter had claimed was already present. In its use of Daniel 7, Revelation in fact stands far closer to the Jewish writings, especially the Pseudepigrapha, than to Jesus, and the Fathers follow its lead.

5. On one point Revelation cannot follow the Jewish interpreters. Jesus had made it abundantly clear that he was the figure presented in verses 13–14, and to this application both the New Testament and the Fathers adhere faithfully. Thus whereas the Jewish writers looked forward to a deliverer to

[196] Revelation gives no separate consideration to the first three kingdoms. Hippolytus is the only early Christian writer to echo the regular Jewish identification of the four kingdoms.

[197] The virtual identification of Rome with Satan in Revelation (see above, p. 202) may be regarded as the source of this development.

overthrow the Roman power, and saw that deliverer in verses 13–14, for Revelation the fulfiller of verses 13–14 has already come, and yet the Roman power is still present. This is perhaps the cause of the atomistic procedure of this author, who does not interpret the vision as a whole, but describes the overthrow of the beast without reference to verses 13–14, and expounds these verses without reference to the rest of the vision.

6. Probably as a result of the above dilemma, Revelation gives a new prominence to what was for Jesus a secondary application of verse 13, *i.e.* to the culmination of his Lordship in the final judgment. The resulting application to the Parousia soon becomes virtually invariable in the Fathers, and only a few incidental applications to the exaltation preserve Jesus' original use of the verse, until it re-emerges in North Africa in the third century.

7. Consequently Jesus' exegesis of the 'coming' in verse 13 as a coming to God to receive power, and never as a coming to earth, while it is still echoed perhaps in Acts 7:55–56 and in Revelation 1:13 and occasional patristic references, is quite overshadowed by the exegesis, first appearing in Revelation 1:7, which sees the coming as the actual 'descent' of the Parousia.

8. Finally we may note that verses 9–10, which were frequently used by the Jews in descriptions of the glory and judgment of God, provide the author of Revelation with details for his picture of the exalted Jesus. Such an application clearly could have no origin in Judaism outside the teaching of Jesus, and is in harmony with Jesus' own claims in Matthew 25:31ff.[198]

(ii) *Zechariah 9:9–10.*

1. The only use of this passage in the New Testament, and the major use in the Fathers, is in making explicit Jesus' 'acted quotation'. In the actual wording quoted in the New Testament, and in the few expository comments found in the Fathers, the emphasis is laid where Jesus' action placed it, on the paradoxical combination of kingship and lowliness. Where Jesus followed the rabbinic use of the verse as against that of the Pseudepigrapha, his followers remained completely true to his use, and no independent use appears until the

[198] See above, pp. 154–155, 157–158.

tendency to allegorize the details begins with Justin.

2. As in the case of Daniel 7:13–14, the New Testament shows a remarkable lack of interest in a verse by which Jesus apparently set some store; there is no reference except where the telling of the Gospel narrative demands it.

(iii) *Zechariah 11:12–13.*

The quotation of these verses by Matthew is entirely original. Jesus never alluded to them, and they find no place in the Pseudepigrapha or at Qumran, while the Rabbis invariably allegorized them. The only parallel to Matthew's application is a single slavish repetition by Irenaeus. The only possible point of dependence is a superficial resemblance to the exegetical devices of the Qumran 'pesharim', but we have seen that here too the contrast is more impressive than the resemblance.

(iv) *Zechariah 12:10–14.*

1. The most striking aspect of Jesus' use of this passage was the application of it to himself, involving the unashamed acceptance of the 'piercing' of the Messiah. The New Testament and the Fathers unanimously follow Jesus in this application, the Fathers laying great stress on the fact of Jesus' suffering at his first coming, and using Zechariah 12:10 as a testimony for this. That the 'piercing' was at the crucifixion is probably implied by Jesus, made explicit by John, and accepted by all early Christian writers except Tertullian.

2. Jesus further departed from Jewish interpretation (and from the intention of Zechariah) in regarding the mourning as an admission of guilt and sign of despair, rather than a repentance leading to salvation. Here again he is followed by the early church. This application is implied in Revelation 1:7, and becomes very clear in the regular use of Zechariah 12:10 in the patristic comparison of the two comings, the one in which Jesus was pierced, the other in which the tables will be turned, and he will triumph over those who pierced him. The combination with Daniel 7:13 by Jesus is also echoed in Revelation 1:7 and in several of the patristic catenae on the second coming.

3. On one point Jesus' application is not followed. The mourning is located by Revelation and the Fathers not at the fall of Jerusalem but at the Parousia. This shift of application,

parallel to that seen in the use of Daniel 7:13, brings the early Christian use closer to the more conventionally eschatological application by the Rabbis.

(v) *Zechariah 13:7.*

1. Like Zechariah 9:9, this verse seems to have played no part in the thought of the New Testament, beyond the actual recording of Jesus' use of it. In the Fathers, with the exception of an eccentric use by Tertullian and a slight difference of emphasis in the letter of Barnabas, it is used exactly as Jesus used it, but again not with any frequency. Jesus' use of the verse was accepted and followed, but it had no prominent place in early Christian thought.

2. The idea of shepherd and flock, which has a large place in these chapters of Zechariah, occurs frequently in the New Testament, modelled, perhaps, on these chapters. In their use of this theme the New Testament writers mirror with remarkable fidelity the different aspects of Jesus' use of it, but show no independent development.

(vi) *Zechariah 14.*

1. The general apocalyptic imagery of the chapter is not used by Jesus, nor by the New Testament as a whole. As in the case of Daniel 7, however, the book of Revelation is again an exception, and in its interest in the apocalyptic scheme shows a closer affinity to the Jewish writings.

2. Jesus' daring and original application of verse 5 to his own angelic retinue at the final judgment is repeated in 1 Thessalonians 3:13, and in a still more daring form in the Didache. There are signs that this attribution to Jesus of an angelic retinue, which for the non-Christian Jew was an exclusive prerogative of God, soon took root in the early church.

(vii) *Summary and conclusion.*

1. *Exegesis.* There is no need to go into detail here. On all points of exegesis, including those at which Jesus differed from current practice, the consensus of Christian exegesis is consistent in its adherence to his usage, with only one exception.[199] That exception is the 'coming' in Daniel 7:13, where,

[199] We do not here take account of such a clearly isolated and eccentric

as we have seen, Jesus differed from most Jewish writers in following the original sense of a coming to God to receive power, not a coming to earth. Traces of Jesus' exegesis survive both in the New Testament (Acts 7:55–56?; Rev. 1:13) and in the Fathers, but beginning with Revelation 1:7 a new exegesis gains ground, taking it as a coming to earth for judgment, and this exegesis, inevitably linked with the application of Daniel 7:13 to the Parousia, is soon established to the virtual exclusion of Jesus' own exegesis. This is in agreement with the predominant Jewish exegesis of the verse, and its introduction may be due especially to the influence of Jewish apocalyptic.

The only other piece of original exegesis we have noted in the New Testament is Matthew's unparalleled use of Zechariah 11:12–13. As we have no record of Jesus' understanding of this passage, this can be classed neither as a deviation from nor a following of his exegesis.

2. *Application.* Again there is an overwhelming preponderance of agreement with Jesus in the Christian application of these chapters, including again the points at which Jesus differed from his contemporaries. That Jesus was the one portrayed in the various Messianic figures of these chapters, and that he has come, and has brought that salvation for which the Old Testament looked, these are agreed assumptions of New Testament and patristic interpretation. The use of an Old Testament passage by the Master was clearly the deciding factor in its use by his followers.[200]

It is more instructive to notice the departures from his usage. They are not many. The originality displayed in Matthew's use of Zechariah 11:12–13 is without parallel elsewhere in in the New Testament within the group of Old Testament passages which we are studying. It is only after the New Testament period that the tendency to allegorize emerges, and leads to a quite new use of Zechariah 9:9. Within the New Testament, new uses of passages alluded to by Jesus do not occur, except in the book of Revelation.

It is in the book of Revelation that the one striking departure

---

interpretation as that of Zc. 13:7 by Tertullian (see above, p. 213).

[200] *Cf.*, with special reference to Matthew, R. H. Gundry, *op. cit.*, pp. 213–215. He concludes, 'The Matthaean quotations not attributed to Jesus do not transgress the hermeneutical boundaries indicated by him.'

from Jesus' application occurs, the shift of Daniel 7:13 and Zechariah 12:10ff. from the fall of Jerusalem to the Parousia. In the period after the fall of Jerusalem this shift is quite understandable. To one well versed in Jewish apocalyptic the events of AD 70, however catastrophic, may not have provided a sufficiently clear fulfilment of Daniel 7:13, of the type expected in apocalyptic thought. Jewish exegesis looked for a descent from heaven to judge and reign. An interpretation of Mark 13:26 (Mt. 24:30), and with it Daniel 7:13 and Zechariah 12:10ff., as referring to the Parousia, and therefore still to be fulfilled, was an attractive solution.

This is perhaps the clearest example of the tendency of this book to work independently of Jesus' use of an Old Testament passage, and to initiate a new application which then becomes a dominant influence on patristic use of the passage concerned. The way it takes is that of Jewish apocalyptic thought. Thus while Jesus and the rest of the New Testament show no interest in the apocalyptic imagery of Daniel 7 and Zechariah 14, Revelation is captivated by it. While Jesus' use of Daniel 7 ignores Jewish discussion of the political identity of the four kingdoms and the time of their final overthrow, and concentrates on the overthrow of spiritual opposition to the purposes of God, Revelation expounds Daniel 7 in terms of the empire of Rome and its imminent downfall. While Jesus claims that in his death and resurrection he has entered into the triumph and exaltation of the Son of man, and received all power in heaven and earth, Revelation sees the opposing kingdom as still rampant, and the triumph of Jesus as future. The attempt to combine the 'consistent eschatology' of Jewish apocalyptic with the 'inaugurated eschatology' of Jesus has led this author into the atomistic interpretation of Daniel 7 which we have noted above, and also into the shift of the fulfilment of Daniel 7:13–14 (except in Rev. 1:13) and Zechariah 12:10ff. from the past to the future, thus giving birth to the patristic application of them to the Parousia.

Revelation excepted, the New Testament shows no departure from Jesus' application of the Old Testament passages studied. But what it does show is a remarkable difference of emphasis. We have seen that Daniel 7 and Zechariah 9–14 provided Jesus with some of the figures most central in his explanation of his mission and, in the case of Daniel 7, most often alluded to. Yet in the whole New Testament we find not a single use of Zechariah 9:9 and 13:7, nor even of Daniel 7:13–14 except in Revelation, beyond simply recording and echoing Jesus' own use of them. The apostolic preaching and teaching made frequent appeal to the Old Testament, but these are not the testimonies which recur. The Christian church dutifully recorded Jesus' use of these passages, and no doubt if questioned would have agreed with it, but it shows no enthusiasm to introduce them into its own message. Even bearing in mind that we possess only a small part of early Christian teaching, and that we have studied the use of only two sections of the Old Testament, the virtual neglect by the Christians of the first century of these favourite passages of their Master is surely remarkable.

3. *A corollary.* We discussed in our first chapter the commonly held view that the 'sayings of Jesus' in the Gospels are the product of the thinking and teaching of the New Testament church. We suggested as one of the data which might justify us in questioning this view the possibility that a distinction might emerge at certain points between the use of the Old Testament ascribed to Jesus in the Gospels and that found in the preaching and writing of the early church.[201] If the teaching ascribed to Jesus is not in fact that on which the New Testament church would have laid its emphasis, it is not likely that the latter was the creative influence behind this teaching. Our last paragraph has now given some substance to this objection, even though in a very limited field. The Messianic figures of Daniel 7 and Zechariah 9–14, which together form such a large part of Jesus' explanation of his mission from the Old Testament, are, with the exception of Zechariah 12:10, virtually ignored by the rest of the New Testament.[202] The most likely reason for the ascription to Jesus of a considerable use of these passages, by a church which did not itself make use of them, is that he did in fact lay emphasis on them.[203]

[201] See above, pp. 23–24.

[202] C. H. Dodd (*Scriptures*, p. 107) lists these passages among the 'primary sources of testimonies' in 'the Bible of the early Church'. Had he distinguished between the reported sayings of Jesus and the church's own use of the OT, these two passages could not have appeared under this heading.

[203] *Cf.* also the argument of S. L. Edgar (*NTS* 9 (1962/3), p. 62), that

At the same point in the first chapter we suggested two other tests of the validity of our presupposition of the substantial authenticity of the use of the Old Testament ascribed to Jesus, *i.e.* the consistency and the originality of the pattern presented. In our final section we shall develop our conclusion that the recorded uses of the Old Testament do in fact display both an originality as against currently-accepted applications, and a consistency in the Messianic character and eschatological scheme which they envisage, which can hardly have arisen by chance. They demand a creative thinker of considerable ability and originality, especially in the conservative milieu of orthodox Judaism. Is there a more likely source for this new approach to the Old Testament than the teacher from Nazareth?

Considering then both the consistency and the originality in the use of the Old Testament in the sayings ascribed to Jesus, and the clear difference in this matter between these sayings and the rest of the New Testament, we feel that the results of our study tend to confirm the hypothesis of the substantial authenticity of the tradition of dominical sayings on which it has proceeded.

IV. THE ORIGINALITY AND INFLUENCE OF JESUS

a. The originality of Jesus

In the Jewish world of the first century AD Jesus of Nazareth was a man apart. This is seen not least in his use of the Old Testament. While second to none in his reverence for the Scriptures, his diligent study of them and his acceptance of their teaching, and while employing an exegesis which differed from that of his contemporaries generally only in a closer adherence to the original sense where misunderstanding or misuse was the rule, he yet applied the Old Testament in a way which was quite unparalleled. The essence of his new application was that he saw the fulfilment of the predictions and foreshadowings of the Old Testament in himself and his work.

From this sprang his constant emphasis on the true character of the Messiah not as a conqueror and ruler, in any worldly or

---

the contrast between the respect for context in OT quotations ascribed to Jesus and the lack of such respect in those by the Evangelists themselves is a mark of the authenticity of the former.

political sense, whether violent or peaceful, but as one who through lowliness and suffering would achieve the spiritual restoration of his people to the blessing and the knowledge of God, and would receive an eternal and universal dominion above and beyond all national and political power, in which he would share the glory, the functions, and indeed the very nature of God himself. It was this conception that governed his selection of and emphasis on aspects of Old Testament Messianism to which his contemporaries gave a secondary place, and his studious avoidance of those passages which could convey the opposite impression; when he did use such passages it was in a way which made misunderstanding of his meaning impossible.

From this same source too sprang his insistence that in his coming 'the time is fulfilled', that there was no need any longer to look to the future for the fulfilment of the hopes of the Old Testament, but that in his coming the day of salvation had come, the last days had arrived, and God had come to bless his people; from this point men would live in the eschatological age, and in the community of his followers the blessings promised to Israel would be realized, until he should come again to bring this age to an end. This 'inaugurated eschatology', which saw the last days as begun, but yet to be completed in the future, is Jesus' unique approach to the soteriological predictions and types of the Old Testament. To his coming the whole Old Testament had looked forward; not only the actual predictions in the prophets and the psalms, but the very pattern of God's working recorded in the Old Testament was preparing for the final and perfect work of God, which in his coming had begun. In him we move from shadows to reality; in him God's purposes are fulfilled at last, and all that now remains is the working out of this fulfilment to its final consummation. Thus Jesus' use of the Old Testament falls into a single coherent scheme, with himself as the focus.

Such a use of the Old Testament was not only original; it was revolutionary. It was such that a Jew who did not accept it must violently oppose it. It is not surprising that a community founded on this teaching soon found itself irreconcilably divided from those Jews who still looked forward to a Messiah.

b. The influence of Jesus

The Christian church was founded on this distinctive and revolutionary use of the Old Testament. With regard to those passages of the Old Testament whose use we have specifically studied in this chapter, we have found, despite a considerable difference of emphasis, an almost unbroken agreement with both the exegesis and the application of Jesus. The Matthean use of Zechariah 11:12–13 was the only original application of any part of these chapters in the New Testament apart from the book of Revelation, nor do the early Fathers seem to have displayed much originality except in the beginning during the second century of a tendency to allegorize. Apart from the book of Revelation, moreover, there is no significant dependence on current Jewish use of the Old Testament. The school in which the writers of the early church learned to use the Old Testament was that of Jesus. If we could have developed our comparative study further we should have found many more evidences of the derivation of the Christian use of the Old Testament from Jesus: the development of the theme of the Servant, the selection of Messianic testimonies, such as Psalm 110:1 and the 'stone' passages, the whole eschatological scheme, and the further development of the sort of typology introduced by Jesus, which reached its full flowering in the letter to the Hebrews. It is all the more remarkable that this distinctive development, often in such strong opposition to traditional Jewish theology, took place entirely, in the earlier period, among Jews. This is the measure of the influence of Jesus.

The only significant attempt to marry Jesus' application of Old Testament passages with a brand of Jewish theology was by the book of Revelation. The result, as we have seen, was the use of Daniel 7 in two quite different ways within the same book, and a new application of Daniel 7:13–14 and Zechariah 12:10ff., which became the dominant one in the early, and indeed the later, church, but which was not that of Jesus. This result is not surprising, for the approach of Jesus to the Old Testament is so clearly contrasted with that of his Jewish contemporaries that they cannot be combined as they stand. The Christian use of the Old Testament is original, and stands inevitably alone.

C. H. Dodd[204] describes the Christian use of the Old Testament as 'a considerable intellectual feat', 'an achievement of interpretative imagination which results in the creation of an entirely new figure'. He continues, in a much-quoted passage, 'This is a piece of genuinely creative thinking. Who was responsible for it? The early Church, we are accustomed to say, and perhaps we can safely say no more. But creative thinking is rarely done by committees. . . . It is individual minds that originate. Whose was the originating mind here?' Various creative thinkers of the New Testament period, known and unknown, are suggested. 'But the New Testament itself avers that it was Jesus Christ Himself who first directed the minds of His followers to certain parts of the scriptures as those in which they might find illumination upon the meaning of His mission and destiny. . . . To account for the beginning of this most original and fruitful process of rethinking the Old Testament we found need to postulate a creative mind. The Gospels offer us one. Are we compelled to reject the offer?'[205]

We believe that our study has given us some grounds for concluding that we not only can but must accept the offer. The source of the distinctive Christian use of the Old Testament was not the creative thinking of the primitive community, but that of its founder. It was not the early church which inscribed its theology on the blank cheque of its Master's teaching, but Jesus whose teaching and life initiated that theology. The church did not create Jesus, but Jesus created the church.

The reason for this was not just that he was a creative thinker with new ideas, but that he was the one 'of whom Moses in the law and also the prophets wrote', and that he himself knew this, and 'beginning with Moses and all the prophets, he interpreted to them in all the scriptures the things concerning himself'.

[204] *Scriptures*, pp. 109–110.

[205] *Cf.* S. Amsler, *op. cit.*, p. 94. He notices 'a common basic orientation' in the NT appeal to the OT, expressed in different forms by the different authors, and concludes that 'we are confronted not with an individual creation by one or other of the authors of the New Testament, but with a datum of the primitive gospel tradition, the origin of which cannot, it seems to us, be elsewhere than in the teaching and the way of life of Jesus himself'. See also E. E. Ellis, *Paul*, pp. 112–113, and for a similar argument, J. A. Baird, *op. cit.*, pp. 30–31.

APPENDIX A

THE REFERENCE OF MARK 13:24–27

We have had to make frequent reference to this passage, which is, in the words of J. A. T. Robinson, 'a pastiche of Old Testament allusions'.[1] The application of the various passages alluded to plainly depends on the intended reference of these verses, and as this is a disputed point, involving several controversial issues, a separate treatment seems necessary.

We shall first try to assess the nature of the problem; then we shall sketch briefly the main solutions which have been proposed; and on this basis we shall proceed to a detailed presentation of the arguments for the solution here adopted.

I. THE PROBLEM

R. A. Knox, writing on Luke 21:25–33, says, 'If the world had come to an end soon after the destruction of Jerusalem in AD 70, the great eschatological chapter (Matthew xxiv, Mark xiii, Luke xxi) would present no difficulty.'[2] It is, he claims, only the verses 25–28 (the Lucan parallel to Mk. 13:24–27) 'that introduce the idea of world catastrophe'. The rest of Luke 21 is, he believes, to the unbiased reader, clearly referring to the destruction of Jerusalem. The same may be said of Mark 13, at least as far as verse 31; the *prima facie* reference of verses 32ff. is to a coming of Christ differentiated from the fall of Jerusalem, and at some unknown time in the future. But Mark 13:24–27 appears either to be out of place, or to place the second coming of Christ at the time of the fall of Jerusalem.

It is this fact as much as any other which has led to the supposition that Mark 13 is a rather unintelligent conflation of oracles, Christian or otherwise, with originally quite different references.[3] Before endorsing any such radical theory, however, it is as well to consider the many attempts to explain the structure of the chapter on the assumption of its essentially dominical origin (whether or not it is regarded as an original unity), to see whether any of them accounts satisfactorily for the evidence.

II. PROPOSED SOLUTIONS

A rough classification of these into four groups will simplify the treatment, even if it means overriding some considerable disagreement between the scholars so associated.

[1] *Jesus and His Coming*, p. 56.

[2] *The Epistles and Gospels for Sundays and Holidays* (London, 1946), p. 11.

[3] Esp. the 'Little Apocalypse' theory, initiated by T. Colani in 1864, and surveyed and criticized in its various ramifications since that time by G. R. Beasley-Murray, *Jesus and the Future* (London, 1954).

(i) The *prima facie* reading is that there is at several points in the chapter an abrupt transition between the fall of Jerusalem and the Parousia. This view is normally combined with an analysis of the material into separate sources, which have been conflated in a rather *gauche* manner.[4] This, of course, is a characteristic of theories of the 'Little Apocalypse' type, but is by no means restricted to those who hold that much of the chapter is from a source other than Jesus. Indeed there are some, though few (at least among biblical scholars: a survey of less erudite opinion might produce a different proportion), who believe that Jesus did in fact utter all these words in the sequence in which Mark records them, with a reference abruptly alternating between AD 70 and the Parousia. The tendency, however, among those who maintain the original unity of the discourse is to minimize the distinction between the two points of reference, seeing a close 'theological' connection between the fall of Jerusalem and the Parousia. This will be treated as the second solution.

The first solution in a pure form is therefore uncommon, and is isolated here primarily for the sake of logical completeness. It is a view which is prompted especially by the embarrassment which verse 30 creates for those who wish to see the whole chapter from verse 24 on as referring to the Parousia. Such subterfuges as the suggestion (going back to Jerome) that γενεά means the Jewish race are now universally condemned, and that word is given its true meaning of 'generation'. The proposed solution is that Jesus speaks first of events leading up to the fall of Jerusalem (verses 5–22; some would, however, see some even of this section as referring to the time preceding the Parousia), then of the Parousia (verses 24–27), returns in verses 28–31 to the fall of Jerusalem, and finally again in verses 32ff. to the Parousia.[5]

(ii) The most popular solution by far among those who see the chapter as being essentially dominical throughout, and one which follows on from the last, is to explain the apparent confusion of the fall of Jerusalem and the Parousia by a doctrine of 'prophetic perspective'. The imminent act of judgment on the Jewish nation is a foreshadowing of the final act of judgment at the Parousia. The long ages between are telescoped in the prophetic perspective to a negligible length, and in the events of AD 70 the Parousia, though clearly conceived as a distinct and more distant event, is already in essence present. G. R. Beasley-Murray[6] lists a large number of modern exponents of this solution, and their number is constantly added to.

There is indeed much to commend the view that Jesus saw the coming fall of Jerusalem as a herald and type of the final judgment. That such an idea was in his mind when uttering the contents of Mark 13, whether piecemeal

[4] See esp. the discussion by M.-J. Lagrange, *RB* n.s. 3 (1906), pp. 382–411.

[5] See, *e.g.*, A. Carr, *The Gospel according to St. Matthew* (Cambridge, 1894), pp. 265–272; A. Plummer, *An Exegetical Commentary on the Gospel according to S. Matthew* (London, 1909), p. 338; P. A. Micklem, *St. Matthew* (London, 1917), p. 235.

[6] *Jesus and the Future*, pp. 131–141, 147–167.

or as a whole, is entirely probable. We may even agree with C. E. B. Cranfield that 'the impending judgement on Jerusalem and the events connected with it are for Jesus as it were a transparent object in the foreground through which he sees the last events before the End, which they indeed foreshadow'.[7]

But this gives us no warrant for ignoring the very definite temporal link which Jesus made between the events of verses 5–22 and those of verses 24–27 ('in those days, after that tribulation', v. 24, accentuated by the Matthean addition of 'immediately'). This is a connection not in principle only, but in time, which is only made more explicit by verse 30. We cannot invoke the typological relation to explain away the chronological juxtaposition which the text makes quite plain.

The difficulties are created entirely by the assumption that verses 24–27 refer to the Parousia, as an eschatological event which is still, for us, in the future. From this arise the awkward transitions in the chapter, and the embarrassment of verses 24a and 30, which leave no room for a time-lag of 2,000 years. This assumption, common to all proponents of solutions (i) and (ii), is questioned and rejected in our two further solutions. In that case there is no time-lag to explain away, and verse 30 loses its terror; the doctrine of 'prophetic perspective' becomes unnecessary as an apologetic device.

(iii) The most radical solution to our problem, while still maintaining the essentially dominical origin of the whole discourse, is that which sees the whole as referring to the events of AD 70, and nothing more. This line of interpretation was fully developed as early as 1878 by J. S. Russell.[8] His view is essentially that the whole of Matthew 24 and 25 describes one and the same period, that of the fall of Jerusalem, the *συντέλεια τοῦ αἰῶνος* ('end of the world', RV; 'close of the age', RSV), which he interprets as meaning the close of the Jewish age. This is the Parousia, and there is no New Testament warrant to look for any other. 'We are compelled, therefore, by all these considerations, and chiefly by regard for the authority of Him whose word cannot be broken, to conclude that the Parousia, or second coming of Christ, with its connected and concomitant events, did take place, according to the Saviour's own prediction, at the period when Jerusalem was destroyed, and before the passing away of "that generation".'[9]

This radical approach has commended itself to others, who do not necessarily share Russell's belief that the second coming of Christ took place in AD 70, but who agree with him in taking the whole of this chapter

[7] *Mark*, p. 405.

[8] *The Parousia*. The first edition (London, 1878) was published anonymously, the second (1887) under the author's name. References are to the second edn. See G. R. Beasley-Murray (*Jesus and the Future*, pp. 167–171) for a discussion of Russell's view.

[9] *Op. cit.*, p. 549. L. Gaston (*op. cit.*, pp. 483–487) suggests that Matthew interpreted Mk. 13 to the same effect, and so believed that the Parousia had occurred in AD 70!

as referring exclusively to the fall of Jerusalem. Such writers are E. P. Gould[10] and A. Feuillet.[11]

The exegetical arguments in favour of this solution, at least with reference to verses 24–27, will be fully considered shortly, for on these verses this solution and the one still to be considered run parallel. On verses 32–37, however, the denial of a reference to a second coming still in the future depends, at least in the most recent exposition by Feuillet, on a quite untenable exegesis of *παρουσία* and *συντέλεια τοῦ αἰῶνος* in Matthew as referring respectively to Christ's judgment on the Jews (in the fall of Jerusalem) and the end of the old (Jewish) era.[12]

But while we must part company with Feuillet on the nature and time of the Parousia, and cannot accept that the whole chapter refers to AD 70, we feel that the exponents of this solution are right to challenge the assumption that verses 24–27 must refer to an event subsequent to and different in character from the destruction of Jerusalem.

(iv) We have quoted above the opinion of R. A. Knox that it is only verses 24–27 of Mark 13 which create the difficulties we are considering. Apart from these verses he maintains that the obvious reference is to the fall of Jerusalem as far as verse 31, and from verse 32 to the Parousia, regarded as a future eschatological event, and distinct from the fall of Jerusalem. It is this observation which has led some, while not questioning the Parousia reference of verses 32ff., to postulate that verses 24–27 do not refer to the Parousia, but are in fact a symbolic description of the fall of Jerusalem and its implications. This fourth solution might, therefore, be described as a mediating position between the first two and the third. In common with the former it recognizes the Parousia reference of the latter part of the chapter, but in common with the latter it denies any such reference in verses 24–27.

[10] *The Gospel according to Saint Mark* (Edinburgh, 1896), pp. 250–255.

[11] 'Le Sens du Mot Parousie dans l'Évangile de Matthieu' in *The Background of the New Testament and its Eschatology*, ed. W. D. Davies and D. Daube (Cambridge, 1956), pp. 261–280. G. R. Beasley-Murray (*Jesus and the Future*, pp. 169–170 n. 4) mentions others who have accepted Russell's position.

[12] Briefly, the following objections stand against Feuillet's exegesis: (i) To argue from the peculiarly Matthean terminology is to begin at the wrong end, if the Matthean account is derived from the Marcan; Mk. 13 must be treated on its own merits. (ii) It is not the word *παρουσία* which leads most people to interpret these verses of the second coming, but the sense of the passage in its Marcan form, where this word does not occur. This renders very improbable Feuillet's proposal of a different exegesis on the basis of a suggested meaning of *παρουσία* which is admittedly different from that in all other NT occurrences (except, he claims, Jas. 5:7–8). (iii) A key point of Feuillet's argument is the interpretation of 'those days' (Mt. 24:29) as referring back to the *παρουσία* mentioned in v. 27. But 'those days' is derived from Mk. 13:24, where there is no equivalent to Mt. 24:27 for it to refer back to. In any case, the whole point of Mt. 24:27 is to *differentiate* the Parousia from the events of AD 70 as described in the previous verses. (iv) The argument on *συντέλεια τοῦ αἰῶνος* depends on a single (incomplete) parallel in Heb. 9:26, against all other NT uses of the phrase.

This view, which was once widely held,[13] is most fully presented in recent times by J. M. Kik,[14] and is advocated by R. A. Knox[15] and R. V. G. Tasker.[16] P. Carrington, who interprets verses 24–27 of the fall of Jerusalem,[17] and then separates off verses 32ff. as a completely new section, 'The Advent Parables',[18] may also be classed under this heading, though he is non-committal on the nature and date of the Parousia.[19]

That it is this solution which is here being advocated will by now be obvious. We proceed to an exegetical study of verses 24–27, especially in terms of the Old Testament passages quoted or alluded to.

III. AN EXEGETICAL STUDY OF MARK 13:24–27

a. *The context*

The disciples' question in Mark is concerned solely with the destruction of the Temple as predicted by Jesus in verse 2, which they summarize as *ταῦτα* ('these things') and *ταῦτα πάντα* ('all these things') (verse 4). The Matthean version introduces the secondary question about the 'Parousia' and the 'close of the age'. Whether or not we see these additions as an editorial attempt to render the question wide enough to cover the whole chapter, the impression is certainly given that we are to expect a statement on the fall of Jerusalem, to which Matthew warns us to expect an additional statement on the Parousia.[20]

Verses 5–13 (Mt. 24:4–14) describe the situation which must obtain before the catastrophe occurs, the coming of false Christs, international upheaval and war, and persecution of the disciples, together with a world-wide proclamation of the gospel. That these events are the preliminaries to the fall of Jerusalem, not to the Parousia, is indicated (a) by the fact that the whole section is couched in terms of what his actual hearers are to witness and experience, the second person being used throughout in warnings and instructions; and (b) by the close link with the following section by 'But when you see. . . .' (Matthew is still clearer: 'Then the end will come. *So* when you see. . . .'), which implies that while all the events of verses 5–13 must occur during the preceding period, the events of verses 14ff. are to be the immediate prelude to the catastrophe envisaged – and it is generally agreed that these verses refer to the events of AD 66–70.

[13] Up to the seventeenth century it was quite commonly held; see M. Poole, *Annotations on the Holy Bible* (1683–1685), reprinted as *A Commentary on the Holy Bible* (London, 1962–1963), vol. 3, pp. 115–116. For a nineteenth-century exposition see J. A. Alexander, *The Gospel according to Mark* (1858, repr. London, 1960), pp. 356–361.

[14] *Matthew Twenty-Four* (Philadelphia, 1948).

[15] *Op. cit.*, pp. 11–13; 278–279.

[16] *The Gospel according to Saint Matthew* (London, 1961), pp. 225–228.

[17] *According to Mark* (Cambridge, 1960), pp. 280–289; *cf.* p. 291.

[18] *Ibid.*, pp. 293–294, 298.

[19] *Ibid.*, pp. 289–291.

[20] G. E. Ladd (*op. cit.*, p. 306) suggests that the *ταῦτα πάντα* of Mk. 13:4 also refers to the 'eschatological consummation'. *Cf.* V. Taylor, *Mark*, p. 502. In the Marcan context this seems improbable.

Verses 14–23 (Mt. 24:15–25) then describe the events connected with the siege of Jerusalem but without describing the actual fall of the city. This leads one to expect a further section which will complete the prophecy by stating that the city will actually be destroyed, and mentioning the significance and effects of this destruction. When one begins to read verse 24 – 'But in those days, after that tribulation, . . .' – the impression is virtually irresistible that one is about to be introduced to the catastrophe to which verses 14–22 have been leading up. The Matthean addition of 'immediately' only strengthens this impression, and lays a heavy burden of proof on those who suggest that verses 24–27 refer to anything other than the fall of Jerusalem.

Verses 28–30 (Mt. 24:32–34) confirm this impression. Not only do they speak still in terms of what his actual hearers are to see and hear, and the way they must react, but they also reintroduce the terms *ταῦτα* and *ταῦτα πάντα* from the disciples' question. If these terms there referred to the fall of Jerusalem, the presumption is that they do so again here. When the signs outlined in the preceding verses (14–22) occur, you may be sure that the catastrophe described in verses 24–27, and summarized as *ταῦτα πάντα*, is at hand. All will be fulfilled within the generation.[21] Given this context, it would take a quite incontestable exegesis of verses 24–27 in terms of the Parousia to shake the conviction that the reference must be to the fall of Jerusalem. As we shall see, such exegesis is not forthcoming.

We maintain then that unless the wording demands it, the introduction of a reference to the Parousia into this chapter before verse 31 is quite gratuitous, and destroys its natural sequence of thought. There is, of course, a reference to the Parousia in Matthew 24:27, but this is with the express purpose of differentiating it from the events under consideration, stating that it is not to be confused with the events at the siege and fall of Jerusalem: it will be no localized event, but universally and unmistakably recognized. The reference to the Parousia here, therefore, further confirms that in this section of the chapter the Parousia is *not* being described.

In verse 32 (Mt. 24:36) we are introduced, it seems, to a new subject. There is, first, the fact that whereas the preceding verses have described an event shortly to occur, and definitely within a generation, this verse introduces an event of the date of which Jesus explicitly disclaims any knowledge. Further, the phrase *περὶ δὲ τῆς ἡμέρας ἐκείνης* ('but of that day') is as clearly as possible setting the day it describes in contrast with what has preceded. The phrase *ἡ ἡμέρα ἐκείνη* ('that day') is a new one in this chapter. The events of AD 66–70 have been described as *ταῦτα πάντα* ('all these things'), and as *ἐκεῖναι αἱ ἡμέραι* ('those days') (verses 17, 19, 24; and Mt. 24:22), but the singular has not yet occurred. The inference is clear that a new and distinct day is being described.[22]

[21] *Cf.* Mt. 23:32–36 and Lk. 23:28–31, in both of which Jesus predicts a judgment on the Jews within the living generation. Mt. 23:36 is closely parallel to Mk. 13:30. These parallel passages support a similar reference here.

[22] *ἡ ἡμέρα ἐκείνη* is used also for the final day of judgment in Mt. 7:22; Lk. 10:12; 17:31; 21:34. Also in the Epistles, *e.g.* 2 Thes. 1:10; 2 Tim.

In both Mark 13:32ff., therefore, and, more obviously still, Matthew 24:36ff., we come to a new section, in which the fall of Jerusalem is left behind, and the Parousia introduced, thus answering the second half of the Matthean version of the disciples' question.[23] In Matthew 24 this section is greatly expanded with Q material, and continues without a break into the peculiarly Matthean chapter 25 with its parables of judgment. Thus Matthew 24:36 – 25:46 is a unity in that it all refers to the final judgment, which coincides with the Parousia.

We conclude, then, that the context suggests strongly that verses 24–27 will describe the fall of Jerusalem, and not the Parousia; indeed, unless the wording makes such an exegesis quite impossible, we might say that the context demands it. But in fact the wording not only allows, but even encourages such an interpretation, when seen against its Old Testament background.

b. Verses 24–25 (Mt. 24:29)

The phrases which make up these verses are part of the stock-in-trade of Old Testament prophecy, and they are used to describe especially political disasters, and the destruction of cities and nations, particularly those which played a leading role. The actual phrases used are drawn from Isaiah 13:10 and 34:4; of these the former predicts the doom of Babylon, the latter that of 'all the nations', but with special reference to Edom.[24] Further examples may be seen in Ezekiel 32:7 (concerning Egypt), Amos 8:9 (concerning the Northern Kingdom of Israel), Joel 2:10 (concerning Judah), and constantly in Joel 3–4 concerning God's judgment on Judah and other nations.

That Jesus' use of such language is intended in the same sense, as a prediction of national disaster(s), is recognized even by many who do not accept the reference of these verses to the fall of Jerusalem. H. B. Swete writes, 'In all these cases physical phenomena are used to describe the upheaval of dynasties, or great moral and spiritual changes; and it is unnecessary to exact any other meaning from the words when they are adopted by Christ.'[25] He goes on to apply the verses to 'dynastic and social revolutions' of the period between AD 70 and the Parousia, though allowing, in defiance of his own stated principle, that they may also refer to 'a collapse of the present order of Nature immediately before the παρουσία'.

1:12, 18; 4:8. *Cf.* also Lk. 17:24, and the singular ἡμέρα κρίσεως in Mt. 10:15; 11:22, 24; 12:36.

[23] So also D. M. Roark, *NT* 7 (1964/5), pp. 123ff.; on pp. 126–127 he makes this same division, though regarding vv. 23–31 (Mt.) as parenthetical, stating what will *not* happen at the fall of Jerusalem: vv. 29–31 therefore describe what the Parousia will be like when it does come, which will *not* be at that time.

[24] This reading is disputed by E. J. Kissane, *The Book of Isaiah*[2] (Dublin, 1960), vol. 1, p. 375, who proposes to read אָדָם for אֱדוֹם. There is no textual support for this alteration, which is well criticized by E. J. Young, *Westminster Theological Journal* 27 (1964/5), pp. 97–100.

[25] *Mark*, p. 311. *Cf.* also B. P. W. S. Hunt, *Primitive Gospel Sources* (London, 1951), pp. 71–72.

More consistent are those who restrict the application of Jesus' words to their Old Testament sphere of reference, *i.e.* to national disaster. And if this is so, it is hard to see a more obvious reference than to the fall of Jerusalem and the eclipse of the Jewish state. J. S. Russell makes the point vividly: 'Is it not reasonable that the doom of Jerusalem should be depicted in language as glowing and rhetorical as the destruction of Babylon, or Bozrah, or Tyre? ... If these symbols therefore were proper to represent the fall of Babylon, why should they be improper to set forth a still greater catastrophe – the destruction of Jerusalem? ... The conclusion then to which we are irresistibly led, is, that the imagery employed by our Lord in this prophetic discourse is not inappropriate to the dissolution of the Jewish state and polity which took place at the destruction of Jerusalem.'[26]

In view of the clear suitability of the language to describe the downfall of the Jewish nation and its capital, there is no need to adopt the intriguing suggestion of R. A. Knox[27] that the reference is to the dynastic changes and revolutions in Rome in the year of the Four Emperors (69 AD). Not only is it far less likely that Jesus would fasten on events in far-off Rome than on what was to him and his hearers of far more significance, the destruction of the Holy City and the eclipse of God's chosen people; it is also to be noted that the Old Testament passages from which these words of Jesus are drawn refer not primarily, or even at all, to dynastic changes, but to the destruction, as an act of divine judgment, of nations. We may therefore confidently conclude that Mark 13:24–25 is a description in the symbolic terms of Old Testament prophecy of the imminent destruction of Jerusalem, and the end of Israel as a nation.

We must therefore protest against the use of such terms as 'celestial signs' and 'cosmic signs' with regard to these verses. C. E. B. Cranfield, who employs these terms, does so in spite of the recognition that 'this is picture-language which we must not attempt to compress into a literal interpretation'.[28] This last observation is correct, and should prevent the use of such misleading terms. Jesus is not predicting that strange astronomical events will occur; he is predicting the judgment of God on the Jewish nation.[29]

[26] *Op. cit.*, pp. 80–81. *Cf.* for a similar interpretation, E. P. Gould, *Mark*, p. 250; A. Plummer, *The Gospel according to St. Mark* (Cambridge, 1914), p. 302; P. P. Levertoff, *St. Matthew* (London, 1940), p. 80; P. Carrington, *Mark*, pp. 280–283; R. V. G. Tasker, *Matthew*, pp. 225–227. Not all of these would agree that the reference is to AD 70, but all would see a reference to political rather than astronomical catastrophe.

[27] *Op. cit.*, pp. 11, 278. *Cf.* R. V. G. Tasker, *Matthew*, p. 226.

[28] *SJT* 6 (1953), pp. 301–302.

[29] 'Only a pitiful prosiness could imagine that Jesus meant an actual dropping of the stars upon the earth' (D. Lamont, *Christ and the World of Thought* (Edinburgh, 1934), p. 266). The strictures of M. S. Terry on nineteenth-century exegetes seem to be still relevant: he writes (*Biblical Hermeneutics*, 1883; new edn. 1890, reprinted Grand Rapids, 1961, p. 466n.), 'We might fill volumes with extracts showing how exegetes and writers on NT doctrine assume as a principle not to be questioned that such highly wrought language as Matt. xxiv, 29–31; 1 Thess. iv, 16; 2 Pet. iii, 10, 12,

c. Verse 26 and the use of Daniel 7:13

Here we come to the crux of the question; for while many are prepared to accept that verses that 24–25 might be a symbolic description of the fall of Jerusalem, verse 26 seems to dispel any such idea. For here is the coming of the Son of man referred to in so many words. We must then either identify the Parousia with the events of AD 70, or admit that the reference is not to the fall of Jerusalem at all.

This argument assumes that Daniel 7:13, and Jesus' quotations of it, must be references to the Parousia, and that this is all that can be intended by the term 'coming'. When, however, we examine both the original meaning of Daniel 7:13, and the various applications of it by Jesus, we are forced to reconsider this assumption.[30]

Our discussion of the meaning of Daniel 7:13 in its Old Testament context[31] led us to the conclusion that its keynote is one of vindication and exaltation to an everlasting dominion, and that the 'coming' of verse 13 was a coming to God to receive power, not a 'descent' to earth. When we studied Jesus' use of these verses, we found that in every case this same theme was the point of the allusion, and in particular that nowhere (unless here) was verse 13 interpreted of his coming to earth at the Parousia.[32] In particular the reference in Mark 14:62, where the wording is clearly parallel to that in the present verse, was to his imminent vindication and power, with a secondary reference to a manifestation of that power in the near future. Thus the expectation that Jesus would in fact use Daniel 7:13 in the sense in which it was written is amply confirmed by his actual allusions. He saw in that verse a prediction of his imminent exaltation to an authority which supersedes that of the earthly powers which have set themselves against God.

We did, however, distinguish three stages in the application of Daniel 7:13–14.[33] It was applied (a) to his exaltation to authority immediately after the resurrection, (b) to a manifestation of that authority in the lifetime of his contemporaries, and (c) to the culmination of the same authority in the final judgment. Which of these three stages of application is here in view the context must decide.

But the context here is quite unambiguous. Jesus is speaking of the fall of

---

taken almost *verbatim* from OT prophecies of judgment on nations and kingdoms which long ago perished, must be literally understood. . . . It will require more than assertion to convince thoughtful men that the figurative language of Isaiah and Daniel, admitted on all hands to be such in those ancient prophets, is to be literally interpreted when used by Jesus or Paul.'

[30] For a similar approach *cf.* G. B. Caird, *op. cit.*, pp. 20–22, arriving at the same exegesis of this passage.

[31] See Excursus 3, above, pp. 169–171.

[32] See above, pp. 145–146, and for details, pp. 139–144. It is extraordinary that L. Gaston (*op. cit.*, pp. 384–392), while arguing persuasively that other allusions to Dn. 7 do not refer to the Parousia, assumes without question that Mk. 13:26 is the one exception to the rule.

[33] See p. 145.

Jerusalem. This is generally admitted of verses 5–23, and we have seen that the context suggests that it is also true of verses 24–27. We must, therefore, accept here, as we have seen reason to postulate elsewhere, that Jesus is using Daniel 7:13 as a prediction of that authority which he exercised when in AD 70 the Jewish nation and its leaders, who had condemned him, were overthrown, and Jesus was vindicated as the recipient of all power from the Ancient of Days.[34] The use is thus closely similar to that in Mark 14:62, except that here the reference to a specific historic manifestation of his authority, which was there secondary, is now primary.[35] Jesus, exalted after his death and resurrection to receive his everlasting dominion, will display it within the generation (verse 30) by an act of judgment on the nation and capital of the authorities who presumed to judge him.[36] Then they will see (ὄψονται; *cf.* Mk. 14:62 ὄψεσθε) for themselves that their time of power is finished, and it is to him that God has given all power in heaven and earth.

What then of the language of verse 26 which seems to demand so inevitably a reference to the Parousia? The 'coming' (ἐρχόμενον) is derived from the אתה (Thdt ἐρχόμενος, LXX ἤρχετο) of Daniel 7:13, and must be interpreted accordingly; and there, as we have seen, it is a coming to God to receive power, not a coming to earth.[37] In any case, Mark 14:62, with its parallelism of 'sitting' and 'coming', warns us against a literal interpretation.[38] The clouds also do not require a quasi-literal interpretation as the vehicles of a descent to earth. Clouds are a common piece of Old Testament symbolism, of the power of God, especially in judgment (Is. 19:1; *cf.* Ps. 97:2, 3; 104:3).[39] In the clouds of Daniel 7:13, and their use by Jesus, there is no need to see any other significance. Where Jesus used the symbolic language of the Old Testament, it is perverse to look for a literal application of his words.[40]

d. The allusion to Zechariah 12:10ff. (Mt. 24:30)

The Matthean parallel to verse 26 includes the words καὶ τότε κόψονται πᾶσαι αἱ φυλαὶ τῆς γῆς, a loose quotation of Zechariah 12:12 וספדה הארץ משפחות משפחות לבד ('the land shall mourn, each family by itself'). The

[34] G. R. Beasley-Murray (*Mark Thirteen*, p. 90) recognizes the emphasis of vv. 26–27 on 'the gathering of the new Israel', and their silence on the usual aspects of the Parousia, and explains this by the context, which is a prediction of the destruction of the Temple. The surprise which he feels at the content of these verses would be dispelled by the recognition that they do not refer to the Parousia at all, but, as both context and content suggest, to the fall of Jerusalem.

[35] So T. F. Glasson (*Advent*, p. 195) argues from the reference in Mk. 14:62 to a similar reference originally intended here.

[36] *Cf.* P. Benoit, *Matthieu*, p. 141.

[37] *Cf.* P. Carrington, *Mark*, pp. 283–284.

[38] *Cf.* J. M. Kik, *op. cit.*, pp. 82–85.

[39] For further examples and discussion see R. H. Gundry, *op. cit.*, p. 231 n. 4; W. K. L. Clarke, *Theology* 31 (1935), pp. 63–65.

[40] *Cf.* E. P. Gould, *Mark*, pp. 251–252; G. B. Caird, *op. cit.*, pp. 21–22.

Matthean text is normally translated 'Then all the tribes of the *earth* will mourn'. But it is pointed out that the reference in Zechariah 12:10–14 is explicitly to a mourning of the tribes of *Israel*, the tribes of David, Nathan, Levi and Shimei being specified, and a final 'all the families that are left' extending the scope to the whole *nation*. It is clear then that in Zechariah 12:12 הארץ means 'the *land* (of Palestine)', and משפחות refers to the tribes or families within the nation. T. W. Manson[41] therefore concludes that in Matthew 24:30 'that original sense has been abandoned', and an international mourning substituted for the national.

It is, however, questionable whether the Matthean wording has any such intention. The terms *γῆ* ('earth' or 'land') and *φυλή* ('tribe') are used in the LXX of Zechariah 12:12 in the full recognition of their limited reference to the tribes of Judah, as verses 13–14 show, and it would seem reasonable to assume that Matthew so understood and used them unless there is evidence to the contrary. Moreover, in the New Testament (except for a formula in the book of Revelation) *φυλή* is invariably a technical term for the tribes of Israel.[42] That *ἡ γῆ* too could refer to Palestine is demonstrated probably by Mark 15:33 (= Mt. 27:45), and certainly by Luke 21:23, and Luke 4:25 (as the Old Testament account of the incident makes clear). It is regularly so used in the LXX. Thus the Matthean wording not only allows but suggests a national mourning, and since this is the clear meaning of both the MT and the LXX of Zechariah 12:10ff., it is hard to see why an international reference has ever been seen in Matthew. Perhaps this is felt to be appropriate to the apocalyptic style of a Parousia context, though it may be noted that the translation 'all the tribes of the land' has been adopted not only by those who accept a reference of these verses to AD 70,[43] but by some who hold that the Parousia is in view.[44]

We find then no justification for the translation 'all the tribes of the earth'. The reference is, as in Zechariah, to a mourning of the Jews. What are the implications of this conclusion for the reference of the verse?

While a mourning of the Jews at the Parousia in fulfilment of Zechariah 12:10ff. is a possible conception, the term 'all the tribes of the land' would be inappropriate to a period envisaged as subsequent to the fall of Jerusalem, as it presupposes a united Jewish people living within their own land. If, however, the reference is to the coming destruction of Jerusalem, seen as a specific act of judgment by the vindicated and exalted Jesus on the people who had rejected him (*cf.* Zc. 12:10, 'they shall look on me whom they have pierced'), the appropriateness of the quotation is clear. A destruction of the city could hardly fail to produce such a lamentation by the Jews.

We conclude then that, while the allusion to Zechariah 12:10ff. does not demand a reference in this verse to the fall of Jerusalem, any other

[41] *The Sayings of Jesus* (London, 1949), p. 242.

[42] *Cf.* also Rev. 5:5; 7:4–8; 21:12; but not the formula of Rev. 5:9; 7:9; 11:9; 13:7; 14:6.

[43] See R. A. Knox, *op. cit.*, p. 279; R. V. G. Tasker, *Matthew*, p. 230.

[44] See W. C. Allen, *The Gospel according to S. Matthew*[3] (Edinburgh, 1912), p. 259; R. H. Gundry, *op. cit.*, p. 234.

reference, and especially a reference to the Parousia, sits very uncomfortably upon it.

e. Verse 27 (Mt. 24:31)

To many, a reference to the Parousia and the end of the world is confirmed by this description of the angels gathering in the elect. This impression is derived from the English version rather than from the original. While ἄγγελος does indeed mean 'angel', its primary meaning is 'messenger'. This is found with reference to human messengers in Luke 7:24; 9:52; James 2:25, and in the three synoptic quotations of Malachi 3:1 (Mk. 1:2; Mt. 11:10; Lk. 7:27). The subject-matter of the New Testament inevitably gives to the secondary meaning 'angel' a large numerical majority over this primary meaning, but this does not necessarily create a presumption in favour of the former; the context must decide.

If our argument hitherto has been correct, the context favours strongly the primary meaning. For this verse describes the sequel to the fall of Jerusalem. The Jews are no longer the people of God; now the true people of God, chosen from all nations, 'from the four winds', will be brought in. The agents of this 'gathering of the elect' will be the preachers of the gospel, God's messengers, his ἄγγελοι.[45]

The language of the latter part of the verse is a compilation of Old Testament phrases concerned with the dispersion and regathering of the people of Israel. The sources seem to be Deuteronomy 30:4 and Zechariah 2:10 (EVV verse 6), with a further reference to Isaiah 27:13 in the 'loud trumpet call' of Matthew.[46] In such passages it is virtually impossible to distinguish between those which envisage a historic regathering of the exiles with no eschatological implications, and those which see this regathering as an accompaniment of the 'day of Yahweh'. But among such prophecies both Deuteronomy 30:4 and Zechariah 2:10 are as free as any from eschatological language, and the context in both suggests a simple prediction of a historic regathering of Israel from exile and dispersion. Isaiah 27:13 falls in a more eschatological passage, but still speaks in specifically local terms of those exiled in Assyria and Egypt returning to worship at Jerusalem. The Old Testament sources, therefore, do not demand any eschatological sense in this verse. As we have seen, they are typologically applied to the gathering of the Christian church, the true Israel; the events of AD 70 demonstrate that the Jewish nation has forfeited its special status, and it is in the community of Jesus' followers that the hopes of Israel are to be fulfilled.

We maintain, therefore, that while verse 27 would bear an eschatological reference, it is not less applicable to the historical gathering of the church in the years following AD 70. In so far as the Old Testament passages

[45] So R. A. Knox, *op. cit.*, p. 278; J. M. Kik, *op. cit.*, pp. 89–92; A. Richardson, *Introduction*, p. 278; P. Carrington, *Mark*, pp. 286–287; R. V. G. Tasker, *Matthew*, p. 227. B. P. W. S. Hunt (*op. cit.*, p. 72) sees this as the original meaning of the verse, but believes that its present position transfers the reference to the Parousia.

[46] See above, pp. 63–64; below, pp. 256–257.

alluded to are concerned with a historical gathering of Israel, this reference is perhaps the easier.

Our study of verses 24–27 has produced no objection to our understanding these verses, as their context virtually demands, as the climax of Jesus' prediction of the destruction of Jerusalem. The special consideration of the various Old Testament passages from which they are compiled adds several strong exegetical arguments in favour of this interpretation.

The symbolism is, of course, extravagant, but it is not more so than in its original use in the Old Testament. Moreover, the significance of the events so described warrants such language. AD 70 marked the end of an era. The nation which, from the days of Abraham, had been the unique people of God, would then be seen to be such no longer; Jesus and his church are the true Israel. The destruction of Jerusalem was more than an act of judgment: it was a symbol, and more than a symbol, of the inauguration of the kingdom of the Son of man.

The contents of Mark 13 now appear in a logical sequence. The abrupt transitions required by our first solution disappear, and there is no need to invoke 'prophetic perspective' to smooth them over. Verses 5–31 are entirely concerned with the events leading up to the destruction of Jerusalem and its Temple, culminating in verses 24–27 in a symbolic description of that event and its implications, with (verses 28–31) a warning of its imminence. The date of the Parousia, however, is unknown (verses 32ff.); it will be sudden and unexpected, and not even Jesus knows when it will be. The clear statement of this contrast in verse 32 rules out the interpretation which takes the whole chapter as referring to the events of AD 70, and justifies the twofold question of Matthew 24:3.

APPENDIX B

A DETAILED STUDY OF THE TEXT-FORM OF THE OLD TESTAMENT QUOTATIONS

We print here the detailed evidence from which the conclusions of chapter 2 above are drawn, arranged under the headings of that chapter.

II. QUOTATIONS WHICH DIFFER FROM BOTH THE LXX AND THE MT

Mark 4:12, quoting Is. 6:9–10. The Marcan free quotation uses the words of the LXX (which here agrees with the MT), except that it contains ἀφεθῇ for LXX ἰάσομαι (= MT ורפא). This corresponds to the Targum וישתביק. The Matthean full quotation (13:14–15) is a pure LXX text, and therefore reads ἰάσομαι. It may be that the Marcan form preserves Jesus' original Aramaic, following the Tg.[1]

Mark 9:48, quoting Is. 66:24. Mark has present tenses (τελευτᾷ, σβέννυται), against LXX futures (τελευτήσει, σβεσθήσεται)[2] which correspond to MT תמות, תכבה (and to futures in Tg).

Mark 10:19 (Mt. 19:18–19; Lk. 18:20), quoting Ex. 20:12–16 = Dt. 5:16–20. Among a rich variation in the order of the commandments in both OT and NT texts, one consistent feature is that all NT texts place the fifth commandment at the end, against all OT versions. It is hard to explain this otherwise than as fidelity to an original alteration of the order by Jesus through all the forms of textual tradition. The addition in Mark of the command, 'Do not defraud', is a further departure from all known OT versions.

Mark 12:30 (Mt. 22:37; Lk. 10:27), quoting Dt. 6:5. Again there is a great variety in both the order and the composition of the list of nouns, in both OT and NT texts. The relevant factor here is the introduction of διανοία into the list in all the Synoptic versions (except the Western text of Mark and Luke, and the old Syriac of Matthew). In both Mark and Luke it is additional to the list καρδία, ψυχή, ἰσχύς, which covers the list in MT and Tg, and corresponds also to the LXX, except that the latter has δύναμις, not ἰσχύς.[3] In Matthew διανοία has replaced ἰσχύς. A possible explanation is

[1] References to 'Tg' in the following pages are to the Targum of Onkelos for the Pentateuch, and the Targum of Jonathan for the Prophets and Writings, unless specified otherwise. 'Tgg' in the Pentateuch refers to the Targums of Onkelos and 'Pseudo-Jonathan' (the Palestinian Targum).

[2] τελευτᾷ is found in LXX A, but there is no parallel to σβέννυται.

[3] διανοία is, however, found in the secondary reading of LXX B, where it replaces καρδία. It seems most likely that this reading is due to assimilation to the Gospels.

that Jesus, like the author of 1QpHab,[4] combined two variants known to him (for there can be little doubt that a text in such constant liturgical use had several variant Aramaic forms[5]), thus extending the list from three to four nouns, in contrast to all known OT texts, which have only three nouns. This fourfold list has been preserved in Mark and Luke, but reduced in Matthew to the familiar three. (The retention of *διανοία* in Matthew indicates his dependence on the fourfold version of Mark.) In the matter of the number of nouns, then, at least, we have a tradition divergent from all known OT texts, which in Mark and Luke has resisted the temptation to assimilate to either the MT or the LXX.

Mark 12:36 (Mt. 22:44; Lk. 20:43), quoting Ps. 110:1. Mark and Matthew read *ὑποκάτω* against LXX *ὑποπόδιον*, which is a literal translation of MT הדום (*cf.* Tg כביש). Luke assimilates to the LXX.

Mark 14:27 (Mt. 26:31), quoting Zc. 13:7. *πατάξω* is a unique reading: MT, LXX, Tg, and all known versions here have an imperative.[6]

Matthew 4:10 (Lk. 4:8), quoting Dt. 6:13. The addition of *μόνῳ* and the reading *προσκυνήσεις* for LXX *φοβηθήσῃ*, MT תירא are peculiar to the Gospels, apart from LXX A, which is probably assimilated to the NT text. The reading תדחל in the Tg (*cf.* Tg Ps-Jon תהוון דחלין) may indicate the source of Jesus' version, since דחל, though primarily meaning 'to fear', is regularly used in the sense 'to reverence, worship'.

Matthew 7:23 (Lk. 13:27), quoting Ps. 6:9 (EVV 6:8). Matthew's omission of *πάντες* differs from the LXX and also from the MT and Tg. Here Luke has assimilated to the LXX, even though in the second half of the quotation he diverges from it.

Luke 4:18–19, quoting Is. 61:1–2. Luke omits the line about healing the broken-hearted, and adds, from Is. 58:6, the line 'to set at liberty those who are oppressed'. There is no support for either alteration in OT texts.

Luke 17:29, quoting Gn. 19:24. 'Fire and brimstone' are in the reverse order from that found in MT, LXX, and Tgg.

Luke 17:31, alluding to Gn. 19:17, 26. *ἐπιστρεψάτω* in Luke replaces LXX *περιβλέψῃς* (v. 17) and *ἐπέβλεψεν* (v. 26) (MT תביט, ותבט; Tg תסתכי, ואסתכיאת). But this is in any case no more than a verbal reminiscence, and the grammar of the sentence in Luke requires the 3rd singular imperative while the context requires the idea of turning, not simply looking, back.

Luke 23:30, quoting Ho. 10:8. Luke reverses the order of the requests 'Cover us' and 'Fall on us'. The only OT authority for this is LXX A, and assimilation to the NT is here at least a possibility.

[4] *Cf.* W. H. Brownlee, *The Biblical Archaeologist* 14 (1951), pp. 61, 63, 64, 68, 69 for examples.

[5] For the probable existence of numerous variant forms in Greek see K. Stendahl, *op. cit.*, p. 76, and for the same in Hebrew and Aramaic see see J. de Waard, *op. cit.*, pp. 63–64, quoting variations both in order and content from 1QH and the Tg. *Cf.* also the expanded paraphrase of Tg. Ps-Jon.

[6] The reading *πατάξω* in LXX V is late, and obviously due to NT influence.

III. QUOTATIONS WHICH AGREE WITH THE MT AGAINST THE LXX

a. Certain or virtually certain quotations

Mark 4:29, alluding to Joel 4:13 (EVV 3:13). Mark's θερισμός (grain harvest) is a correct and literal translation of MT קציר, where the LXX has τρύγητος (vintage), a possible but very unusual sense of קציר, no doubt suggested to the LXX translator by the vintage metaphor in the second half of the verse. (Tg קיצהון here supports the LXX against the MT, no doubt for the same reason.)[7]

Mark 10:19 (Mt. 19:18–19; Lk. 18:20), quoting Ex. 20:12–16 = Dt. 5:16–20. The order of the commandments after the fifth in Matthew and (probably) Mark is that of the MT and Tgg against LXX B; LXX A has the MT order. Luke has the order of LXX B at Dt. 5:16–20. Further, Mark and Luke have the form μή with subjunctive, whereas Matthew has assimilated to the LXX οὐ with indicative.

Mark 12:30 (Mt. 22:37; Lk. 10:27), quoting Dt. 6:5. The use of ἰσχύς in Mark and Luke[8] has no parallel in the LXX at Dt. 6:5. It has been suggested that it comes from the LXX of 2 Ki. 23:25, where it occurs in a similar formula, but it is more likely to be an independent translation of MT מאד, or some Aramaic equivalent. The Tg rendering נכסך 'your property' (*cf.* Tg Ps-Jon ממונכון 'your wealth') has no parallel in the LXX or the NT.

Mark 13:24–25 (Mt. 24:29). This passage will be more fully considered later.[9] The wording is derived essentially from Is. 13:10 and 34:4. In Is. 13:10 MT and Tg have השמש as subject of the main verb, as has the NT, whereas in the LXX it is in a dependent phrase in the genitive absolute. Further, Mark translates MT אורו by τὸ φέγγος αὐτῆς as against LXX τὸ φῶς αὐτῆς.[10]

Matthew 11:10 (Lk. 7:27; Mk. 1:2 – in the Marcan version it is not given as a quotation by Jesus), quoting Mal. 3:1 conflated with Ex. 23:20. Two points may be noted: (a) Matthew correctly translates וּפִנָּה־דרך by ὅς κατασκευάσει, against the LXX καὶ ἐπιβλέψεται, which depends on reading the verb as Qal (וּפָנָה־דרך), not Piel.[11] (b) The conflation is most likely to have

[7] The Marcan singular δρέπανον also corresponds to a singular in the MT and Tg, against LXX plural. Since, however, the verb in Joel is plural, whereas in Mark it is singular, this may be no more than a grammatical adaptation to the context.

[8] Matthew omits this noun to leave room for the new διανοία; see above, pp. 240–241.

[9] See below, pp. 255–256.

[10] Note, however, that both these features are present in LXX Joel 2:10, a passage which uses similar imagery; the influence of this verse on the NT text is not impossible.

[11] The combination of this conflated text with Is. 40:3 in Mk. 1:2–3 depends on the occurrence in both of the phrase פַּנּוּ־דֶרֶךְ, which occurs only four times in the OT. This link is absent in the LXX, which renders the

been made from a Semitic text, not from the LXX. It is true that the two verses are closer in Greek in that in both the LXX reads τὸν ἄγγελόν μου, whereas the MT in Ex. 23:20 has מלאך (Tg מלאכא), and in Mal. 3:1 מלאכי (Tg מלאכי). On the other hand, the opening words correspond more closely in the Semitic texts: in the MT both verses have the participle שלח with a first singular pronoun (Mal. 3:1 הנני, Ex. 23:20 הנה אנכי), and in the Tgg the correspondence is exact, both verses having האנא שלח, whereas the LXX reads in Ex. 23:20 ἐγὼ ἀποστέλλω, and in Mal. 3:1 ἐξαποστέλλω (without ἐγώ).[12] That the conflation in fact took place in a Semitic milieu is further suggested by the fact that the two verses were used together (with Mal. 3:23–24) in synagogue preaching, probably already in pre-Christian times, and in rabbinic teaching.[13]

Matthew 11:23 (Lk. 10:15), alluding to Is. 14:13, 15. The text in both Matthew and Luke is too uncertain to build firmly on; if καταβήσῃ is the right reading the correspondence is with the LXX, but if καταβιβασθήσῃ is right, it will correspond to the passive verb in the MT (תורד) and in Tg (תיתחת). The manuscript evidence in Matthew seems slightly weighted in favour of καταβήσῃ; in Luke the balance probably inclines the other way. But the state of the text suggests a process of conscious assimilation to some textual form, and it seems more probable that assimilation should be towards the LXX than to the MT.[14] Hence it is reasonable to see the reading καταβιβασθήσῃ as the original; if so, the correspondence is with the MT against the LXX.

Matthew 11:29, quoting Je. 6:16. Matthew's ἀνάπαυσιν translates MT מרגוע (hapax legomenon, but by derivation it must mean 'rest'; so Tg ניח). and bears no relation to LXX ἁγνισμόν (ἁγιασμόν in LXX A).

Matthew 18:16, quoting Dt. 19:15. Considerable variety in the text of both Matthew and the LXX yields one solid fact, that Matthew reads ἤ, corresponding to MT and Tgg או against LXX καί.

Luke 4:19, quoting Is. 61:2. MT לקרא is rendered by Luke κηρῦξαι, and by the LXX καλέσαι. Despite the LXX character of the remainder of this quotation, this rendering is independent of the LXX, and its dependence on the MT is confirmed by noting that Luke has κηρῦξαι for לקרא again in the previous verse; here the LXX too has κηρῦξαι, but whereas the LXX has varied its translation of the MT, Luke has remained consistent.

Luke 13:27 (Mt. 7:23), quoting Ps. 6:9 (EVV 6:8). Matthew follows the LXX in translating פעלי־און by οἱ ἐργαζόμενοι τὴν ἀνομίαν. Luke's ἐργάται

---

verb by ἐπιβλέψεται in Mal. 3:1, and by ἑτοιμάσατε in Is. 40:3. This combination was therefore made with a Semitic text.

[12] So Bא*; the addition of ἐγώ in other LXX texts seems clearly to be a later correction to agree with the MT and NT.

[13] *Cf.* J. Mann, *The Bible as Read and Preached in the Old Synagogue*, vol. I (Cincinnati, 1940), pp. 479–480. Also K. Stendahl, *op. cit.*, p. 50, and references *ad loc.*

[14] For the tendency to assimilate to the LXX see above, p. 26 n. 3.

ἀδικίας is independent of the LXX, and in form slightly closer to the construct state of the MT and Tg.

Luke 20:18 (?Mt. 21:44), alluding to Is. 8:14–15.[15] The difficult MT text causes the LXX to negative the description of Yahweh as a stone of offence and a rock of stumbling, and to paraphrase verse 15 (Tg also paraphrases, making the Memra a stone of smiting, and the divided people of Israel the cause of stumbling). The idea of stumbling on the stone, which is the point of the allusion, is thus found in the MT alone.

Luke 22:37, quoting Is. 53:12. Luke translates MT את־פשעים by *μετὰ ἀνόμων*, which is both independent of LXX *ἐν τοῖς ἀνόμοις* and a more literal translation of the MT. (Tg takes the את as the mark of the direct object, not as the preposition.)

b. Less certain allusions

Mark 8:38 (Mt. 16:27; Lk. 9:26), alluding to Dn. 7:13–14.[16] The word *δόξα* probably reflects MT יקר, which LXX omits, and Thdt renders by *τιμή*. (It is generally agreed that the version of Daniel used by the first century church was not our present LXX, but a version underlying the later Theodotion.)

Mark 11:15 (Mt. 21:12; Lk. 19:45). This is not strictly a saying of Jesus, but his action in casting out traders from the Temple is clearly reminiscent of Zc. 14:21; it is virtually a quotation in action.[17] The LXX, however, translates MT כנעני (*cf.* Tg. עביד תגרא) by *Χαναναῖος*, a rendering which would entirely lose the point of Jesus' symbolic action.

Mark 13:8 (Mt. 24:7; Lk. 21:10), alluding to Is. 19:2. The NT *βασιλεία ἐπὶ βασιλείαν* is a very likely allusion to the corresponding MT ממלכה בממלכה, which the LXX renders by *νομὸς ἐπὶνομόν*. Tg here corresponds to the MT and the NT, viz. מלכו במלכו.

Mark 14:24 (Mt. 26:28), alluding to Is. 53:12. The allusion has been seen not only in the phrase *ὑπὲρ πολλῶν*, but also in the word *ἐκχυννόμενον*, which echoes MT הערה, where the LXX has *παρεδόθη*, with no idea of 'pouring out'.[18]

Matthew 6:11 (Lk. 11:3), alluding to Pr. 30:8. *τὸν ἄρτον τὸν ἐπιούσιον*

[15] For the allusion see above, p. 152.

[16] For details of the allusion see above, p. 139.

[17] See above, pp. 92–93.

[18] M. D. Hooker (*Servant*, p. 82) denies the allusion on the ground that the Hiphil of ערה means 'to lay bare'. See, however, BDB, p. 788, where for each mood in which the verb occurs the meaning 'pour out' is given as well as 'lay bare'. For the Niphal, which BDB characterize as 'pass. of Hiph. 2' (where Is. 53:12 is listed), the meaning 'pour out' is essential in its one occurrence, Is. 32:15. It seems then that BDB have good reason for giving the meaning in Is. 53:12 as 'pour out'. Tg מסר ('deliver', 'surrender') is, like the LXX, a prosaic interpretation, which does not help us to determine the metaphor of the MT. For this allusion see further above, p. 122.

echoes the לחם חקי of the MT (*cf.* Tg לחמא מסתי), where the LXX *τὰ δέοντα καὶ τὰ αὐτάρκη* has no reference to bread.

Matthew 6:23 (Lk. 11:34), alluding to Pr. 28:22. The fact that both passages occur in contexts of preoccupation with wealth makes the allusion likely. The phrase *ὀφθαλμὸς πονηρός* would then correspond literally to MT רע עין (*cf.* Tg ביש עיניה), where the LXX has *βάσκανος*. Even if the allusion were not accepted, the NT phrase is clearly Semitic in origin, for the idea of the 'evil eye', common as it is in many cultures, always refers elsewhere to powers of bewitching.[19] (This is possibly implied also by the LXX *βάσκανος* here.) The use of 'evil eye' in the sense of niggardliness or envy, as here in the NT and in Pr. 28:22, is a purely Semitic idea.

Matthew 13:41, alluding to Zp. 1:3. *τὰ σκάνδαλα καὶ τοὺς ποιοῦντας τὴν ἀνομίαν* is an echo of MT והמכשלות את־הרשעים, a phrase which is missing from the LXX.[20]

Luke 16:15, alluding to Pr. 16:5. For MT תועבה LXX has *ἀκάθαρτος*, Luke the more literal *βδέλυγμα* (used by the LXX for תועבה in v. 12). The similar passage, Pr. 6:16–17, is possibly also in mind, containing the same idea of God's abhorrence for pride, and the same word תועבה; here the LXX is quite different from the MT, but again LXX *ἀκαθαρσία* corresponds to תועבה.

Luke 22:31, possibly alluding to Am. 9:9. If so, Luke's *σινιάσαι ὡς τὸν σῖτον* would correspond to MT והנעותי כאשר ינוע בכברה, for which the LXX has *λικμιῶ ὃν τρόπον λικμᾶται ἐν τῷ λικμῷ*. The Lucan version is a literal rendering of the 'sieving' metaphor of the MT (*cf.* Tg ואבדר כמא דמחזרין בערבלא), whereas the *λικμᾶν* of the LXX substitutes the more familiar process of winnowing.

c. A textual variant

Matthew 4:4 (Lk. 4:4), quoting Dt. 8:3. The Western reading in Matthew, which in Luke gains also the support of A and the Caesarean MSS, discards the cumbersome LXX *παντὶ ῥήματι τῷ ἐκπορευομένῳ διὰ στόματος Θεοῦ* for the simpler *παντὶ ῥήματι Θεοῦ*, which is certainly not LXX, but might be derived from the terse MT expression כל־מוצא פי־יהוה. The non-LXX character of this reading is in its favour.[21]

IV. QUOTATIONS WHICH AGREE WITH ONE TEXT OF THE LXX AGAINST ANOTHER

Mark 7:6 (Mt. 15:8), quoting Is. 29:13, follows אAQ in omitting *ἐν τῷ στόματι αὐτοῦ καὶ ἐν*.

[19] *Cf.* J. H. Moulton and G. Milligan, *The Vocabulary of the Greek Testament* (London, 1930), *s.v. βασκαίνω*.

[20] For a detailed textual and exegetical study of this allusion see above, pp. 156–157.

[21] See above, p. 26 n. 3. For a defence of the shorter reading see G. D. Kilpatrick, *JTS* 45 (1944), p. 176; R. H. Gundry, *op. cit.*, p. 67.

Mark 7:10 (Mt. 15:4), quoting Ex. 21:17 (LXX 21:16), follows A in reading *θανάτῳ τελευτάτω* for *τελευτήσει θανάτῳ*.

Mark 9:48, quoting Is. 66:24, follows A in reading *τελευτᾷ* for *τελευτήσει*.

Mark 10:7 (Mt. 19:5) quoting Gn. 2:24; while Mark (probably: the text is doubtful) follows B and all other texts in reading *πρὸς τὴν γυναῖκα*, Matthew has *τῇ γυναῖκι*, with A.

Mark 10:19 (Mt. 19:18–19; Lk. 18:20), quoting Ex. 20:12–16 = Dt. 5:16–20. The order of the sixth to ninth commandments in Matthew and (probably) Mark is that of A (= MT). Luke follows B at Dt. 5:16–20 in reversing the sixth and seventh commandments.

Mark 12:26 (Mt. 22:32; Lk. 20:37), quoting Ex. 3:6. B has no articles before *Θεός*, whereas A has before *Θεὸς Αβρααμ* only. Mark here follows A (as does Luke, though grammatically adapted to work it into his sentence). Matthew extends the use of the article to all three uses of *Θεός*.

Mark 12:30 (Mt. 22:37; Lk. 10:27), quoting Dt. 6:5. A has *καρδία* as the first noun, in which all NT versions agree; B here reads *διανοία*, but the reading is secondary, and the original is indecipherable. This case is therefore doubtful.

Mark 13:25 (Mt. 24:29; Lk. 21:26). The reference to *αἱ δυνάμεις τῶν οὐρανῶν* (or *αἱ ἐν τοῖς οὐρανοῖς*, Mk.) derives from Is. 34:4 LXX B, a reading found also in the Lucianic revision, and inserted by Origen under an asterisk (indicating that it was not in the LXX as it came down to him), but absent from other MSS.

Mark 14:27 (Mt. 26:31), quoting Zc. 13:7. The LXX text is very rich in variants. The following stand out: the text of Bא*W is unique, and utterly different from that quoted in the NT – it runs *πατάξατε τοὺς ποιμένας καὶ ἐκσπάσατε τὰ πρόβατα* (the sections underlined show where the NT differs from this text); the NT *πατάξω*, as we have seen, has *no* LXX support, though it is nearer to the singular imperative of AQ than to the plural of Bא*; *τὸν ποιμένα* is in *all* other texts; *διασκορπισθήσονται* is in A and Q (the latter conflating the A and B texts, and therefore also including *ἐκσπάσατε*); finally, Matthew's addition of *τῆς ποίμνης* is supported by A. In short, the NT text is as far as possible from B, and is in agreement with A in all respects except *πατάξω*.

Matthew 4:10 (Lk. 4:8), quoting Dt. 6:13, follows A *προσκυνήσεις* against all other texts *φοβηθήσῃ*, and follows A in adding *μόνῳ*, again against all other texts except the second-century papyrus 963.

Matthew 9:13 and 12:7, quoting Ho. 6:6, has *καὶ οὐ*, the reading of A and other MSS against B and some MSS of the Lucianic revision, which have *ἤ*.

Matthew 18:16, quoting Dt. 19:15, has *σταθῇ*, a necessary grammatical alteration from *σταθήσεται*, since in Matthew the clause is introduced by *ἵνα*; B alone reads *στήσεται*. This is, however, probably a scribal error, not a question of variant textual traditions.

Luke 23:30, quoting Ho. 10:8. The transposition of the two requests in Luke is supported by A alone.

V. QUOTATIONS WHICH AGREE WITH THE LXX AGAINST THE MT

a. Quotations where the LXX form does not affect the sense or the application of the passage

Mark 4:29, alluding to Joel 4:13 (EVV 3:13). Mark has LXX *παρέστηκεν* against MT בשל. There is, however, no difference in sense between the 'arrival' and the 'ripening' of the harvest (Tg מטא זמן קיצהון 'the time of his harvest is ripe' virtually combines the two conceptions). The quotation is in any case at other points clearly independent of the LXX, and closer to the MT.[22]

Mark 10:8 (Mt. 19:5) quoting Gn. 2:24. *οἱ δύο* in the NT is derived from the LXX, but is not in our MT. It is a gloss which in no way affects the sense, only heightening its effect. However, T. W. Manson[23] believes that here the LXX preserves the true Hebrew text, since the MT is supported only by Tg Onkelos and a quotation in Jubilees 3:7, while the addition of *οἱ δύο* is attested not only by the LXX, but by the Samaritan, Peshitta, and Vg versions, and the Palestinian Targum Pseudo-Jonathan, as well as by quotations here, in 1 Cor. 6:16; Eph. 5:31, and in Philo. The case is convincing, and this passage too must therefore be discounted.

Mark 10:19 (Mt. 19:18–19; Lk. 18:20), quoting Ex. 20:12–16 = Dt. 5:16–20. The order of the commandments is very confused. Apart from the transposition of the fifth to the end in all NT texts, Matthew and Mark (ℵ^{c}Bsy^{s}, *etc.*) follow the order of the MT, Tgg, and LXX A, while Luke and Mark (AWΘf13lat, *etc.*) follow that of LXX B in Dt. 5. This complicated textual problem need not detain us, since the order of the commandments clearly makes no difference at all to the sense of the passage.

Mark 12:1 (Mt. 21:33), alluding to Is. 5:1–2. The language is basically that of the LXX (though by no means a word for word quotation), and includes the phrase *φραγμὸν περιέθηκεν* (*–θηκα* in LXX); this translates MT ויעזקהו, which is probably to be translated 'and he dug it carefully about' (so BDB).[24] This is therefore probably a case of agreement with the LXX against the MT, but the discrepancy is in a minor point of agricultural detail, which cannot possibly affect the sense of the passage as a whole, which is to convey the elaborate care of the owner for his vineyard.

Matthew 4:7 (Lk. 4:12), quoting Dt. 6:16. The NT follows the LXX singular *ἐκπειράσεις* against the MT plural תנסו (*cf.* Tg תנסון). Here it may be said that the quotation is more clearly applicable in its LXX form, but even in the MT form it is a relevant quotation, its sense being quite

[22] See above, p. 242.

[23] *BJRL* 34 (1951/2), pp. 315, 317. NEB accepts this reading.

[24] The verb is hapax legomenon. According to BDB its use in New Hebrew includes the meaning 'surround', 'enclose', and the cognate Aramaic עזקתא means 'ring'. (Tg gives an interpretative paraphrase which does not help with the literal meaning.) There is therefore a possibility that the LXX does give the true meaning of the MT, in which case this passage too must be discounted.

unaffected by the number of the verb. A translator confronted by a plural Aramaic verb would naturally use the LXX without altering its singular to plural, since it not only left the sense unaffected, but also made the application more sharply obvious.

Matthew 18:16, quoting Dt. 19:15. The gloss πᾶν in the LXX is repeated in Matthew.[25] As in Mk. 10:8, the LXX addition simply clarifies and emphasizes what is already the meaning of the Hebrew (the word כל does in fact occur three times earlier in the verse in the MT and Tgg); the use of the text by Jesus in no way depends on it.

Matthew 18:22, alluding to Gn. 4:24. It has been suggested that Matthew, in writing ἑβδομηκοντάκις ἑπτά, is repeating a mistake of the LXX, substituting the number 490 for the MT 77 (שבעים ושבעה). It is, however, probable that the form in both the LXX and the MT does in fact express '77 times'.[26] Even if the rendering '490 times' were preferred, the LXX form would clearly not affect the sense, the figure being merely symbolic for an unlimited number of times in contrast to the limited number seven.

Matthew 25:31, alluding to Zc. 14:5. Matthew follows LXX μετ' αὐτοῦ against MT עמך. The allusion is, however, at another point divergent from the LXX (ἄγγελοι for ἅγιοι), and the 'emendation' to the third person is found also in the Tg (עמיה) and other versions, so that a Semitic original is equally likely. In any case, the grammar of the NT context demands the third person.[27]

Luke 4:18, quoting Is. 61:1–2. Despite the variations noted above from the LXX, both in agreement with the MT and against it, the text of the quotation is basically LXX. Four points of difference from the MT may be noted, one of which may affect the use of the quotation by Jesus, and is therefore treated in the next section. The other three are as follows: *Κυρίου* for MT אדוני יהוה; οὗ εἵνεκεν for MT יען; and ἔχρισέν με for MT משח יהוה אתי. In the remainder of the quotation the LXX is a literal translation of the MT. It is clear that these minor deviations do not in the least affect the sense or the applicability of the quotation.

Luke 23:46, quoting Ps. 31:6 (EVV 31:5). Luke follows the LXX plural εἰς χεῖράς σου against the MT singular בידך. Here again is a purely stylistic matter which does not affect the meaning.

b. Quotations whose appropriateness may be said to depend on their LXX form

Mark 7:6–7 (Mt. 15:8–9), quoting Is. 29:13. Here Stendahl states positively that 'the function of the quotation presupposes its LXX form. . . . The line of thought in the quotation is wholly dependent upon the LXX's

[25] *Cf.*, however, R. H. Gundry, *op. cit.*, p. 76 n. 2: 'כל was often inserted into or deleted from the Hebrew text.' Jesus may, therefore, have known the word 'all' in his Aramaic version, though it does not appear in the existing Tgg.

[26] See E. J. Goodspeed, *Problems of New Testament Translation* (Chicago, 1945), pp. 29–31. Also Blass-Debrunner §248:2; AG, p. 212.

[27] On the reality and textual origin of the allusion see above, p. 157.

translation of *μάτην*'.[28] From this the conclusion is drawn either that Jesus was speaking in Greek (improbable at all times, and surely impossible in discussion with Pharisees and scribes), or that the quotation was not made by Jesus. Does the evidence carry the weight of this conclusion?

The significant divergence is in the second half of the quotation. The MT reads ותהי יראתם אתי מצות אנשים מלמדה ('and their fear of me is a commandment of men learned by rote' RSV). The LXX reads *μάτην δὲ σέβονταί με διδάσκοντες ἐντάλματα ἀνθρώπων καὶ διδασκαλίας* ('but in vain do they worship me, teaching commandments of men and (human) teachings'). The Tg is essentially in agreement with the MT.[29] Mark and Matthew quote the LXX, except for the grammatical tidying up of the final words to *διδάσκοντες διδασκαλίας ἐντάλματα ἀνθρώπων*, which clearly does not affect the meaning. The differences in the LXX are therefore (a) the introduction of *μάτην*, due no doubt to a reading וְתֹהוּ for וַתְּהִי;[30] (b) the consequent reorganization of the rest of the sentence: מצות can no longer be predicate after ותהי, and so *διδάσκοντες* is introduced as a verb on which it may depend. At the same time, מלמדה is read substantivally, and made into a second object by the addition of *καί*, producing a reasonable translation of the Hebrew, though an ugly piece of Greek! Of these two differences, the latter has little effect on the sense: it is expressing in other words the same point of a worship consisting of human ordinances. The former is more serious, as it introduces into the verse the new idea of their worship being 'in vain'.

Is this peculiarly LXX idea of the vanity of their worship essential to the alleged use of the quotation by Jesus? This must be decided by the NT context. The quotation introduces a denunciation of the religion of the Pharisees: verses 8–9 specify their error, which is that they have abandoned the commandment of God and hold fast to human tradition; verses 10–12 give an example of this, whereby a human ruling had been used to set aside the plain commands of God; verse 13 sums up the point – by their human traditions they have annulled God's word. And all this is in respect to their question about ritual cleansing. It is therefore concerned with their

[28] *Op. cit.*, pp. 57–58.

[29] The final phrase כתפקידת גברין מלפין 'like a commandment of men who teach' is a stylistic improvement of the awkward final participle of the Hebrew, and lends no support to the LXX version or to that of the NT.

[30] So E. Nestle, *ExpT* 11 (1899/1900), p. 330, and many others. It might be argued that the OT text used by Jesus had וְתֹהוּ or its equivalent in Aramaic, hence the use of the LXX by the translator, but this is unlikely. The MT is supported by both Tg and Syriac, and וְתֹהוּ has no support outside the LXX and the NT. Besides, it is relatively easy to imagine the misreading of וַתְּהִי as וְתֹהוּ, which conveys the idea of the passage so well, and the addition of the extra verb would then be essential. This is more probable than the misreading of וְתֹהוּ *and* at the same time the loss of the second verb. We must, therefore, accept the MT as representing the Palestinian text of the first century.

idea of worship: they have allowed their human ritual requirements to replace God's spiritual requirements.

Now the striking point in all this is that the specifically LXX point of the *vanity* of such worship is nowhere explicitly taken up; the argument centres entirely upon the substitution of human for divine standards in worship, *i.e.* that part of the quotation which is unaffected by the LXX form. The MT makes this point quite as forcibly: perhaps even more so, for it states that their very worship *is* mere human commandment, whereas the LXX states rather that their human tradition makes their worship vain. In other words, Jesus' use of the quotation rests firmly upon the sense of the Hebrew, and makes no use of the LXX addition of *μάτην*. It may, of course, be admitted that the LXX version gives added force to Jesus' denunciation, but this is not the question at issue. Jesus' explicit argument depends on the Hebrew text. (This is clearly seen by disregarding the LXX version and asking whether a quotation of Is. 29:13 MT would have been appropriate in this context: an affirmative answer is inevitable.) A Greek translator, however, seeing the appropriateness of the LXX, would naturally use it, and in so doing sharpen the point of the attack; but this is no reason to postulate a Greek *origin* for the saying.[31]

Mark 9:12 (Mt. 17:11), alluding to Mal. 3:23–24 (LXX 3:22–23; EVV 4:5–6). Matthew's *ἀποκαταστήσει* certainly, and Mark's *ἀποκαθιστάνει* almost certainly, are derived from the LXX *ἀποκαταστήσει*. This is a fair translation of the MT והשיב (Tg ויתיב), but it is questionable whether the extension of the sense in the NT could derive from the Hebrew. Whereas in Malachi the meaning is 'to cause to turn back', the object being 'the hearts of fathers to their children', in the NT the object is *πάντα*, which seems to demand a different sense of *ἀποκαθιστάνω*, viz. 'to restore, re-establish'. Both senses of *ἀποκαθιστάνω* are attested in the period, but it is doubtful whether והשיב can bear the latter sense; at least in this context in Malachi it is not the meaning. It would appear, therefore, that the extension of Malachi's concept of the restoration of family solidarity to an idea of a general renewal or restoration can be based only on the LXX wording.

Here again a reference to the context casts doubt on the argument against authenticity. Jesus is answering a reference to scribal expectations, and the words in question are his quotation of the scribes' interpretation of Malachi[32] (whether to endorse it or to reject it is here not the issue).[33]

[31] *Cf.* V. Taylor, *Mark*, pp. 337–338. Even Stendahl, despite the statements recorded above, admits the force of this argument: 'It is impossible to decide whether Jesus referred to this passage in its Semitic form, or if the quotation is added in a church where the LXX scriptures were used. In the former case we must suppose that the LXX form appeared to fit even better than the Semitic one, and thus influenced the Greek rendering' (*op. cit.*, p. 58).

[32] This is indicated by the presence of *μέν*, answered by the *ἀλλά* (Mt. *δέ*) of the next verse, which introduces Jesus' own contrasting teaching that Elijah has *already* come. *Cf.* V. Taylor, *Sacrifice*, pp. 93–94.

[33] For the view that he here endorsed the scribal estimate of the task of

This extension of the sense of Malachi by the scribes is well attested. Its beginning may be seen in Ecclus. 48:10, and in the Mishnah it has come to include quite diverse functions of restoration.[34] We are therefore justified in concluding that *ἀποκαθιστάνει πάντα* was a fair summary of scribal expectations with regard to Elijah at the time of Jesus. How Jewish thought came to this conclusion on the basis of Mal. 3:23–24 is outside our scope, but that it was not on the basis of the LXX may be taken as certain. We conclude then that in this saying of Jesus we have not, as appeared at first, an extension of the meaning of Malachi based on the LXX, but a quotation of scribal tradition, which made this extension in the purely Semitic milieu of Ecclesiasticus and the Mishnah. A Greek origin for the allusion to this tradition by Jesus is therefore quite improbable. That the translator found in the LXX *ἀποκαταστήσει* a suitable verb to render whatever Aramaic term Jesus used, and made use of it, is of course to be recognized, in accordance with our previous discussion of the use of the LXX in translating the words of Jesus; but that the saying arose on the basis of the LXX cannot be maintained.

Matthew 21:16, quoting Ps. 8:3 (EVV 8:2). Matthew follows the LXX *αἶνον* against MT עז and Tg עושנא. There is no doubt that Jesus' quotation requires the meaning 'praise': it is the praise by the children that he is using it to defend. And at first sight the meanings of *αἶνον* and עז seem irreconcilable. But a study of the use of עז in the OT requires a modification of this impression, for it is frequently used in contexts of praise, as in the phrase עזי וזמרת יה (Ex. 15:2; Ps. 118:14; Is. 12:2). The phrase בכלי־עז in 2 Ch. 30:21, describing the act of praise by Levites and priests, is best translated 'with instruments of praise'. Especially prominent is the repeated call to ascribe or give עז to God (Ps. 29:1 = Ps. 96:7 = 1 Ch. 16:28; Pss. 59:17; 68:35 (EVV 59:16; 68:34)), where in each case the context makes plain that what is called for is an ascription of praise; indeed, in the last two references the translation 'praise' seems preferable.[35] עז essentially means 'strength', but strength is often attributed to God as a cause for praise, and hence עז comes to mean something like 'praise for his strength'. That the LXX understood it in this sense is indicated by its use of *δόξα* (Ps. 68:35; Is. 12:2) and *τίμη* (Pss. 29:1; 96:7) to translate עז. Here in Ps. 8 the context is again of praise and wonder at the greatness and glory of God. Verse 3 depicts God, confronted by his enemies, confounding them by means of עז brought from the mouths of babes and sucklings. The translation 'stronghold' given by BDB seems quite inappropriate. What

Elijah see C. E. B. Cranfield, *Mark*, p. 298. *Contra* A. H. McNeile, *Matthew*, p. 253.

[34] Sot. 9:15; B.M. 1:8; 2:8; 3:4, 5; Eduy. 8:7. For these and the later rabbinic development of the idea see J. Jeremias, *TDNT* II, pp. 928–934; W. D. Davies, *Sermon*, pp. 159–161.

[35] K. Stendahl (*op. cit.*, p. 134 n. 1) cites the translation given in Gesenius-Buhl *Wörterbuch*: 'Verherrlichung, Lobpreis, nur von Gott.'

comes from the mouths of babes and sucklings must surely be something like praise. In view of the uses of עז mentioned above it seems best to see the picture as one of the disarming of the opposition by the infants' cry עז ליהוה: it is their *ascription* of strength which is in view. So the LXX must have thought, and it is for this reason that Stendahl describes *αἶνον* as 'a peculiar, though possible translation'. Can we not go further and say that it expresses, no doubt with an element of paraphrase, what the Hebrew intended?[36]

Jesus' aim in making the quotation is to vindicate the children's praise against his enemies. Even in its MT form Ps. 8:3 is appropriate to such an occasion.[37] *αἶνον* is not essential to this application, if we recognize the meaning of עז as 'praise for his strength', 'ascription of strength', which the OT context demands. No single Greek word would adequately convey this idea, but the LXX *αἶνον* effectively preserves the intention of the original.[38] As in Mk. 7:6–7 the Hebrew text is appropriate to the occasion, but the use of the LXX in the Greek version gives added point to the quotation.

Luke 4:18, quoting Is. 61:1. This quotation has already come up for consideration several times, since at different points it goes with the MT against the LXX, with the LXX against the MT in minor details, and against both at once. This in itself must lead us to suspect any argument which would suggest that we deny the authenticity of the saying on the grounds of agreement with the LXX. But there is one phrase of which the appropriateness may be said to depend on its LXX form. This is the phrase *τυφλοῖς ἀνάβλεψιν*, for MT לאסורים פקח־קוח, rendered by RSV 'the opening of the prison to those who are bound'. However, פקח־קוח is a reduplicated form from פקח, which is invariably used of the opening of eyes (except the transferred use in Is. 42:20 for opening ears); neither in Hebrew nor in the cognate languages is there evidence for its use for opening doors, prisons, *etc.* אסור, on the other hand, as definitely means a 'prisoner', 'one bound'. The Hebrew is therefore a mixed metaphor. Either we must see פקח־קוח as used 'figuratively as freeing from dark prison' (BDB), or we must see אסור as figurative for 'blind' (*i.e.* one whose eyes are bound). Either figure would be unique, and there is no good reason for preferring the former. The Tg, sensing the difficulty, has produced a similar mixed metaphor in its version, לדאסירין אתגלו לניהור '(to say) to the prisoners, "Be exposed to the light" '.[39] (ניהור is frequently used to mean 'eyesight'.) The LXX

[36] For a defence of the LXX translation see R. H. Gundry, *op. cit.*, pp. 121–122.

[37] *Cf.* H.-J. Kraus, *Psalmen*[2] (Neukirchen Kreis Moers, 1961), vol. 1, pp. 68–69.

[38] T. Zahn (*Einleitung in das NT*[2] (Leipzig, 1900), vol. 2, p. 318) notices the Tg rendering עושנא for עז, and suggests an original pun in the words of Jesus with the *ὡσαννά* of v. 15, which the Greek translator attempted to render by the LXX *αἶνον*.

[39] Stenning's translation 'Come forth to the light' is dictated more by the

has unambiguously preferred the latter alternative in translating τυφλοῖς ἀνάβλεψιν. In this it is supported by a closely parallel passage, Is. 42:7, where the ideas of opening blind eyes and releasing prisoners are combined as functions of the one on whom is the Spirit of Yahweh (*cf.* Is. 42:1); the LXX version gives a closely parallel set of ideas here. There is then good reason for believing that the LXX version, used by Luke, conveys at least a part of the sense of the MT.[40]

The reference to the healing of the blind is not, in any case, essential to Jesus' purpose. The passage is a metaphorical description of merciful relief and deliverance, and even if the RSV translation of the MT could be proved to be right, the LXX would be a different metaphor to express the same idea. The point of the quotation in Jesus' sermon at Nazareth does not depend on the details, but on the picture as a whole.[41] His assertion is that in himself God's appointed redeemer has come, and this is as well expressed by either version. If we add to this the fact already mentioned that the quotation shows divergence from the LXX at other points, clearly no argument against the authenticity of the passage as a saying of Jesus can be based on its textual form.

Matthew 11:5 (Lk. 7:22), quoting Is. 61:1–2. This may be treated with the preceding passage, as it is the same phrase of the LXX which is in question. The occurrence of πτωχοὶ εὐαγγελίζονται later in the verse makes it certain that τυφλοὶ ἀναβλέπουσιν here is derived from the LXX τυφλοῖς ἀνάβλεψιν, though the verse alludes also to Is. 35:5–6, where the healing of the blind is mentioned again in different words. The difference here from Lk. 4:18 is that whereas there the use of τυφλοῖς ἀνάβλεψιν is clearly metaphorical, here the reference is as clearly to the literal healing of the blind. (Luke makes this explicit in v. 21.) If, then, the RSV translation of Is. 61:1 is right, this verse would seem to depend on the LXX. We have, however, argued above that the LXX may in fact be a fair translation of the Hebrew. Even if it were not, though the words may be drawn from the LXX of Is. 61:1, the idea of the healing of the blind is provided by both the LXX and the MT of Is. 35:5, which is also a source of Jesus' words; in that case the LXX words would not be importing a sense foreign to the MT, but rather providing a useful Greek paraphrase of the thought of the MT of Is. 35:5. This is in fact exactly what the rest of the verse is doing, though it is not elsewhere using LXX words for the purpose. So whether what Jesus originally said was an Aramaic paraphrase of Is. 35:5a[42] or an Aramaic

---

traditional interpretation of the MT than by any possible meaning of the Ithpeel of גלי.

[40] *Cf.* RSV mg. 'the opening of the eyes'. F. Delitzsch (*Isaiah*, vol. 2, p. 395) translates 'removal of blindness to the prisoners', and quotes (*ibid.*, p. 397) Luzzatto's rendering 'ed ai carcerati il vedere la luce' ('and to the prisoners to see the light').

[41] A literal application of this phrase would in any case be inappropriate, as Luke has not up to this point recorded the healing of the blind.

[42] The Tg, which applies the restoration of sight metaphorically to a recovery of Israel's knowledge of the law, would not be appropriate.

version of the פקח־קוח of Is. 61:1, taking it in the sense of 'opening of eyes' (which is the only sense which would be relevant and would warrant a reference to the verse in this context), in either case the Greek version *τυφλοὶ ἀναβλέπουσιν* would be a faithful rendering of the original.

c. The Apocalyptic Discourse

Mark 13:7 (Mt. 24:6; Lk. 21:9). *δεῖ γενέσθαι* is said to allude to Dn. 2:28–29 (LXX and Thdt), where the MT (Aramaic) מה די להוא means simply 'what *shall* come to pass'. This is a hazardous reference. It is true that the term *ἃ δεῖ γενέσθαι* seems to be a standard one in apocalyptic: see Rev. 1:1; 4:1; 22:6, where, as in Dn. 2:28–29, it is a description of the content of the revelation, and may therefore very well be based on the Daniel passage. However, none of the Gospels gives the full *ἃ δεῖ γενέσθαι*, and it is not here a description of what is revealed. We must, therefore, class this allusion as, at the most, possible. Further, it is hard to see much, or indeed any, difference in meaning between what 'shall' and what 'must' happen in a context of apocalyptic: the whole ethos of apocalyptic is to equate the two, and it is hardly by accident that both the LXX and Thdt consistently translate מה די להוא by *ἃ δεῖ γενέσθαι*. In other words, if Jesus in fact said להוא or the equivalent (which would adequately express the idea of necessary preliminaries to the *τέλος*), it is hard to imagine a Greek translator using a translation other than *δεῖ γενέσθαι*, if he recognized it as an allusion to Dn. 2:28–29.

Mark 13:13 (Mt. 24:13). *ὁ δὲ ὑπομείνας εἰς τέλος οὗτος σωθήσεται* is seen as an allusion to Dn. 12:12. The only actual verbal correspondence with Thdt is his *ὑπομένων*, for MT מחכה 'waiting for'. It is claimed that the idea of endurance in *ὑπομείνας* is derived from the Greek, not the Hebrew. The finding of an allusion here is even more hazardous than in the previous case, and once again the supposed difference in sense between Thdt and the MT is more apparent than real, for the MT המחכה ויגיע includes both the ideas of waiting and of attaining, or 'coming up to'. *ὑπομένων* is really an excellent translation of the idea in the Hebrew. Clearly this case need not detain us.

Mark 13:14 (Mt. 24:15), alluding to Dn. 11:31; 12:11. *τὸ βδέλυγμα τῆς ἐρημώσεως* follows the LXX and Thdt A in 12:11 (*cf. βδέλυγμα ἐρημώσεως*, LXX 11:31 and Thdt B 12:11). This is said not to be an exact translation of the MT השקוץ משומם (11:31), שקוץ שמם (12:11). This is not obvious. *βδέλυγμα* is the regular LXX translation of שקוץ, 'an abominable thing', generally used of something idolatrous. שמם has as its primary meaning 'to be desolate', and then 'to be appalled': both meanings run through all its moods, and the Poel in Daniel seems to mean that the שקוץ 'desolates' or 'lays waste' the Temple;[43] *ἐρήμωσις* could not be more appropriate. Is the

[43] According to BDB the primary meaning ('to be desolate') enjoys a considerable numerical preponderance. They give no reason for restricting

objection then to the Greek use of a genitive ('of desolation') to render a participle ('that makes desolate')? This is, however, a not unparallelled use of the genitive,[44] and was clearly how the LXX and Thdt intended it to be understood. It is, therefore, pedantic to postulate any difference in meaning between the MT and the LXX or Thdt. The use and meaning of the quotation do not in any way depend on the use of the Greek version.

Mark 13:19 (Mt. 24:21), alluding to Dn. 12:1. This case is not relevant to our enquiry, as Glasson himself admits that 'the Greek words represent quite fairly the meaning of the Hebrew, but they are not the only words possible'. We could ask no more!

Mark 13:24–25 (Mt. 24:29; Lk. 21:25–26), using regular OT apocalyptic imagery, but drawn specifically from Is. 13:10; 34:4. Of Is. 13:10 Glasson says that it 'need not detain us'; we have shown above that the agreement of the NT is here with the Hebrew against the LXX.[45] But Is. 34:4 seems more to support his thesis. He finds three discrepancies between the MT and the LXX, in all three of which the NT follows the LXX.

(a) Mark's *αἱ δυνάμεις αἱ ἐν τοῖς οὐρανοῖς* (Mt. *αἱ δυνάμεις τῶν οὐρανῶν* – so also in Mark, Western text) follows the LXX *πᾶσαι αἱ δυνάμεις τῶν οὐρανῶν* rather than the MT כל־צבא השמים. This clause in the LXX is read by B and the Lucianic revision, and by Origen under an asterisk (indicating that it was not in the LXX text as he received it); it is missing from other LXX texts, notably from A, which we saw above to be the text followed by the NT writers in almost all cases of discrepancy. This might well cause us to doubt whether the words in Mark were drawn from the LXX. And even if one grants a use of the LXX text, this is no mistranslation of the Hebrew. צבא means basically 'an army', but is frequently applied to the stars, which are called, as here, צבא־השמים. The LXX translation of this phrase is varied; *στρατία* and *κόσμος* are common, but *δύναμις* occurs in the following passages besides this one: 2 Ki. 17:16; 21:3, 5; 23:4, 5; 2 Ch. 18:18; Pss. 33:6; 103:21; 148:2; Dn. 8:10 Thdt (bis).[46] It was evidently a recognized Greek rendering of the phrase, and as such was rightly used by the translator of Jesus' words here.[47]

(b) Mark's *οἱ ἀστέρες* follows the LXX *πάντα τὰ ἄστρα* against the MT

---

the Poel (occurring transitively only in Dn. 8:13; 9:27; 11:31; 12:11) to the second meaning. The primary meaning gives a better sense, and is adopted by LXX, Thdt, and 1 Macc. 1:54, as well as by Matthew and Mark (and by almost all EVV).

[44] *Cf.* Dn. 8:13, where הפשע שמם is translated by both the LXX and Thdt as *ἡ ἁμαρτία ἐρημώσεως*.

[45] See above, p. 242.

[46] *δύναμις* is generally used in the singular, but in Pss. 103:21; 148:2 the plural is used, the latter (probably) in translation of a Hebrew singular, as in Is. 34:4.

[47] The rendering חילי שמיא in the Tg may indicate that the word used by Jesus was in fact not far from *δύναμις*, since the primary meaning of חיל is 'strength', hence 'army'.

כל־צבאם and Tg משריתהון 'their armies'. But here we must first note that Mark's noun is not that of the LXX, but a cognate. Secondly, there are numerous references in the OT to prove that צבא־השמים does in fact mean the stars (see, *e.g.*, Dt. 4:19; 17:3; 2 Ki. 23:5; Is. 40:26; Je. 8:2; 33:22; Dn. 8:10); in at least one other place (Is. 45:12) the LXX has again translated it by *ἄστρα*. The NT is here, therefore, a correct translation of the sense of the MT, and is in fact slightly different from the LXX.

(c) Mark's *ἔσονται πίπτοντες* (Mt. *πεσοῦνται*) follows the LXX *πεσεῖται* against the MT יבול. Again, as in each of the previous cases, we must notice that Mark's translation is not verbally identical with the LXX. And again we find that the supposed difference in meaning between the LXX and the MT is an artificial one. For though Glasson's translation of נבל as 'to fade' is possible, the verb means essentially to fall through exhaustion or withering. BDB give its meanings as follows: '1. *sink* or *drop down*, from exhaustion; from discouragement; of a mountain. 2. usually *fall* like a leaf, or flower, *wither and fall, fade*. . . .' In eleven of its sixteen uses it is specifically of the falling of dead leaves, flowers, or grass, and in six of these cases the LXX translates by some form of *πίπτω*.[48] Here in Is. 34:4, therefore, the LXX gives the true sense of the Hebrew, which is, 'All their host shall fall, as the leaf falls from the vine and like a falling (leaf) from a fig tree.' The use of the preposition מן in the Hebrew surely necessitates the translation 'to fall from'.[49] Undoubtedly the idea of the leaf being withered and faded is present, but the point of comparison is the falling. Here again, then, there is no discrepancy between the MT and either the LXX or the NT.

Mark 13:27 (Mt. 24:31). Mark's *ἐπισυνάξει . . . ἐκ τῶν τεσσάρων ἀνέμων ἀπ' ἄκρου γῆς ἕως ἄκρου οὐρανοῦ* is seen, with considerable probability, as based on LXX Zc. 2:10 (EVV 2:6) *ἐκ τῶν τεσσάρων ἀνέμων τοῦ οὐρανοῦ συνάξω ὑμᾶς*. This differs from the MT כארבע רוחות השמים פרשתי אתכם, both in the verb (פרשׂ means 'to spread out', the opposite of *συνάξω*) and in the consequent difference of preposition (כ for *ἐκ*). Here for the first time is a clear case of the LXX differing in meaning from the MT. Here, it would seem, is real support for Glasson's thesis, a case where the NT statement could not have been drawn from the Hebrew text. But Glasson has omitted to notice another equally probable OT source,[50] viz. Dt. 30:4. Here the LXX reads . . . *ἀπ' ἄκρου τοῦ οὐρανοῦ ἕως ἄκρου τοῦ οὐρανοῦ, ἐκεῖθεν συνάξει σε Κύριος ὁ Θεός σου*. This is a straight translation of the MT, except that the first eight words are an expansion of MT בקצה־השמים. The verb is יקבצך. The first words of this quotation (which are a legitimate expansion of the Hebrew, and add nothing to its meaning) explain the *ἀπ' ἄκρου γῆς ἕως*

[48] Other LXX translations are forms of *ἀποβάλλω*, *ἐκρέω*, and *καταρρέω*; only the use of *παλαιοῦν* in Ezk. 47:12 suggests the translation 'fade'.

[49] Thus RSV, which usually translates נבל by 'wither', here corrects RV 'fade' to 'fall'. *Cf.* JB.

[50] He had done so in *Advent*, p. 196, the first edition of which was published in 1945, but failed to draw any conclusion from it.

ἄκρου οὐρανοῦ of Mark (*cf.* the even closer Matthean form ἀπ' ἄκρων οὐρανῶν ἕως τῶν ἄκρων αὐτῶν), which was not drawn from Zc. 2:10. So it seems necessary to see here a composite allusion (as we postulated also in Mk. 13:24, above) to at least these two OT passages which contain the idea of world-wide dispersion and ingathering, and in one of these, Dt. 30:4, the LXX συνάξει is a correct translation of the Hebrew. It would be arbitrary to postulate as the sole source of the NT words the OT passage to which they bear less resemblance.[51]

Matthew 24:30, alluding to Zc. 12:10–14. It could be argued that the application of this quotation depends on the LXX words γῆ and φυλαί, corresponding to the MT ארץ and משפחות. The Hebrew words, as is shown by the listing of the tribes, refer to the mourning of the *land* of Judaea and of the *tribes* or clans of Israel. The LXX is a fair translation of this, but the words it uses could bear a wider meaning, and it is suggested that they are used in Mt. 24 to refer to a world-wide mourning, commensurate to a cosmic view of the Parousia.[52] In that case the use of this quotation would follow more easily from the LXX wording. But we have argued[53] that no such extension of the meaning is intended, since the verses refer not to the Parousia, but to the fall of Jerusalem. If that is so, the use of Zc. 12:10ff. is in its original sense, referring to the mourning of the tribes of Judaea.

It must also be noted that, even if this interpretation is not accepted, it is wrong to speak here of an application based on the LXX, for the LXX, no less than the Hebrew, has the list of individual tribes, which makes it quite unambiguous that only the tribes of Judaea are in view. If the Matthean version refers to 'all the nations of the earth', it is a deliberate extension of the meaning, whether based on the Hebrew text or on the LXX. The objections to this interpretation are, however, in any case formidable.[54]

The use of Zc. 12:10ff. is not, therefore, dependent on the LXX.

Luke 21:24. 'Ἱερουσαλημ ἔσται πατουμένη ὑπὸ ἐθνῶν is said by Glasson[55] to be modelled on LXX Zc. 12:3 θήσομαι τὴν 'Ἱερουσαλημ λίθον καταπατούμενον πᾶσιν τοῖς ἔθνεσιν. The participle corresponds to the MT מעמסה, a 'burden', 'load', 'something carried'. But, as in Mk. 13:27, this is not a reference to a single OT passage, but to a frequent idea in the OT, the desolation and trampling down of God's sanctuary or of Jerusalem; see, *e.g.*, Is. 22:5; 63:18; Je. 12:10 for the trampling down of Jerusalem, the root here being בוס, and also Is. 5:5; 10:6; 28:18; Dn. 8:13 for the same idea with the

[51] Note the eschatological application of Dt. 30:4 in Tg Ps-Jon, with the insertion of Elijah and the Royal Messiah.

[52] See T. W. Manson, *Sayings*, p. 242.

[53] See above, Appendix A; on this particular quotation see pp. 236–238.

[54] See above, pp. 237–238.

[55] *Advent*, p. 201.

noun מרמס, 'trampling-place'.[56] We have argued[57] that the principal OT source is in fact Dn. 8:13, where the context is, as in Lk. 21:24, of a limited period of desecration of the sanctuary, not, as in Zc. 12:3, of the triumph of Jerusalem over its attackers, who will besiege but not capture and desecrate it. Here there is no discrepancy between the MT and the LXX.

[56] The reason for the LXX version of Zc. 12:3 is no doubt the readings מרמס and רמסיה for the far less common מעמסה (which is hapax legomenon) and עמסיה. (Tg has also substituted the more familiar אבן תקלא for the uncommon MT expression, andh as interpreted עמסיה by אנסתא, 'oppressing' or 'robbing'.) It is not impossible that Jesus knew such a text.

[57] Above, p. 73.

APPENDIX C

A TABLE OF USES OF THE OLD TESTAMENT ATTRIBUTED TO JESUS IN THE SYNOPTIC GOSPELS

We distinguish the following classes:

A. *Verbatim* quotations with introductory formula.
B. *Verbatim* quotations without introductory formula.
C. Clear verbal allusions.
D. Clear references without verbal allusion.
E. Possible verbal allusions.
F. Possible references without verbal allusion.

A quotation formula sometimes occurs with other than *verbatim* quotations; in such cases * is added to the classification.

A measure of arbitrariness in the classification is inevitable. In some cases more than one classification might seem appropriate, and in others the form of the allusion differs in the three Gospels. In the following table details of such variations are kept to a minimum. Alternative OT sources are listed where the exact source of a reference is not clear, but we have avoided listing all possible parallels.

Gospel Reference	*Gospel Parallels*	*OT Source*	*Class*
Mk. 1:44	Mt. 8:4; Lk. 5:14	Lv. 14:2–32	D
2:25–26	Mt. 12:3–4; Lk. 6:3–4	1 Sa. 21: 2–7 (EVV vv. 1–6)	D
2:26	Mt. 12:4; Lk. 6:4	Lv. 24:9	D
3:27	Mt. 12:29; Lk. 11:21–22	Is. 49:24	E
4:12	Mt. 13:13; Lk. 8:10	Is. 6:9–10	C
4:29		Joel 4:13 (EVV 3:13)	C
4:32	Mt. 13:32; Lk. 13:19	Dn. 4:18 (EVV v. 21)	E
6:35–44	Mt. 14:15–21; Lk. 9:12–17	2 Ki. 4:42–44	F
7:6–7	Mt. 15:8–9	Is. 29:13	A
7:10	Mt. 15:4	Ex. 20:12	A
		Ex. 21:17 (LXX v. 16)	A
8:18		Je. 5:21; Ezk. 12:2	E
8:31	The predictions of the resurrection.[1]	Ho. 6:2 Jon. 2:1 (EVV 1:17)	C*

[1] For details see above, p. 53 notes 47–49. The OT sources given in the table above are those for the prediction of 'the third day', not for the resurrection in general.

Gospel Reference	*Gospel Parallels*	*OT Source*	*Class*
Mk. 8:38	Mt. 16:27; Lk. 9:26	Dn. 7:13–14	E
		Zc. 14:5	E
9:12		Is. 53:3	E*
9:12–13	Mt. 17:11–12	Mal. 3:23–24 (EVV 4:5–6)	C
9:13		1 Ki. 19:2, 10	F*
9:48		Is. 66:24	B
10:5	Mt. 19:8	Dt. 24:1	D
10:6	Mt. 19:4	Gn. 1:27	B
10:7–8	Mt. 19:5	Gn. 2:24	B
10:19	Mt. 19:18–19; Lk. 18:20	Ex. 20:12–16; Dt. 5:16–20	B
10:27	Mt. 19:26; Lk. 18:27	Gn. 18:14	E
10:45	Mt. 20:28	Is. 53:10–12	C
11:1ff.	Mt. 21:1ff.; Lk. 19:29ff.	Zc. 9:9	D
11:15–16	Mt. 21:12; Lk. 19:45	Zc. 14:21	F
		Mal. 3:1–4	F
11:17	Mt. 21:13; Lk. 19:46	Is. 56:7	A
		Je. 7:11	C
12:1	Mt. 21:33 (Lk. 20:9)	Is. 5:1–2	C
12:10–11	Mt. 21:42; Lk. 20:17	Ps. 118:22–23	A
12:26	Mt. 22:32; Lk. 20:37	Ex. 3:6	A
12:29–30	Mt. 22:37 (Lk. 10:27)	Dt. 6:4–5	B
12:31	Mt. 22:39 (Lk. 10:27)	Lv. 19:18	B
12:36	Mt. 22:44; Lk. 20:42–43	Ps. 110:1	A
13:7	Mt. 24:6; Lk. 21:9	Dn. 2:28–29	E
13:8	Mt. 24:7; Lk. 21:10	Is. 19:2	E
13:14	Mt. 24:15	Dn. 11:31; 12:11 (9:27)	C
13:19	Mt. 24:21	Dn. 12:1	E
13:22	Mt. 24:24	Dt. 13:2 (EVV v. 1)	E
13:24–25	Mt. 24:29 (Lk. 21:25–26)	Is. 13:10	C
		Is. 34:4	C
13:26	Mt. 24:30; Lk. 21:27	Dn. 7:13	C
13:27	Mt. 24:31	Dt. 30:4	E
		Zc. 2:10 (EVV v. 6)	E
13:31	Mt. 24:35; Lk. 21:33	Is. 40:8	F
14:18	(Mt. 26:21)	Ps. 41:10 (EVV v. 9)	E
14:24	Mt. 26:28 (Lk. 22:20)	Ex. 24:8	C
		Is. 53:10, 12	E
		Je. 31:31	F
14:27	Mt. 26:31	Zc. 13:7	A
14:34	Mt. 26:38	Ps. 42:6 (EVV v. 5) & parr.	E
14:58	Mt. 26:61	Zc. 6:12–13	E

Gospel Reference	*Gospel Parallels*	*OT Source*	*Class*
Mk. 14:62	Mt. 26:64; Lk. 22:69	Ps. 110:1	C
		Dn. 7:13	C
15:34	Mt. 27:46	Ps. 22:2 (EVV v. 1)	B
Mt. 3:15		Is. 53:11	E
4:4	Lk. 4:4	Dt. 8:3	A
4:7	Lk. 4:12	Dt. 6:16	A
4:10	Lk. 4:8	Dt. 6:13	A
5:3	Lk. 6:20	Is. 61:1	E
5:4		Is. 61:2	E
5:5		Ps. 37:11	C
5:8		Ps. 24:4	E
5:21		Ex. 20:13; Dt. 5:17	A
		Ex. 21:12; Lv. 24:17, *etc.*	D
5:27		Ex. 20:14; Dt. 5:18	A
5:31		Dt. 24:1	C*
5:33		Ex. 20:7; Lv. 19:12	F
		Dt. 23:22 (EVV v. 21); Ps. 50:14, *etc.*	C*
5:34–35		Is. 66:1	C
5:35		Ps. 48:3 (EVV v. 2)	C
5:38		Ex. 21:24; Lv. 24:20, *etc.*	A
5:43		Lv. 19:18	A
5:48	(Lk. 6:36)	Lv. 19:2 & parr.	E
6:6		Is. 26:20	E
6:8		Is. 65:24	F
6:11	Lk. 11:3	Pr. 30:8	E
6:23	Lk. 11:34	Pr. 28:22	E
6:26	Lk. 12:24	Ps. 147:9; Jb. 38:41	F
6:29	Lk. 12:27	1 Ki. 10:4ff., *etc.*	D
7:7–8	Lk. 11:9–10	Dt. 4:29; Je. 29:13, *etc.*	E
7:15		Ezk. 22:27	E
7:23	Lk. 13:27	Ps. 6:9 (EVV v. 8)	B
7:24–27	Lk. 6:47–49	Ezk. 13:10–14	F
8:11–12	Lk. 13:28–29	Is. 43:5–6; Ps. 107:3, *etc.*[2]	E
		Is. 2:2–3, *etc.*	F
9:13		Ho. 6:6	B
10:6		Je. 50:6, *etc.*	E
10:15	Lk. 10:12	Gn. 19	D
10:16		Gn. 3:1	E
10:23		Dn. 7:13	E
10:35–36	Lk. 12:53	Mi. 7:6	C

[2] For details see above, p. 63.

Gospel Reference	*Gospel Parallels*	*OT Source*	*Class*
Mt. 11:5	Lk. 7:22	Is. 35:5–6	C
		Is. 61:1	C
		Is. 26:19	E
11:10	Lk. 7:27 (Mk. 1:2)	Mal. 3:1	A
		Ex. 23:20	E
11:14		Mal. 3:23 (EVV 4:5)	D
11:21–22	Lk. 10:13–14	Is. 23; Ezk. 26–28, *etc.*	D
11:23	Lk. 10:15	Is. 14:13, 15	C
11:23–24	(*cf.* Mt. 10:15)	Gn. 19	D
11:29		Je. 6:16	C
12:5		Nu. 28:9–10, *etc.*	D*
12:7	(*cf.* Mt. 9:13)	Ho. 6:6	B
12:40	(Lk. 11:30)	Jon. 2:1 (EVV 1:17)	B
12:41	Lk. 11:32	Jon. 3:5–9	D
12:42	Lk. 11:31	1 Ki. 10:1–13	D
13:14–15		Is. 6:9–10	A
13:39		Joel 4:13 (EVV 3:13)	E
13:41		Zp. 1:3	E
13:43		Dn. 12:3 (Jdg. 5:31)	E
15:13		Is. 61:3 (60:21)	E
16:4	(*cf.* Mt. 12:39)	Jonah	D
16:18		Is. 38:10; Jb. 38:17	E
17:17	Lk. 9:41	Dt. 32:5	E
18:16		Dt. 19:15	B
18:22		Gn. 4:24	E
19:17	(*cf.* Lk. 10:28)	Lv. 18:5	E
19:19		Lv. 19:18	B
19:28	(Lk. 22:29–30)	Dn. 7:13ff.	E
21:16		Ps. 8:3 (EVV v. 2)	A
23:17, 19		Ex. 29:37; 30:29	D
23:23	(Lk. 11:42)	Mi. 6:8	E
23:35	Lk. 11:51	Gn. 4:1ff.	D
		2 Ch. 24:20–22	D
23:38	Lk. 13:35	Je. 22:5 (12:7)	E
23:39	Lk. 13:35	Ps. 118:26	B
24:30		Zc. 12:12	C
24:31		Is. 27:13	E
24:37–39	Lk. 17:26–27	Gn. 6–7	D
25:31		Dn. 7:13–14	E
		Zc. 14:5	E
25:32		Joel 4:2 (EVV 3:2)	E
25:46		Dn. 12:2	E
28:18		Dn. 7:14	E

Gospel Reference	*Gospel Parallels*	*OT Source*	*Class*
Lk. 4:18–19		Is. 61:1–2	A
4:18		Is. 58:6	B
4:25–26		1 Ki. 17	D
4:27		2 Ki. 5	D
10:18		Is. 14:12	E
10:19		Ps. 91:13	E
11:20		Ex. 8:15 (EVV v. 19)	E
11:22		Is. 53:12	E
12:47–48		Dt. 25:2	F
14:10		Pr. 25:6–7	F
16:15		Pr. 16:5 (6:16–17)	E
17:14		Lv. 13–14	D
17:28–29, 32		Gn. 19	D
17:29		Gn. 19:24	C
17:31		Gn. 19:17, 26	E
19:10		Ezk. 34:16, 22	E
19:43		Is. 29:3; Ezk. 4:2	E
20:18	(Mt. 21:44)	Is. 8:14–15	C
		Dn. 2:34–35, 44–45	E
21:24		Dn. 8:13, *etc.*	E
22:31		Am. 9:9	E
22:37		Is. 53:12	A
23:30		Ho. 10:8	B
23:46		Ps. 31:6 (EVV v. 5)	B
24:49		Is. 32:15	E

In addition to the quotations and allusions listed, there are a large number of sayings which state, without explicit reference to any one OT passage, that it is written that the Messiah must suffer, die and rise again. For these passages see above, pp. 125–126.

INDEX OF REFERENCES

1. BIBLICAL

Old Testament references are to chapter and verse of the Hebrew text.

The main discussions of passages in the Synoptic Gospels are indicated by references in italics.

Synoptic parallels are not listed: for a passage which occurs in Mark, only the Marcan reference is given; for those which occur only in Matthew and Luke, the Matthean.

References in Appendix C are not included here.

2. JEWISH LITERATURE

(a) TARGUMS

Citations of Targums as witnesses to the OT text in Appendix B are not listed here.

(b) APOCRYPHA

(c) PSEUDEPIGRAPHA

(d) QUMRAN LITERATURE

(e) RABBINIC LITERATURE

3. EARLY CHRISTIAN LITERATURE

INDEX OF MODERN AUTHORS

References in italics indicate the first citation of a work; bibliographical details will be found in the notes so indicated.